THE LITERARY HISTORY

OF ENGLAND

THE

LITERARY HISTORY

OF

ENGLAND

IN THE END OF THE EIGHTEENTH AND BEGINNING

OF THE NINETEENTH CENTURY

BY MRS. OLIPHANT

AUTHOR OF 'MAKERS OF FLORENCE,' ETC.

" Reading maketh a full man."—BACON, *On Study*.
" A good book is the precious life‑blood of a master spirit embalmed and
    treasured up on purpose to a life beyond life."—MILTON, *Areopagitica*.
" Je ne voyage sans livres, ny en paix, ny en guerre. C'est la meilleure munition
    que j'aye trouvé à cet humain voyage."—MONTAIGNE, Livre iii. Chap. iii.
" Books are the legacies that a great genius leaves to mankind." — ADDISON,
    Spectator.

IN THREE VOLUMES

VOL. I.

New York

MACMILLAN AND CO.

1882

PREFACE.

It is with diffidence that the Author of the following volumes offers them to the public. The subject is a great one, and so manifold in its details that it is impossible not to have made omissions in various quarters: and especially in those on which she can pretend to least knowledge, in the graver literature of Science and Philosophy. It was intended originally that the work should extend farther, and come down to the elder figures even of our own times, the poets who are now regnant in England, and the many eminent writers who have but just departed; but the period before our own, which has formed them and us, and which reaches into our own by so many survivals, was found too rich and ample to allow of further additions. The aim of the Author has been throughout rather to give, as fully as she was able, a history of the new departures, in poetry above all, in criticism, in fiction, and, to the extent of her ability, to indicate those which have occurred in history and philosophy—than to undertake an absolute commentary upon every individual writer. She is prepared to be told that she has passed too lightly over some important names; and if some lesser ones have escaped her altogether, to receive with humility any strictures which may be pronounced upon her on this account. Her aim has been to set forth the remarkable outburst of new and noble genius by which the end of last century and the beginning of our own was distinguished, and made into a great and individual age in literature. It is hard to cut the line clear across all those intertwinings of human life and influence by which one generation links itself to another; and consequently the story will be found to overlap the boundaries on both sides, now going too far back, now reaching too far forward. The kind and sympathetic reader will see how this comes about, and how the uneven lines of life—some cut so sadly short, some holding on their course up to old age — cannot fail to leave an irregular outline. For all faults of omission or redundancy, she makes her apology beforehand, with the hope of being able to amend them at some future time.

CONTENTS.

CHAPTER VI.

CHAPTER VII.

CHAPTER VIII.

THE LITERARY HISTORY OF ENGLAND.

INTRODUCTORY.

THE literary history of every country follows a course of its own. It is independent to a great measure of the political existence of the race in which it is developed, and except in so far as a period of remarkable intellectual activity in other ways is generally distinguished also by one of the great outbursts of literary genius which recur from time to time, it cannot be said to follow any of the rules of historical progress known to us. Even in this respect there is no fixed rule; for though the glory of the Elizabethan age was a sort of universal flood-tide, swelling the veins of every manner of man, and communicating greatness to every section of the national life, there was no public soul whatever in Germany when the great literature of that country arose at a bound; and few ages have seen more vigour and grace in letters than the period, so little remarkable otherwise, in which Louis Philippe reigned in France. Neither does Literature develop historically as national life does. In the history of men and of commonwealths there is a slow progression, which, however faint, however deferred, yet gradually goes on, leaving one generation always a trifle better than that which preceded it, with some scrap of new possession, some right assured, some small inheritance gained. From age to age the advance may be small, yet it is appreciable. Great statesmen and little, together work out something for us that we had not possessed before. Even in the countries most behindhand in the race, things which were easy and invariable a hundred years ago have now become impossible. New modifications and conditions arise continually, the public sense is awakened, or it is cultivated, or at all events it is changed. There will of course always be a large and respectable portion of mankind, to whose ideas progress is a mistake, and the old always better than the new; but even this class so far recognises the reality of the new, as to agree that the civilised races cannot retrace their steps, and that the old order, if it remains a thing to sigh for, yet cannot be brought back. " Our little systems have their day;" but that day being over, humanity passes on and cannot return. The reforms from which we have hoped most, the advances for which we have struggled most strenuously, do not produce all the good we expected; but we cannot, nor would we, undo them. In everything there is a current onward, perhaps downward, but never back. In individual life, and all its personal manifestations, it is true enough that the thing that hath been is that that shall be; but in history there is a gradual working out and working on, a certain logic, and some traceable principle of development. The principle indeed changes from time. It comes to a climax. It is a despotism growing and ripening towards a great catastrophe; it is a hot democracy, dropping asunder into anarchy and confusion; it is a struggle of force against force, of kings and populace, of nobles and adventurers, of those who have and those who would have—each working towards destruction or towards consolidation, by means which are dimly or grandly traceable across the ages, but each leading to something, intended or unintended, which was not before, and which turns the current slowly another way, alters the channel, overflows the boundaries, makes a wilderness of a fruitful field, or turns the sandy desert into shocks of standing corn. All is not absolute good or advantage to the human race; but yet the race is stepping onward, it discovers new powers, it learns new ameliorations, and if it also makes proof of novel sufferings and dangers, it finds new defences and medicines for them. Whether progress makes the general mass of mankind really happier or better, will always be a moot question; but yet it improves their position from one generation to another. It goes on making certain sorts of evil obsolete, as well as certain sorts of good; it overcomes the coarser conditions of life, gives universal protection, better shelter, opportunities before unknown. It is in fact a real progress, even through a thousand drawbacks, and every age leaves some foundation upon which the next can build.

But in the history of literature no such development can be traced. Since the age of Elizabeth how much has been altered in the national life, what convulsions have been gone through, what constitutional changes achieved! From insurrections and beheadings without number, to a constitutional calm, in which a hot word is the fiercest weapon ever used among Englishmen, and an indignation meeting the wildest attempt of the rebellious; from a set of pirate sea-knights robbing the Spanish galleons, to peaceful navies that fill all the ports of the world; from a half settled plantation amid the western mists, to colonies and conquests that circle the whole earth around, what a difference! And perhaps most wonderful of all, if not so imposing, from the rude and homely life in which few softnesses existed, to a miraculous comfort which pervades all classes, even the poorest, and carries to the humblest house conveniences and ameliorations of living of which great Elizabeth herself had no thought. All this is true; but we have not advanced upon Shakspeare; Bacon is still our fountain-head of philosophy, nay, even old Chaucer remains the "well of English undefiled." All the generations of poets and prose writers who have flourished since, and who have had it in their power to start from the point where these great authorities left off, have failed to improve upon their masters.

This is a problem, we think, harder to solve than the scientific puzzles which occupy so many minds; but it is one to which no philosopher has ever yet attempted a solution. In art this strange contradiction of all rules is equally patent, and we are tempted to quote an illustrative anecdote, not *ben trovato* only, like the vanities of Mr. Punch's æsthetic victims, but simply true. " Do you think, perhaps," said an amused critic listening to the condescending comments of a young artist upon Fra Angelico, " that you could do as well?" The youth was modest; he took nothing upon himself; but he knew something about the long results of time, the infinite study which has been given to all the conditions of art since Fra Angelico's time. " I think," he said, " that considering all the progress that has been made since then, and the laws of perspective, and the mysteries of light and shade that we have mastered, and all the work of the generations, it would be no credit to one if one could not aspire to do—better." The hope was most reasonable—nothing could be better founded; surely a highly-trained painter of the nineteenth century must be a small creature indeed if he cannot do better than a poor monk of the fourteenth. And surely a young poet of the same period, trained in all the learning of all the ages, with classic examples at his finger-ends, and all the wealth of native literature to form his standing ground, and the full

command of an enriched and refined language—surely, by
all the laws of progress, and every canon of nature, he
ought to do better than a poor player of three hundred
years ago, with few models, no rules of composition, and
no particular training at all.

And yet somehow it is not so. The expectation is
not in reality presumptuous, though it seems presumptuous to the point of ridicule.   Why?   But to this
question we can give no answer. The processes of Development or Evolution, of which we have heard so much, are
manifestly suspended in Physics since the age of history
began, so that nowhere, since men have been able to
report or perceive their own progress, has an inch been
added to their stature, or a joint to their fingers—a result
which must be confusing to the scientific student even on
his own ground; but the development of mind has not
even remained stationary like that of the body. It has
been regulated by some spasmodic force which no one has
tried to define, and which acts by great unforeseen impulses
of irregular recurrence, of which no one has succeeded in
calculating the times or seasons. We scarcely venture, in
these days of certainty as to the laws which regulate everything, to quote the old divine description of the wind that
bloweth where it listeth. In the nineteenth century it is
more philosophical to say that the movements of literary
genius are determined by some force of which we have
not as yet discovered the conditions, some influence of a
volcanic order which lies and broods and smoulders in the
bowels of the earth, until the moment comes when its
flames burst forth and fling themselves to the skies, and
the molten metal pours over hill and plain. But when
this eruption may occur, or how it comes about, is unknown to man; neither is it possible to predict—as with
its physical parallel it sometimes is possible — by any
heavings of the soil or subterraneous moan of force re-

strained, about what time or in what direction the
mysterious impulse may be given.

To leave similes aside, nothing is more remarkable in
the history of humanity, or less capable of reduction to
rule, than are the waves of literary impulse.   They
neither resemble each other, nor do they move at
regular intervals; nor has one, so far as we can perceive, any natural connection in the way of cause and
effect with another, or resemblance to it.   No two
spirits that have ever inhabited this earth have less
mental kindred than has Milton to Shakspeare, though
he was the natural heir upon whom the mantle of poetry
descended, and who wore the crown after our sovereign
poet.   And through all the succession of the ages the
same fact is apparent: Dryden had it next, then Pope
—inferior princes, with no such imperial rank as their
predecessors, but equally unlike them; and who could
estimate the unsimilarity, the antagonism on every point,
between Pope and Wordsworth?   The mind and the
form and the meaning change from one generation to
another so entirely, that in each it seems a new thing, a
separate creation, instead of a succession and hereditary
kingdom.   Now and then, appearing obliquely through
the course of the ages, certain indications of kinship will
appear, to remind us accidentally of a possible connection
too subtle for our tracing.   But every singer is a new
miracle—created if nothing else is created—no growth
developed out of precedent poets, but something sprung
from an impulse which is not reducible to law—a being
without father, without mother, like the mysterious
patriot-king and priest upon the old Chaldean plains.
How this is, is as difficult to find out as how human
identity is, the most secret of all wonders.   Science, so
far as we are aware, has not even attempted to fathom
this strangest of all the strange caprices in the universe;

but it is very curious, and very well worth the profoundest study.

The history of England from a literary point of view may be broadly divided into three great epochs, which are not so much the three centuries in which modern literature may almost be said to originate and run its course, as they are three eras which may be distinguished as the age of Elizabeth, the age of Anne, and, we should be glad to say for the sake of euphony and delightful equipoise, the age of Victoria; but, alas! though a number of the great names which made the last epoch illustrious lasted into her day, truth compels us to admit that the last flood-tide of intellectual wealth and genius came in the age of George, most unpoetical of patrons. If in this we seem to omit the great autocracy, or rather theocracy, administered by a severe and splendid deputy, of Milton, we do so with no want of veneration, but solely because his period was himself, and the gentle songsters around him, sweet as they were, had no title to the rank of princes, or sharers of his supremacy. But in the others we have named, genius is poured forth in a full and overflowing stream, and the leading spirit of the time is but the chief among equals. Nor does Dryden, his contemporary and successor, give sufficient wealth to the epoch to make it compete in greatness with the other groups. In the eighteenth century, however, a host of writers arose, following the same fashions and partaking the same influence, with a unity which links them together, as the writers of the Elizabethan age were linked. It will probably always remain a question for discussion what is the comparative importance of this period as coming between the others which have created English literature; but that it was an epoch of the most marked character there can never be any doubt. In its own opinion it was the climax and sublimest development of

English genius.   The prodigious wealth and freedom of
the preceding age were, to its fastidious eyes, license and
savagery.   It was the age of taste, of critics, of style as
an elaborate art, a thing cultivated for its own sake ; and
as nothing worthy to be regarded had come before it, so
it was hard to see what could come after it.   Pope brought
its poetical utterance to perfection ; and beyond perfection
even the archangels cannot reach.   After him were echoes
and repetitions ; but the world was resigned to a kind of
elegant certainty that all that could be aimed at was
attained.

And, like the style, the subjects fit for poetry and imaginative writing of every kind were already tabulated
and understood.   The world, which had been so vast and
broad, contracted into a narrow sphere where satire was
the highest art and social manners the only subject.   To
correct society in its vices, and hold up the mirror to its
foibles, was the great and only end of literature,   " An
unfortunate lady," the victim of some Lovelace, or an impersonation of avarice or envy, were the emblems of the
passions.   Such landscapes as existed were made up of
velvet lawns and savage torrents, with Dryads and Naiads,
and urns and fountains ; and when the chief poet of the
age would charm the world with delicate fancy and heroic
verse, the pleasant theft of a lady's curl was the subject
of his muse.   Thus everything was artificial in the sphere
where once the loftiest imagination reigned.   Titania's
fairies, so well met by moonlight, the airy creatures of the
woods and groves, turned into legions of sly little imps
full of knowing adjustments, who kept safe the magic
circle of Belinda's petticoat ; and hoops and patches took
the place of hearts and thoughts.   To be sure, there was
a good deal of philosophy and instruction of various sorts
conveyed in the medium of that melodious verse—sharp
and distinct thinkings, character cut with a diamond,

classic eclogues, and fine sentiment. There was nothing
wanting, in short, which the mind of that time could
think of; and all enunciated with clear unhesitating voice
in rhymes as correct as Boileau could have desired. It
was not according to the genius of the English language;
but it was as excellent a rendering of the rules of classic
French into English, with a vigorous admixture of English
force and robustness, into the foreign medium, as could
have been desired. It was a fighting age, and never were
the French more distinctively the national enemies of our
island : but France was absolute in letters, if not on the
field of battle, and from Twickenham to Grub Street
everything owned her power.

This great literary epoch was, however, an anomaly.
It was foreign from head to foot. Its laws and regulations were all those of another race. We are so much
more liberal in our ideas than they were, that nobody
attempts to ignore the just claim of the magnates of this
period as they did those of their predecessors. However
our affections may lie towards Pope, we do justice to his
importance and his power ; but his art was that of another
atmosphere, and when he himself was wound up and
accomplished like his verse, the state of affairs left behind
was dismal and hopeless as it has rarely been before.
Beyond him in his own method nothing more was possible.
He had gone as far as man may go in the polish, the
finish, the exact and faultless balance of poetical composition, and his art came to an end in him. The Augustan
age was accomplished and over, and a dreary interregnum
followed. During this interregnum a few fine but faint
voices were heard by intervals, belonging neither to the
age that was past nor to the new epoch which was still
unrevealed. Goldsmith, with a fresh and genial note ;
Gray, delicate, melodious, and refined ; Collins, too classic
for the general — like stray birds waking in the night,

belated nightingales left solitary, their season over, or
thrushes prematurely awakened by some too early gleam
of the unaccomplished dawn.   But in spite of those mild
unintentional rebels, the tradition of the ended age bound
England still with a bondage difficult to throw off.   The
poets were gone, but the critics were left; and those
précieuses, who belong to a still lower depth, echoes and
shadows of the critics, had formed themselves into little
elegant coteries all over the country to hatch such stray
germs of poetry as might be coming into being, and keep
them correct, and frame them after the best models.   If
ever any freeborn thing stirred in the obscurity, they did
their best to clip its wings.

Things were not much better in the other regions of
literature.   Johnson still reigned there an autocrat of the
severest sway, imposing the clumsy grandeur of his own
mode of expression upon the language, and overawing all
beginners into imitation of those defects of his ponderous
genius which they had no better gift to redeem.   He
had given much to his generation—a rugged uprightness
and scorn for all meaner arts — a noble spirit which
would not brook the servility to which literature had so
long been bound; but in return he tyrannised over it,
and permitted no voice to be heard in his presence,
objecting in others to the independence which was his
own great title to the respect and admiration of his time.
He, too, had exhausted the soil that bore him, and
brought its capabilities to an end; and literature, crushed
under his weight, could only feebly moan out an allegiance to him, which in its heart it did not feel.   The age
was dying away ingloriously, failing in all those manifestations of the imagination which are the heart of
literature.   History, indeed, and philosophy still throve
and flourished; but the last had flitted northwards, and
the first, when not in Edinburgh, was over the Channel,

hugging herself upon her quiet by the shore of Lake
Leman. Richardson, Fielding, and, at a distance, Smollett,
had given vigorous life to the novel, a new form of
literature in England ; but that, too, had fallen silent,
though the lively voice of Miss Burney awakened some
of the old echoes. The world of English literature was
frost-bound ; it made small things into great. It had
lost the true standard of English, and had learned to
measure all merit by the stature of a few individuals,
and constrain all voices into one monotonous and imitated
tone.

Our present object is to trace the awakening of the
new epoch in literature which dawned in the end of the
eighteenth century, stretching forward into our own, and
not only creating a new code and new laws, but changing
the very atmosphere, the scene, the firmament, and bringing in a purer moral, and a higher soul. For this
development of higher genius and purified life, the way
was prepared by two poets, whom we may call the
precursors of the new age. These heralds of the day
arose spontaneously at very nearly the same moment to
the sight of men, though one was already in the decline
of life, and another in the perfect bloom of youthful manhood. From no quarter was it less likely that the new
impulse should come than from the rural places in which
William Cowper, an invalid and recluse, sick and sad,
and sometimes more deeply disabled still, with a cloud of
incipient insanity hovering over him, hid himself from
the conflicts of the world : or where Robert Burns, a
young and vigorous farm-labourer, went whistling after
his plough along the Ayrshire furrows. He who took to
the solace of verse in order to forget himself and his
troubles, and he who " rhymed for fun " as he went about
his daily work, were not the leaders any critic would
have chosen for the revolution which was to change the

face of literature.   But happily critics are not consulted
on such matters.   Spontaneously, to sweeten a life of
suffering on one side and of toil on the other, thinking
little of any result to follow, inspired by no rebellion or
discontent with the mediums used before, and altogether
without consent or knowledge of each other, these two
strangely chosen reformers awoke to a sense of the power
that was in them.   To Burns it was a passion, but to
Cowper not much more than a pastime.   They awoke
each in his covert, shadowed over with foliage and greenness, and——far apart from each other, in conditions of
life as different as it is possible to conceive, stretched
forth each his hand to the worthy work.   A hypochondriac
and a ploughman !   The looker-on might well have
laughed at the suggestion that imperial interests of any
kind were to be affected by anything they could say or
do ; but yet between them they set the lamp alight which
was to pass to so many gifted hands and lighten all the
attentive skies.   Fifteen years of the century were yet to
run, when almost simultaneously these two poets—precursors of the greatest tide of genius that has flowed into
our country since Shakspeare—began their public work ;
but we must step back into the shadows—into the actual
meridian of the past age, to trace out to the reader what
has already been so often done, the training and course of
existence which prepared them for their mission.

CHAPTER I.

WILLIAM COWPER.

WILLIAM COWPER was born in 1731 in the vicarage of
Great Berkhampstead in Hertfordshire. At the time of
his birth all the former generation of poets was still
living and in full utterance. Pope, decrepit and waning,
but not in power or in fame, was making his grotto and
polishing his verses on his river-side, while Thames flowed
sweetly by, but not to the accompaniment of any such
song of love and beauty as that which Spenser sang.
His Essay on Man, and several of his most important
works, were being produced while the Hertfordshire
parson's boy, a little weakly fellow,

> "Delighted with his bauble coach, and wrapped
> In scarlet mantle warm, and velvet-capped,"

was drawn by the gardener Robin " to school along the
public way ; " Thomson, fat, amiable, and indolent, was
manufacturing bad plays, and thinking lazily of the
" pleasant land of drowsyhed," which afterwards grew
into the " Castle of Indolence ; " Gray was scarcely out of
those Eton fields to which he has given one of their
tenderest recollections. In another region of literature,
good Samuel Richardson was beginning to think of
writing letters that should teach the common people, and
especially " handsome girls obliged to go out to service,"

how to conduct themselves in the difficulties in their
career, as well as how to frame epistles to their friends;
in the fulfilment of which modest design the honest bookseller stumbled somehow into Pamela, and, more wonderful
still, into Clarissa, strange product of some occult inspiration, the child of dulness and unsuspected genius ; and
in this undertaking roused and found out the keener
metal of Fielding, who, fired by derision and indignant
sense of superiority, placed his hardy tale by the side of
the old proser's sentiment—but in so doing was betrayed,
he too, by his good angel, into Parson Adams, though all
he meant was Joseph Andrews to start with. The
works of both come within the period of Cowper's youth.
And Johnson, the autocrat of letters, was a poor usher
in a school, as yet unwitting of the reign before him.
Goldsmith was but just born in another parsonage, in
Ireland, though his career was over some years before
that of Cowper began in poetry. Such were the existing
lights at the moment when this little timid child came
into being. They were all congregated in the dingy old
London of those days, as he grew towards manhood.
And beyond that busy scene the larger world extended
full of event and commotion. The reign was that of
George II., or rather of Caroline, a nobler sovereign.
Sir Robert Walpole was in the midst of his long and
steady sway as Prime Minister, and Bolingbroke was
assailing him with vigorous wit and logic. Handel was
in Windsor, associating the English name with a new
development of grave and noble music, a loan from
Germany more harmonious than that of the royal family,
still scarcely acclimatised among us ; and Garrick, still
little known, was directing his thoughts to the elevation
of the stage. Beyond the Channel there were plenty of
notable figures revealed or on the point of revelation :
Frederick the Great, awaiting the event which was to

bring about the seven years' war — the death of the emperor; Maria Theresa, that emperor's daughter, one of the greatest sovereigns of her race, and not likely to turn out so easy a victim as a young woman ought to have done; Louis XV. in France, lost in depravity and bankruptcy, fostering those seeds of the revolution which his father had sown. Fontenoy and Dettingen, and also —a miserable parallel to battles of which Englishmen are still proud—Culloden, were all fought when Cowper was a boy. The young Chevalier, hapless adventurer, stormed through the one historical moment of his life, had his hour of triumph in faithful Scotland, and half seized England by surprise, during the same peaceful childhood. It was an exciting age, with news by every lumbering post and slow-paced waggon, such as set men's hearts beating; news that was sometimes of victory, yet some-times also of trouble: the French interfering with our trade, the Spanish pirates maltreating our seamen on the high seas; our footing on the American continent, and faint beginning of our empire in India, kept in check by the nimble and adroit neighbour who was our national enemy : and England standing at bay, holding her own in all parts of her dominion, somewhat desperately abroad, and often with a panic at home, with melancholy prophets declaring loudly that her greatness was at an end, and her ruin near.

It is a very peaceful little vignette of life which rises before us against that stormy background, when we turn to Cowper's own tender recollections of his childhood, that picture made after fifty years, of the only home that had ever belonged to him, the "pastoral house" of which nobody now remembered that it had once been his. The memories of so young a child—for he was not six when his mother died, and its happiness was over—never per-haps were the foundation of so perfect a picture : the

child so truly infantile, the mother so vague and benign
a vision, the pensive and shadowy sweetness of the recollection, carry it direct to the reader's heart.

> "Thy maidens, grieved themselves at my concern
> Oft gave me promise of thy quick return,
> What ardently I wished, I long believed,
> And disappointed still, was still deceived ;
> By expectation every day beguiled,
> Dupe of to-morrow even from a child.
> Thus many a sad to-morrow came and went
> Till all my stock of infant sorrow spent,
> I learnt at last submission to my lot,
> And though I less deplored thee, ne'er forgot."

Thus sorrow and disappointment ended the first brief
chapter of his baby-life.   He had not a happy youth, for
he had no home, no natural shelter to return to in the
little troubles of his school career; and no doubt this
want gave double bitterness to the childish unhappiness
which the gloom of his maturer days exaggerated in its
turn.   Unfortunately, the only record of his boyhood is
the sombre account of it given by himself in after years,
when the disposition to increase all the darker shades in
his unregenerate days was strong upon him, as it was in
most of those who thought as he did.   From this account
the credulous reader might be led to suppose that the
poor little timid boy was depraved from his earliest years,
and had been brought up by a succession of wicked people,
all conspiring to heighten the natural blackness of his
character, and put him beyond the reach of amendment.
He grew wickeder and wickeder in his schoolboy days,
he became an adept "in the infernal art of lying ;" he
had no sentiments of contrition, nor thoughts of God and
eternity.   About all this there seems a curious, but very
evident self-delusion.   Poet though he was, Cowper's
power of realising his own distant past seems to have
failed him.   He remembered the child in the gentle quiet

of the nursery, the mother's nightly visits and morning ministrations; but he forgot the boy who had played in the shadow of the Abbey, and rattled over the stony pavement in Dean's Yard; for there are other indications artlessly afforded by the very story itself, which prove that he was neither very sad nor very wicked. He played cricket and football, and excelled in these manly games; he formed a number of friendships which lasted into mature life; and to all appearance led his little existence in a harmless gentle way, liked by everybody, and with no tragical melancholy about him. Even the horror of public schools, which he expresses in his poems, is modified by unconscious admissions, " We love the play place of our infant days," he is betrayed into saying, even in the midst of his denunciations; and, beguiled from theory into recollection, lets his fancy stray to that charming picture of " the little ones unbuttoned, glowing hot " in full tide of those enjoyments which he too shared, before it occurred to him that he was depraved and miserable—

"The pleasing spectacle at once excites
Such recollections of our own delights,
That viewing it, we seem almost to attain
Our innocent, sweet, simple years again."

Thus poetry rights the balance against the gloomy theory of life which swallowed up so much of Cowper's manhood; and he who has just maligned his childhood in prose inadvertently vindicates it in verse.

Of his youth we have the same dark description, with the same breaks and openings in it to show a different reality below. When he left Westminster School, he entered an attorney's office, where he was again miserable enough, to take his own jaundiced account of it; but when we correct this by the inadvertent admissions made at cheerful moments, the picture undergoes a pleasant change. The formal narrative continues to give us

gloomy glimpses of a weak and wretched youth, but the
unintentional revelation is of a much more cheerful
character. If he was idle and foolish, he was at the
same time happy and gay, shirking his work perhaps,
but for no more reprehensible indulgence than that of
hanging about the pleasant house of his uncle, where
there were girls and innocent diversion. " I did actually
live three years with Mr. Chapman," he writes afterwards to Lady Hesketh, one of those girls, "that is to
say, I slept three years in his house; but I lived, that is
to say I spent my days, in Southampton Row, as you
very well remember. There was I and the future Lord
Chancellor constantly employed from morning to night in
giggling, and making giggle, instead of following the law.
Oh fie, cousin! how could you do so?" That Thurlow,
the stern and saturnine, should have been his companion
in happy levity, is as remarkable as that the laughing
boy should afterwards have seen this careless episode
under so gloomy a light. Thurlow's giggle is far more
unaccountable than Cowper's, who kept the faculty of
laughter all his life; and it is astonishing that the constant companionship of such a vigorous and dominant
spirit should not have had more influence upon his gentle
companion. But Cowper, being indisposed to effort by
nature, was in circumstances which made his idleness as
excusable as idleness can ever be. These were the days
of sinecures and patronage. And he had influential connections, and in all probability felt his future to be assured.
He was free to dally in the primrose paths, and happy
in doing so. He helped to keep his uncle's house full
of gentle mirth and frolic; and he fell in love, as was
natural, with his uncle's daughter. When his appren-
ticeship to the attorney was over, and he began to live
alone in chambers in the Temple, his biographers seem
to agree that the coming cloud threw its first shadow

over him ; but then they are all painfully on the outlook
for this coming cloud ; and it is hard to believe that a
man could lead a very gloomy life who was a member of
the "Nonsense Club, consisting of seven Westminster
men, who dined together every Thursday," and who was
distinguished by what was then called "restlessness," but
which we should now call love of change and variety.
His letters of this period represent him in anything but
a dismal light.   He tells us, indeed, that his life was
"spent in an uninterrupted course of sinful indulgence,"
but that is a vague phrase which may mean anything,
from actual vice to absence from church and dislike of
early rising.   He was, however—which is more fatal even
than actual transgression—destitute of personal power
and energy to an extraordinary extent, amiable and loving,
but incapable of any sacrifice, honourable and honest, yet
content to be dependent : a paradox not uncommon, but
always involving misery.   He loved, as such men love,
his cousin Theodora ; but her father having objected to
the marriage, the lover seems to have made no effort to
render it possible.   All that we know of her, which is
little enough, denotes a high-spirited girl who would have
been capable of bearing the burden of her companion's
helplessness.   But Cowper had not the courage or the
earnestness to overcome his uncle's scruples.   Ashley
Cowper was not a stern or alarming parent.   When he
died, his nephew's hand records his character in terms of
gentle enthusiasm—

> " Endowed with all that could engage
> All hearts to love thee both in youth and age ;
> In prime of life for sprightliness enrolled,
> Among the gay, yet virtuous as the old ;
> In life's last stage (oh, blessings rarely found !)
> Pleasant as youth with all its blossoms crowned ;
> Through every period of this changeful state,
> Unchanged thyself—wise, good, affectionate."

This was not a man to refuse to hear reason; but it is evident all through his life that William Cowper was not capable of great and generous effort, even for one he loved. Throughout his life he accepts but never makes sacrifices. He is affectionate, sweet, and caressing, no one more pleasant to serve, more grateful, more tender. Whatever was done for him, he was most delightfully ready to acknowledge; but all this is quite consistent with a kind of selfishness to which people generally shrink from giving its right name—a selfishness so refined and exquisite that the very sufferers by it often adore the amiable attractive weakness. No indication of any effort on his part to overcome the opposition of the family appears in the record—

> " Her, through tedious years of doubt and pain,
>   Fixed in her choice, and faithful, but in vain "—

he does indeed give one poetical tear to: but he does not seem to have paid Theodora even the compliment of faithfulness, since very soon after their separation he writes to a friend of a certain " lovely and beloved little girl," with whom he had spent a blessed three days, though he adds with the same resignation, that the approaching return of this " bright star" to the West Indies, in which region " it had risen," will leave him " nothing but sighs and tears." He was very willing to be loved and happy, but not to secure the possession even of happiness by the sacrifice of ease or leisure, or any personal comfort. He was, however, of the celibate class, which is as clearly indicated by nature as any other division of humanity, born to know no passion, but to be affectionately dependent upon the affection of women in all relations of life save one.

The " seven Westminster men " who formed the Nonsense Club brought Cowper at least within the circle

of the literary life of the period. Among them were
Bonnel Thornton and George Colman the dramatist, who
edited, or rather wrote between them, a paper called the
Connoisseur, to which Cowper is believed to have contributed several short articles. He was thus attached to
literature as most young men of literary tastes who have
come with fair repute through their preliminary education
are so likely to be, by a link of association at least and
sympathy, and perhaps some mild pleasure in seeing
themselves in print. He wrote verses too, as so many
do, without special promise, or any indication that he
was in the future to surpass, or even to attain to an
equality with his two companions, who gave him the
chance of helping them in their more ambitious efforts.
The literary profession may be said to consist rather of
men like these, who take up the art of writing as a
trade, with considerable immediate fluency, but no particular inspiration, nor any faculty of continuance in
them, than of the greater writers, who so often fall to
their work by a different impulse altogether, often without any distinct intention in their minds, or consciousness
of what is coming. Thornton and Colman were of the
same class as that large and flourishing branch of the
profession which is now occupied in journalistic work ;
but their productions were curiously different in form.
The *Connoisseur* was one of the successors of the *Rambler*,
and Johnson himself is said to have contributed to it ;
it was a little brochure filled with little essays upon
general subjects, upon classical literature, and upon the
manners and morals of the time. A big broadsheet
such as occupies us now, full of news and political
events, had then no existence : and this was the form of
the periodical press in those days. It was the ebb of the
wave which the *Spectator* had begun, and which Johnson
had revived. Cowper contributed to the *Connoisseur* a

playful little paper upon the art of keeping secrets, just as now-a-days he might have sent a disquisition on the Irish land laws or sanitary science. The two editors, however, produced it almost entirely by their own exertions. "We have not only joined in the work taken together, but almost every single paper is the joint product of both," they announced in their concluding number; and it is curious to see the inexperienced young Templar, who was their schoolfellow, but had none of their pretensions in literature, adventuring the pen which afterwards produced work so much more important than theirs in the little essays of this short-lived periodical, without any prevision in his mind or theirs of the very different level upon which he and they should stand hereafter.

Another pair of Cowper's literary schoolfellows were Lloyd and Churchill, persons much less safe and respectable than the others, but, like them, Westminster men. Long years after, when Cowper had gone to the other extreme of feeling, and might have been supposed to be entirely alienated from a man so profane both in literature and life, he still admired Churchill and his poetry with that loyal support of the school hero, which is one of the most tenacious and faithful of prejudices. Lloyd was the son of a Westminster master, under whom Cowper had worked as a boy, and for whom he in after years wrote a touching epitaph; and he too was the editor of a little weekly periodical, the *St. James's Magazine*, which he was apparently expected to compose entirely himself, with what little gratuitous assistance he could receive from his friends. He had taken refuge in letters (so called), in this curious journalism and trade of essay-writing, as his only means of escape from the life of a schoolmaster, which he found intolerable; but the magazine was apparently more doleful drudgery still. Cowper

was also a modest contributor to this periodical.   He
wrote in it a dissertation on the modern ode, signed with
his initials ; but he is not referred to in the list of names
which are quoted in the preliminary poetical dialogue
between the author and the bookseller, nor is there the
slightest reason to believe that he was even thought of
as likely to be of serious importance in any literary
undertaking.   The following scrap, out of a rhymed letter
addressed by him to Lloyd, will show the modesty of his
own ideas, and the unobtrusive position he was acknowledged to occupy beside his friend.   It is interesting also
as giving almost the earliest intimation of that despond-
ency which later seized upon Cowper with such infernal
force :—

> " 'Tis not that I design to rob
>   Thee of thy birthright, gentle Bob.
> For thou art born sole heir, and single,
>   Of dear Mat Prior's easy jingle ;
> Not that I mean, while thus I knit
>   My threadbare sentiments together,
> To show my genius or my wit,
>   When God and you know, I have neither ;
> Or such, as might be better shown
>   By letting poetry alone.
> 'Tis not with either of these views,
>   That I presumed t' address the Muse :
> But to divert a fierce banditti,
>   (Sworn foes to everything that's witty !)
> That, with a black, infernal train,
>   Make cruel inroads in my brain,
> And daily threaten to drive thence
>   My little garrison of sense :
> The fierce banditti, which I mean,
>   Are gloomy thoughts, led on by spleen."

He was living alone in his chambers in the Temple
when these lines were written, in cheerful intercourse
with this set of clever, ingenious, and by no means strait-
laced young men, all bound together by the most natural

of ties—eyeing their perturbations and excitement with
the eye of an interested spectator, but by no means
embarking in the same risky career, or venturing upon
anything but the occasional little essay of an amateur,
doing not much of anything indeed, apparently making
no attempt to practise the profession to which he
nominally belonged ; for he had been called to the bar,
little as that meant in those days. " My resolution is,"
he says in one of his early letters to another of his youthful friends, " never to be melancholy while I have a
hundred pounds in the world to keep up my spirits."
Apparently nothing could have been more reckless and
imprudent than this happy-go-lucky existence, especially
as he proposed to follow it as a matter of principle and
philosophy.   " This provokes me," he writes, " that a
covetous dog who will work by candlelight in a morning
to get what he does not want shall be praised for his
thriftiness, while a gentleman shall be abused for sub-
mitting to his wants rather than work like an ass to
relieve them.   Did you ever in your life know a man
who was guided in the general course of his actions by
anything but his natural temper ? "   Cowper was over
thirty when he asked this pregnant question, so that it
was no bravado of extreme youth.   He was not rich
enough to live such a life, and at that age it was a somewhat wretched way to be spending those precious sands
of existence which run so quickly through careless fingers.
So far as appears he had never made an honest effort of
any kind in his life.   His money was streaming thrift-
lessly away, and so were his best years ; the schoolboy
pranks of the Nonsense Club, the *pococurante* existence
growing stale in its uselessness—and underneath all, it is
scarcely possible to doubt, an under-current of that self-
contempt which saps all energy, and engenders a listless
hopelessness not energetic enough to be called despair,

but even more dismal——were all he had to represent life.
It is scarcely possible to believe that such an existence
could have gone on without some crisis to come.

Few events in history are better known than this
crisis when it did come. The story has been told over
and over again, and almost always, so attractive is the
character of the man, with tenderness and sympathy.
As a matter of fact, he who was to glorify and idealise
the domestic routine of the most secluded life was up to
this period of mature manhood living in a way as little
praiseworthy or respectable as can be imagined, doing
nothing, attempting nothing, and shutting his eyes to the
future as far as was possible ; but the principle of his
existence afterwards was little changed, though the result
was so different. The letter from which we have quoted
is full of a subtle consciousness that his position is a
false one. His self-excuses are self-accusations——" There
is a degree of poverty which has no disgrace belonging to
it," he says ; " that degree, I mean, in which a man
enjoys clean linen and good company ; and if I never
sink below this degree of it, I care not if I ever rise
above it." But his " natural temper," that which he concludes with terrible justice to be the only rule by which
a man is ever guided, was not more entirely the inspiration of his life in the Temple, than it was of the very
different life at Olney, which he would have professed
and believed to be governed by rules entirely opposite.
He is quite consistent throughout. He would not if he
could, and, as it turned out, he could not if he would,
take his fate in his own hands. He could flow on with
the stream that caught him, whatever it might be. His
fits of insanity give a tragic piteousness to the story, and
the extreme misery involved takes all power of judgment
and wish to exercise it from the sympathetic spectator ;
but still the fact remains that Cowper had trained him-

self to incapacity, as other men do to work. He had let everything go from him ; nothing in the world, not love itself, not independence, far less ambition, were worth to him the effort of seizing them. In all probability his appointment, if it had come to him at twenty-two instead of thirty-two, would have found him by no means so tragically helpless; but this is a useless conjecture. " Many years ago, cousin," he writes, while the crisis was impending, to Lady Hesketh, " there was a possibility I might prove a very different thing from what I am at present. My character is now fixed and riveted fast upon me." Nothing could be more sad or more true.

The event which brought this aimless existence to a climax was one to which all Cowper's training, such as it was, had tended—the piece of looked-for good fortune which had been the only justification of his previous indolence. All this time a lucrative and important office had been destined for him, and the time had now come when he could enter upon it. The place of Clerk to the Journals in the House of Lords, which was in the gift of his relation, Major Cowper, fell vacant by the death of the previous occupant, while at the same time two other offices of greater value, and held conjointly, were resigned by their holder. Major Cowper, by one of those inexplicable arrangements common at that period, was " the patentee of these appointments," and he at once, as no doubt was fully expected of him, offered the best paid and most important of them to his kinsman. " Dazzled by so splendid a proposal, and not immediately reflecting upon my incapacity to execute a business of so public a nature, I at once accepted it," he says ; but the very next moment " seemed to receive a dagger in my heart." It was the lesser appointment, that of Clerk to the Journals, which he had hoped for, chiefly, as it would seem, because " the business of the place was transacted

in private ;" and as he had been, or fancied himself to
have been, so wicked as to "express an earnest wish"
for the death of the official then holding it, it was perfectly natural to him afterwards to believe that "the
spirit of a murderer" was in his heart, and that all the
misery that followed was sent to him as "an immediate
punishment of my crime." After a week of dismal
ponderings over the great prospect before him, Cowper
at last entreated his kinsman to give the better appointment to another friend, and allow him to drop into the
safer obscurity of the place he had originally desired.
This expedient laid both Major Cowper and his nominee
open to the imputation of a job, "since nothing would
be so likely to bring a suspicion of bargain and sale upon
his nomination, which the Lords would not have endured,
as his appointment of so near a relative to the least profitable office, while the most valuable was allotted to a
stranger." The risk, however, had to be run; and a
"momentary calm" took possession of Cowper's mind
when he saw this safe and quiet position behind backs
opening to him. But whether "the Lords" suspected, as
was supposed likely, a disgraceful transaction behind
(*bien entendu*, it was neither disgraceful nor undesirable
that the "patentee" should use his power for the advantage of one of his own blood, natural affection in this
important particular being fully recognised as the rule of
the public service), it is certain that an opposition arose,
and Cowper "was bid to expect an examination at the
bar of the House, touching my sufficiency for the post I
had taken." This unforeseen and unprecedented ordeal
drove him frantic. Nobody, so far as we are aware, has
instanced the proposal as a proof either of the advantages
or disadvantages of the principle of examination, which is
now the key to every door—yet it affords a curious com
mentary upon the uses of that method. It drove Cowper

into insanity ; but perhaps even in this elementary and
arbitrary stage of its existence it was beneficial in its
way. Had he stolen in quietly to his place, and reaped
its placid advantages without any such alarming preliminary, he might perhaps never have been insane, never
have gone to Olney, never written poetry to console a
spirit, which in that case might neither have been sick
nor sorry. There is no end to conjecture, and everything,
as the poet himself would have been the first to allow,
works for good. The world pays cheaply for a great
work and influence when the sufferings of one forlorn
individual are all the price that is demanded. It was
hard upon the poet, but good for the race. The "Task"
was of far more importance to the general welfare than
the happiness of one young man about town ; and his
happiness was not of a very warm or genuine description
that its temporary extinction should have called forth so
many moans.

Thus the unfortunate young man was out of the
pleasant indolence and carelessness of his unthrifty life,
plunged all unprepared and incapable into that mäelstrom
which now, under the easy title of " going in for an
examination," is so universally known to the youth of
our time. In those days slang was not, at least in this
kind ; and that fact of itself made everything more
serious. No pleasing levity, no light-hearted calculations
of chance, modified the terrible ordeal. " A thunderbolt
would have been as welcome to me as this intelligence,"
he says. " I knew to demonstration that upon these
terms the clerkship of the journals was no place for me.
To require my attendance at the bar of the House, that I
might there publicly qualify myself for the office, was in
fact to exclude me from it. In the meantime, the interest
of my friend, the honour of his choice, my own reputation
and circumstances, all urged me forward—all pressed me

to undertake that which I saw to be impracticable. They whose spirits are formed like mine, to whom a public exhibition of themselves on any occasion is mortal poison, may have some idea of the horrors of my situation: others can have none."

In this state of mind he began to study the work that would be required of him, going daily to the office, trying to extort information from the books, without help, without capacity or habit of investigation—and exposed, as he thought rightly or wrongly, to the hostility of all the inferior clerks and everybody around. The state of mind into which he gradually worked himself can, as he says, only be divined by those to whom the same conditions of mental enervation, feebleness, self-indulgence, and excited imagination are possible. The robust mind, or even that which, weak in itself, is braced by habits of self-subordination, would, but for the pity of it, be disposed to turn with a certain contempt from the pitiable sight. But the issue gives to this hopeless struggle the solemnity of a tragedy; and it is impossible to read Cowper's account of his growing madness, the gradual subjection of all his powers to the one fixed horror, from which he could not escape, the gloomy door of suicide that seemed to open and shut, as by a fitful wind, in front of him; his attempts, always feeble, and restrained by the very weakness that moved him to it, to push that door wide, and make his frightened exit thereby —without feeling the strange fascination of the struggle. A hunted soul in restless conflict with its own delusions, sometimes flying before the dark crowd of excited fancies which might be spirits of darkness for anything he could tell or see, sometimes standing miserably at bay; the world shut out from that strange solitude in which he moved alone, turning every incident vaguely perceived through the mist, every encounter of men's faces and

voices, into agents in the chase to which he was subject,
driving him nearer and nearer to the precipice—this
strange and wild picture forms the greatest contrast to
the tranquil pictures he was to leave to us as his contribution to the wealth of England ; but it has in it a force
of passionate feeling which they do not possess, and which
will always make it painfully interesting to the student
of humanity and life.

And nothing can be more strange than to realise the
background of busy and cheerful and trivial existence
upon which this agony stands out. The Nonsense Club
continued its existence as long at least as Cowper kept
above water, and its pranks were sometimes amusing
enough. Among them was an exhibition of signboards,
got up by Thornton in ridicule of the annual exhibitions
of pictures which preceded the establishment of the Royal
Academy and its yearly show. It may be easily imagined
how the names of taverns would lend themselves to this
facile joke, and all the fun that might be got out of it—
fun of a poor order, but yet suiting the broad and easy
fancy of the time, and in which Hogarth, the master of a
mode of expression more terrible and withering than this,
took a part. And the little company of wits who were
Cowper's chief companions were writing their little essays
and composing their verses, and as busy about their
magazines as if the existence of the world depended upon
the getting up of so many monthly pages, while he was
going through all this delirious struggle. No doubt these
young adventurers thought him better off than any of
them, and envied his fate, with his competence to step
into, and his powerful friends behind him. One of them
came to see him at the very blackest of the struggle, to
congratulate him—just after in the revulsion of his distracted heart he had flung the laudanum out of the window.
" We conversed awhile with a real cheerfulness on his

part, and an affected one on mine ; and when he left me
I said in my heart, I shall see him no more." The other
Westminster lads who had been at school with him, had,
to all appearance, a great deal more cause for uneasiness
than Cowper : Lloyd breaking down under his work—
Churchill writing violent and powerful verse, in bad
odour with the authorities, and wretched in remorseful
vice at home—were both drawing near the end of their
tragedy, and were in every external respect far more to be
pitied than their old schoolfellow. They died about a
year after, the one of a broken heart for the loss of the
other, having wasted their faculties, and stained their
names in the brief career through which they had stormed
so wildly. Churchill was exactly Cowper's age, his
friend a little younger. And thus they dropped before
either was half-way over the path of life. On the other
hand Colman had turned his efforts to the stage, and had
become a successful writer of plays, a friend of Garrick.
At the same time, though altogether outside of this little
society, Goldsmith was going through his serio-comic
troubles, impounded by his landlady, liberated by Johnson,
writing some of the most immortal works of the age, but
smiled if not laughed at by all the contemporaries who
were so much wiser than the reckless Irishman, who
" wrote like an angel, and talked like poor Poll." It is
curious that the two circles should have flourished so
near to each other without touching, and that no echo of
Johnson's heavy foot and autocratic speech should have
sounded into the precincts in which Cowper was inclosed.
Yet from Fleet Street to the Temple was not far, and no
doubt the sweet-tempered and courteous young idler from
that hive of gaiety and folly, wit and wisdom, must have
stood aside upon the busy pavement many a time, while
the big frame of " the great lexicographer " lumbered
along, scarcely guided by his dim eyes. But they might

have been in different worlds for all we hear mutually of
their existence—Cowper, always the very embodiment of
gentle manners and suave consideration, was very probably repelled by Johnson's rude superiority—and Goldsmith's vanity and swagger would be still less to the
taste of the well-born and fastidious gentleman. They
would seem never to have crossed each other—a thing
which gives us a strange perception of the coteries into
which London was divided.

It was on the very morning of the day on which he
was to make his appearance at the bar of the House of
Lords for the dreaded examination, that Cowper made
his last and most strenuous effort at suicide. The previous ones had been but intentions, but this was carried
the length of action, and when it failed by the breaking
of the cord with which he had hanged himself, the unfortunate young man, on recovering consciousness, sent
with the courage of desperation for his kinsman and
patron. Major Cowper seems to have been as prompt as
his young relation was weak. He asked at once for the
papers of nomination, and carried them off with him on
the spot. And so the dreaded ordeal was averted, but
not the consequences of all this excitement and misery.
The one immediate cause of anguish being removed,
Cowper's mind, now thoroughly astray, and excited into
a habit of self-torture, sought about it for another. It
was only then that his sufferings took the turn of religion.
The magnitude of the sin he had been about to commit
suddenly became evident to him, and the misery of earthly
panic turned into an agony of remorse. He had " felt no
concern of a spiritual kind up to this time "—but now
the sense of the crime he had almost committed seized
upon him like a lion. In every book he opened—not
the Bible only, but every printed page, even those of the
old dramatists—he found some winged words which trans-

fixed him. Never man had been so guilty—never man had sinned so terribly. God was against him and all good angels, as well as men. He had committed the unpardonable sin, the sin against the Holy Ghost. Life was better than death, only because it delayed a little the burning fire of eternal punishment. This gradually heightening horror, coming not from without but within, rolling upwards in heavy vapours that hid both sky and sun, out of his perturbed and anguished being, came at last the length of unmistakable madness. While he was still capable of some effort of mind he sent for a friend and family connection, Martin Madan, who was one of the new sect of Evangelicals, roused by Wesley and his associates to make a new and much-needed revolution in the religious life of the country, and got some temporary consolation from him; but the evil by this time had gone too far to be cured. A copy of Sapphics, to which he gave vent at this terrible moment, places before us in tuneless tumultuous lines the horror that possessed his soul. Not poetry but misery produced them; he had not as yet found out the way to speak in his own voice and manner. A forlorn echo of his studies, the artificial utterance of the schools had to suffice him in his wretchedness.

> " Hatred and vengeance,—my eternal portion
> Scarce can endure delay of execution,
> Wait with impatient readiness to seize my
> Soul in a moment.
>
> " Damned below Judas ; more abhorred than he was
> Who for a few pence sold his holy Master !
> Twice betrayed, Jesus, me, the last delinquent
> Deems the profanest.
>
> " Man disavows and Deity disowns me,
> Hell might afford my miseries a shelter ;
> Therefore, Hell keeps her ever-hungry mouths all
> Bolted against me."

"It will be proper," he says, "to draw a veil over the secrets of my prison-house." It would be a curious question, could we in pity for the woeful spectacle thus set before us, have the heart to investigate it, how much the habit of continual self-reference and unconscious egotism have to do with this peculiar form of mental disease. Individual character is far more involved in intellectual aberration than most people are disposed to admit, and it is our conviction that self-will and self-love will almost invariably be found at the bottom of such failures of the brain. A man of generous temper and large heart — one habitually more occupied with the happiness and comfort of others than with his own, has an armour of proof against this mysterious and terrible disease. But Cowper had laid himself open to its attacks; he had lived the life of a careless egotist for years. He had let everything go from him rather than make the necessary effort to secure anything; and, accordingly, he was quite defenceless when the strain came.

And it was all the more miserable that his malady should have taken a religious form, from the fact that the newly awakened religious feeling of the age was almost entirely introspective. Wesley had awakened his countrymen to a consciousness that this world was not everything—that the unseen and eternal were not only of some importance, but of supreme importance, far exceeding the seen and temporal; but he had not stopped there. He had turned the current of religious feeling, both within and without his own community, into the channel of severe and constant self-examination. He had taught his disciples—and almost every pious person of the time was more or less his disciple—to weigh every feeling and impulse which arose in their minds, and to allow no movement of the affections or fancy to escape their scrutiny. They were intent (in theory) upon them-

selves as a surgeon is on the subject he is dissecting.
The simile is unsavoury, but we know no other so exact.
Such a theory is by nature injurious only to the few individuals who are predisposed to enter into its full meaning. Most men have too many clogs of flesh and blood
about them, too many sympathies and emotions, too much
instinctive and unreasoning confidence in the God that
made them, to be driven frantic by it; and accordingly,
the good it does to the mass, by teaching them the profound importance of right feelings, motives, and wishes,
and by putting spiritual religion in its true place, as
something above and beyond mere external observances,
is probably tenfold more than the harm it has done in
creating the sin of spiritual selfishness. But Cowper had
not the safeguards that protect the mass of humanity.
This form of religion tended to increase by every means,
and as it were to legitimatise and give a heavenly sanc-
tion to those habits of mind from which his madness
came. To cure him of that tragic self-importance which
made him perceive in himself a kind of antagonist to
God, pursued implacably by divine wrath and contended
for by all the powers of darkness—an enemy so important that heaven departed from its usual rules and made
war against him *à outrance*—the religion of his day set
him to self-examination. It taught him to regard God as
perpetually watchful of his smallest movements, noting
everything with a vigilant eye, more easily angered than
a jealous woman, insisting on a share in every thought.
Instead of the " larger, other eyes than ours," with which
the gentler philosophy of to-day endows even the departed
spirits of human race, the sign of God's greatness to
Wesley and to Newton was the minuteness of His all-
inspection, the ceaseless, breathless watch He kept upon
every word and every thought. And when it is fully
realised what this means; when the reader represents to

himself the effect upon a sensitive mind of such a constant unremitting surveillance; when he thinks of the
poor solitary half-insane human creature feeling himself
surrounded by the austere, all-penetrating light of eyes
that watch him waking and sleeping, watch him in his
weakness, in his dreams, at the table, among his books,
whatever he does or thinks or says, taking account of
everything and laying up an awful score of uncon-
sidered sins against the judgment day,—can he wonder
that Cowper's madness came back again and again, and
was the persistent shadow of his life? This was how the
most pious men of his time regarded God. It is how
human nature, at all times, is most apt to regard Him,
being so seldom able to divest itself of a deep consciousness of guilt towards Him. These men spoke much of the
Saviour and spiritual joy; but it did not occur to them
that God's loving and large comprehension of our confused ways and works must be not less but infinitely
more indulgent and tender than that of any man. Yet
this was the theory of existence which such a mind as
Cowper's wanted, and in which was its only hope.

He was placed under the charge of Dr. Cotton in St.
Alban's, an excellent physician, a good man, and, according to the fashion of his time, a creditable poet, who
sympathised as deeply with his religious anxieties as a
perfectly sane man could do, and did what he could to
help the anguished spirit not only by medical care and
treatment, but by spiritual counsel. It is impossible for
us to discriminate in such a case the delicate line which
separates disease of the body from trouble of the soul,
but at the same time it is very difficult (though it happens
to be the fashion of the present moment) to obliterate
that line altogether, and accept Cowper's malady as purely
physical. To say of his recovery what his latest biographer, Mr. Goldwin Smith, says, in an essay which is

discriminative and just on most points—that Cowper's recovery " was brought about, as we can plainly see, by medical treatment wisely applied ; but it came in the form of a burst of religious faith and hope,"—seems to us somewhat absurd, and not a little unscientific, though supposed to be in accordance with the latest scientific tenets. At the best it is but a conjecture that religious faith and hope can be produced by a regulation of the digestive organs. Few people manage to buy happiness even in smaller matters by such inexpensive means. However, by whatsoever means attained—in all probability by many means acting together—by calm, and the absence of causes of external irritation ; by the wearing out of the paroxysm of insane delusion, by the soothing influence of religious intercourse: and, finally, by that inexplicable power which nobody may understand, but which it is impossible to ignore—called grace, conversion, light from heaven, by the associates whom Cowper now chiefly prized, and only very lamely and vaguely accounted for by the philosophers as a reformed digestion—the sick man got well. He did more than get well ; a tremulous and exquisite happiness took the place of his anguish and despair. We may safely say that if any physician could promise to his patients by any kind of physical treatment, such a result of blessedness as that attained by this weak and troubled spirit, no sanitary establishment in the world would be so crowded, no ministrant to the mind diseased so richly and amply rewarded as that physician would be.

Had his history ended here, it would scarcely have been more remarkable than that of a host of converts whose transition from a profane and secular to a religious life, has been marked by not unsimilar agonies. But Cowper was not altogether delivered, and his career had still many dark vicissitudes. He was " converted " and

happy, but he had still the same indolent and unoccupied
being, the same limited sphere of gentle self-absorption,
as before; and never escaped out of that narrow circle
into the wider influences even of a family, where egotism
has at least the excuse of being doubled or quadrupled,
and where self must give way to other selves, if not to
any broad rule of generous self-abandonment. He was
two years at St. Alban's under the charge of Dr. Cotton;
and when he leaves that scene of his sufferings and recovery there is a touching air of subdued tranquillity and
convalescence about him, which forms a tender background
to the ecstasies which have now taken the place of his
former fits of intolerable anguish. He came to Huntingdon in the year 1765. No particular reason seems to
have influenced his brother in making choice of this place
of residence for him, except that it was near—and happily
not too near—to Cambridge, where John Cowper, the only
surviving member of the family, a Fellow of his college,
usually resided. He was a kind brother, but probably
he was not prepared to take upon him the entire charge
of such an invalid, or to wear out his own spirit with the
constant sight of one who had become an embarrassment
to all his friends. Huntingdon was near enough to permit
frequent visits—the brothers saw each other every week,
we are told—but it was not too near. There was not at
this time any sympathy between them on the religious
topics of which William Cowper's mind was now full.
His brother contemplated his new rapture, as he had
contemplated his former sufferings, with the uneasiness
of a spectator who was by no means sure that there was
not something more important than all else in heaven and
earth, in those convulsions of the spirit—which, nevertheless, were madness to his common sense, and offensive
to the beliefs he had held during all his life. Four
years later, John Cowper was himself converted, and died

with something of the same rapture of religious certainty
which now and then glorified his brother's life.

This choice, however, so inadvertent as it seems to
have been, of Huntingdon as the future home of the con-
valescent, led to remarkable results. Here Cowper dropped
apparently by hazard into the strange little dull town
(yet not so dull either; but possessed of diversions such as
put the economy of little towns in our own day to shame),
without introductions, without an acquaintance, found
what he might have sought over a whole world without
finding, had he sought it consciously—the one friend in
the world from whom he was never to be separated more.
It seems a strange kind of discipline for an invalid, to
set him down thus in an obscure corner, without occupation, or amusement, or companions; but in all likelihood his friends were at their wits' end what to do with
him, and glad to have him peaceably put out of sight
anywhere, as the kindest friends are apt to do with an
amiable but impracticable dependant of this class. Cowper had been proved incapable of taking care of himself,
or enduring the ordinary struggles of life; he had not
nearly enough to live on, yet he was expensive and generous in a way which no man without money has a right
to be. He had a man-servant in attendance upon him,
and he had also taken up and was providing for a boy
who had interested him. Most likely all the Cowpers,
though very kind and faithful to him, were thankful that
he should be safely withdrawn out of the way. And his
friends in London seem either to have dropped from him,
or been dropped by him, in the time of his illness. The
only one with whom he continued to correspond was
Joseph Hill, one of the least-known members of the
Nonsense Club, an undistinguished, good man, who had
taken charge of his friend's affairs and stood by him all
his life. Nonsense Clubs and all such follies were far

from Cowper's thoughts now. His cousin, Lady Hesketh, the sister of Theodora, who had always been his faithful friend, resumed correspondence with him when he re-emerged out of the cloud. But except these two and his brother, he brought no old alliances with him out of his former life. He was the more ready for the new tie which awaited him here.

A great deal has been said about the poet's connection with Mrs. Unwin, and perhaps the greater proportion of the public from his day to this have entertained the idea that the love between them was more or less the love of lovers, and that it might (and in the opinion of many ought to) have led to marriage. Except one statement brought forward by Mr. Benham in the biography pre-fixed to the Globe edition of Cowper's works—a state-ment of something which Mr. Bull remembered to have "heard his father say," backed by an extract from an unpublished diary of Newton's—there seems no evidence, except that he was a man and she a woman, for this idea. The relations between them were evidently as calm, as sober, and as simply affectionate as if their bond had been one not of choice but of nature. And in all the revela-tions of himself and his ways which he poured forth dur-ing their long companionship—revelations in which the most sacred things of life are conjoined with the most trivial—there is not one word which could lend the most far-away support to this notion. Not the least shade of shyness or self-consciousness is upon either of the friends : their connection was so simply a matter of fact, so clearly recognised by all who belonged to them on both sides, exciting no jealousy or alarm on either, that nothing but the popular prejudice against the possibility of such friendship could, in our opinion, have suggested the thought. It is the most perfect example on record of a relationship so difficult, yet so beautiful ; and perhaps only under circumstances so peculiar—circumstances in which the man owed everything to the woman, and never was otherwise than dependent upon her support and affection—could it be possible to maintain it. The vulgar mind rejects it altogether, and the experienced though not vulgar, doubt; but it begins to be more possible in the present day, when our Protestant deification of marriage has ceased to be polemical, to realise the existence of a class which is celibate by nature, and neither wishes nor requires to marry—a class to which, we are convinced, Cowper belonged. The reader, perhaps, will always decide the question according to his own bias, but we by no means agree that it is settled by the piece of evidence above quoted. Here is a man most voluminous in letter-writing, who has babbled (charmingly, delightfully, in a way few men can do—yet the word is not unjust) about everything that happened to him, great and small. Yet we have to wait a century, until somebody chooses to print an extract from a friend's diary, for information of what might have been the most important step in his life. However, we do not suppose that argument is likely to affect the question one way or another

When Cowper first made acquaintance with the Unwins, Mr. Unwin was still alive, and the family consisted of four persons, son and daughter, as well as the father and mother. His first friend was the son; but it was the mother always whose society attracted him the most. " She and I walked together near two hours in the garden, and had a conversation which did me more good than I should have received from an audience of the first prince in Europe. That woman is a blessing to me, and I never see her without being the better for her company," he says. He was thus brought within reach of an influence which was more suited to his wants than any other. He who at fifty could say that his mother,

whom he lost at six, had never been out of his thoughts
for a week together, thus recovered in a moment the
maternal aid of which his enfeebled life stood in need.
It is ridiculous to speak of the relationship of mother
and son, between a man of thirty-six and a woman of
forty-three; but so are many other things ridiculous,
which at the same time are the source of great individual
happiness.   There are cases in which a very young woman
is capable of occupying the position of a mother to
brothers and sisters who may even be older than herself.
Mrs. Unwin took this feeble soul in hand, not in the
right of superior strength, but of benignity and kindness,
understanding all that he most wanted.   He had no
woman belonging to him, no one to whom he could give
the thousand confidences which, kept within himself,
wounded and overwhelmed him—and to whom he could
look for that sympathy, which penetrated to every act of
his life and every crevice of his thoughts.   She did not
ask more than he could give in return.   His shy bachelor-
hood was never invaded.   Till their last breath he was
Mr. Cowper to the serene matron, who was his Mary,
the object of a perpetual claim and demand on his part,
the claim of weakness and dependence.   But one great
charm of the relationship to such a man no doubt lay in
the fact that there was no balancing claim upon her
side.   She wanted nothing from him but the tranquil
companionship which was his happiness.

When her husband died the two were left alone
together, the son going out into life into a sphere of his
own, the daughter marrying, and following her husband
and separate fortunes.   The widow and her harmless
lodger chose Olney as their place of refuge, not from any
attraction in the dull and unlovely village, but for the
sake of John Newton, the curate of the place—a man
who belongs to the history of literature in one of its

lesser walks, but whose strong and notable individuality
has more to do with the religious excitement of the time
than with any other of its developments. He was the
true type of a converted sinner turned into a saint; a
man of strong character and ceaseless activity, whose
early life had gone through all manner of violent changes.
His stormy youth had veered from the pious exercises
taught him by his mother, to the rude infidelity which
was the first reaction from it. He had gone to sea at
eleven, in the collier smack of which his father was the
skipper; had been impressed under the horrible system
then existing, and after various experiences in the pan-
demonium of a man-o'-war, had entered the slave service;
and without any special perception of the evils of that
abominable trade, had serenely commanded a slaver for
several voyages before illness and some dislike of his profession induced him to return home. Nothing would
serve this energetic person then—having already gone
through all the preliminaries of conversion, and being as
determined, as vehement, and as powerful in this new
development as he had been in the old—but to enter
the Church of England, and take part in the Evangelical
crusade then organising everywhere, and universally
opposed by all that thought itself cultivated or learned
in society. When he at last attained his desire he
became curate of the little Buckinghamshire town, where,
among the lace-workers and straw-plaiters there was
much work to be done, and much reformation needed.
Newton wrote some spiritual treatises, and had a principal part in the collection of Olney hymns, familiar to
the Evangelical party, and the Dissenters who fraternised
with it for many years. His acquaintance with Cowper
and Mrs. Unwin was of recent date. He had gone to
see them at a moment when their hearts were very open
to sympathy, immediately after Mr. Unwin's death; and

probably out of pity for their forlorn condition, and with an impetuous adoption of them as fellow-saints and congenial spirits, had immediately proposed to take a house for them at Olney, where they could have the consolation of his own spiritual counsel and direction. The attraction must have been great on both sides, for an extreme intimacy, as of members of one family, arose at once between them.

They settled accordingly at Olney. The life the family had lived at Huntingdon had been almost monastic in its routine. Two hours of religious reading or converse in the morning, then morning prayer in church, then religious conversation in the evening, and a concert of hymns to wind up with, had been their regular daily round—a routine which discloses as much absolute leisure and power to do as they pleased, as devotional feeling. But in Olney the time spent in devotion was greatly increased. Instead of the morning service came infinite preaching, prayer meetings in which Cowper himself, notwithstanding his natural timidity and horror of all public appearances, was constantly called upon to officiate, and visiting of the sick and poor. Newton thus inspired his new parishioner to undertake duties more difficult and alarming than those which he had been unable to face, and for fear of which he had all but destroyed himself in London; and it would be difficult to imagine anything more absorbing than such a routine. An infinity of small duties and observances are, next to hard work, the most complete of common expedients for satisfying the restless. Cowper became wholly absorbed in this ceaseless round. Nothing was talked of, nothing thought of, but saving souls and urging the careless over the threshold of conversion. For such an object, what pains could be too much? Cowper was made solemnly happy by the conversion of his brother, though grieved by that brother's death; but what, indeed, could have happened better to him or to any man than to be snatched into heaven, in all the freshness and bloom of feeling, at the moment almost when his darkness was turned into light! Newton furnished the energy, the movement, the power, which was necessary to keep the whole in motion. There was a door made in the wall which separated Cowper's house from that of his friend. Into that life of narrow yet lofty aspiration, where perpetual meditation, prayer, and the pernicious researches of self-examination, were enlivened only by those little bits of village gossip which now represented all the outside world to the cultivated mind and tender sportive fancy of a man once used to surroundings so different—Cowper was more and more closely shut up. He became a kind of curate to his energetic companion, who probably had not the slightest idea of the risk the gentler soul beside him was running. The pot of iron and the pot of porcelain thus swayed along together upon the quickening stream till finally the crash came.

It was in 1771, ten years after his first attack, that the second overwhelmed him. Up to this time his estrangement from all interests but those of the parish and religious life had gradually grown and increased. He who had taken so warm an interest in all passing events, that he "leaped for joy" at the news of "Boscawen's success," and whose "rapture nothing could express when Wolfe made the conquest of Quebec," says coldly now—" Whether the nation is worshipping Mr. Wilkes or any other idol is of little moment to one who hopes and believes he shall shortly stand in the presence of the great and blessed God;" he whose power of letter-writing has by many critics been considered almost as remarkable as his poetry, sends a brief spare note, half-a-dozen lines and no more, with long intervals between, to the one only friend, Joseph Hill, who still insisted upon writing to him. He read little, having no books, nor any time to give to them. Now and then he wrote a few hymns for Newton's collection, and obeyed Newton's will, and followed Newton's ways, with a miserable docility. The lurking demon which pursued him was not long in taking advantage of circumstances so congenial. Cowper was in the vicarage when the final outburst came, and such was the obstinacy of the attack, that months elapsed before he could be got to return to his house, though it was only next door—an extraordinary trial of his friend's affection. We have no particular account of the events of this terrible time. Newton was overwhelmed with sorrow and sympathy—a sympathy which was naturally soon tinctured by a sense of the extraordinary burden thus cast upon him. Mrs. Unwin alone stood by the man who had thrown himself like a child upon her companionship; uttering no word out of the terrible vigil, making no attempt to deliver herself; wearing her life out in attendance upon him, in humouring all his sick fancies, and watching all his troubled ways.

Cowper recovered from this second attack as a child might have recovered from a severe illness, with no rapture of light and joy such as attended his former recovery, but a gentle and languid return to the possibility of existence. He came slowly to life out of doors. The spiritual and intellectual man which had been strained to death dropped from him, and a harmless gentle creature, with the tastes of a child, came out into the silent sunshine instead. He pruned the trees, he fed the fowls, smiling, "for the first time for sixteen months," at some touch of nature among them. When he at last consented to go home, the flickering life grew a little stronger; he became a carpenter, made bird-cages and tables, and built himself a greenhouse, like a boy come

home for the holidays. "As long as he is occupied,"
says Newton, "he is tolerably easy." As the process
advanced he tried a little drawing, and, when he began
to approach complete amendment, books. But he was
not fully restored (if, indeed, he can ever have been said
to be fully restored) until his spiritual director was
removed from Olney. It seems almost cruel to the real
friendship and affection subsisting between them, to note
the new spring which came to Cowper as soon as he was
left to himself. Probably he was quite unconscious of
it, and the friendship remained as warm as ever; but the
fact is certain that Newton was no sooner out of the way
than the first break appeared in the sky of the poet.
Newton left Olney in the end of 1779, and in May
1780 Cowper sent to his friend Hill, with whom he had
resumed correspondence, a copy of the pleasant verses
entitled "Report of an Adjudged Case not to be found
in any of the Books;" the case of "Nose *versus* Eyes."
The coincidence is singular, if it is no more; and it is
singular, too, to note the innocent unconscious hypocrisy
with which he keeps up to Newton the semblance of
entire darkness after the invasion of this spark of light.
The interposition of "a sportive thought" is, he says,
" as if harlequin should intrude himself into the ghastly
chamber where a corpse is deposited in state "— a saying
which his biographers in general take for a proof of the
continuance of his darker mood, but which looks much
more like that maintenance of the habitual gloom expected from a sufferer, which is one of the commonest
and most excusable traits of humanity. " You think I
am merry, and have got over it," we all say when we
are surprised by our first laugh; "but if you only knew
how my outward appearance mocks the woe within."
Thus Cowper kept on his sables, his melancholy countenance, knowing that these glooms would gain him a certain

credit in his friends' eyes which a laugh would dissipate;
but, all the same, felt the warm tide of renewed life
stealing into his heart.

And now there dawned upon him brighter days—
the brightest days in his life. He begins not only to
write to his friends, but to send verses to them; now
sportive, now moralising, but all disclosing a new tide
in his mind. His letters to Newton still display, with
a certain half-sad, half-amusing persistency, the black
mask of woe unutterable in which that friend had been
accustomed to see him; but he puts it on to no other of
his correspondents. Thus, while he writes to Unwin of
his favourite pursuits, it is in cheerfulest tones. " I
never received a little pleasure in my life; if I am
delighted, it is in the extreme;" but he recurs to the
fictitious solemnity habitual to their intercourse when he
tells Newton of the very same pleasures, assuring him
that when he has paid his greenhouse, his latest toy,
" the accustomed visit, and watered it and given it air, I
say to myself—' This is not mine, it is a plaything lent
me for the present; I must leave it soon.'" The solemnity here is almost ludicrous; he could not have spoken
more seriously had " the plaything lent him" been a
favourite child. But it becomes amusing to note this
entire change of tone according to the correspondent. It
is as if Newton and Cowper were compelled to use a
different language from that of ordinary men, and kept
up their proficiency in it, as they might have done with
a foreign tongue, by practising it between themselves.
But in the meantime his bondage to unnatural duties
was over, and all about him learned to humour and
soothe, no longer to make claims upon, the gentle invalid.
How to keep him amused and quietly employed was now
the chief problem, not how to make use of him, and turn
his gifts and graces to account.

This then was the training which made a poet of
Cowper, one of the most popular in England—in his way
a transforming influence, a new beginning of intellectual
life and power. Had we been left to conjecture what
lines of education would have been the best on which to
raise up for us the precursor of a new poetical age, certainly these are not the lines which we would have
chosen. Nor, had we been asked to prophesy what were
the works to be expected from a man so exceptionally
circumstanced—with a past so strangely chequered, a
future so painfully uncertain, a mind so sensitive, and
which had passed through so many passionate struggles
—could we have hit upon anything half so unlikely as
the actual issue. What we should have looked for would
have been some profound and morbid study of a despairing soul, some terrible pictures like those of Job, some
confusion of gloomy skies and storms, and convulsions of
nature. That anatomy of the heart which he gives us in
his various narratives of his own feelings, that minute
dissection of quivering nerve and tissue, would have been
what we should have looked for in his poetry. But lo,
when the moment came, and the prophet was softly
persuaded and guided into the delivery of his burden, it
was no such wild exposition of the terrors and pangs of
the soul that came to his lips. These heavy vapours
melted and dispersed from the infinite sweet blueness of
the heavens : he forgot himself as if he had never been
—and forgot all those miseries of the imagination, those
bitter pangs and sorrows, the despair and darkness through
which he had stumbled blindly for years. A soft and
genial freedom entered into his soul, involuntary smiles
came to him, light to his eyes, and to his steps such
wandering careless grace, such devious gentle ways, as no
one had dreamed of. The country through which the
lazy Ouse meandered was new-discovered by the new

poet. It was a torpid, flat, damp midland district; and
he a convulsed and sorrow-stricken soul. But ere any
one knew the dull fields turned into a fresh and fragrant
landscape, a homely sweet epitome of nature, and the
man into a new see-er according to the ancient meaning
of the word, a spectator full of that happy wonder and
surprise as at a new sight never revealed to man before,
which is the privilege of genius. Something miraculous
is in every such revelation. In Cowper it was doubly
so ; for this new country which he discovered, like Col-
umbus, was old and familiar, and himself long past all
the novelties of life.

His first beginning, however, belonged more to the
old generation in which he was born than the new, for
which he was to prepare the way. It was at the suggestion of Mrs. Unwin, urgently seeking occupation for
her patient, and tremulously hopeful that making poetry,
even better than making bird-cages would draw him out
of himself, that he began the composition of something
more important than fugitive verses. It seems to have
been necessary for Cowper to have a suggestion from
some one to impel him into every exertion, and no doubt
in that religious circle it was said and thought that great
good might be done, and the best of all causes advanced
by poetical discussion of the evils abroad in the world
and the cure for them. He was disabled from Evangelical
work in the personal way, but here was something which
he could do. He took up the suggestion with so much
relish that his first volume was entirely written in the
cold and gloomy winter days, between December and
March, probably the time of the year which alarmed his
kind nurses most. It was composed of several poems on
abstract subjects—the " Progress of Error," " Truth,"
" Expostulation," " Hope," " Charity," " Retirement," and
" Conversation "—with a poetical dialogue called " Table

Talk," which was supposed to be the most light and amusing, in the front, to beguile the public into the more serious moralities behind. The poetical importance of these productions was small, and there was no novelty either in the treatment or in the subjects to call for special attention. Had he written no more, he would scarcely have found a place with his biographer Hayley, and would have been far from reaching the elevation of his school-fellows Lloyd or Churchill—both of them dead nearly twenty years before. "These poems," says a record of the day, "are written by Mr. Cowper of the Inner Temple, who seems to be a man of a sober and religious tone of mind, with a benevolent heart and a serious wish to inculcate the precepts of morality. He is not, however, possessed of any superior abilities, or the power of genius requisite for so arduous an undertaking." Daring though this seems, it was not any such instance of critical temerity as the attempted slaughter, in later times, of Wordsworth or Keats. The reviewer had solid reason for his opinion. Good sense and virtuous feeling, with a somewhat sectarian onslaught upon phases of society, of which the poet knew little or nothing, charac- terise these efforts. They are like their titles, essays in verse, containing nothing that had not been said before, nothing that gave any promise of the new fountain of poetry, which was about to spring in so unlooked-for a spot. It may be curious, however, in a literary history, to give the summary made by this respectable and sober Mr. Cowper of the Inner Temple, of the history of literature—

> "Ages elapsed ere Homer's lamp appeared,
> And ages ere the Mantuan swan was heard,
> To carry nature lengths unknown before,
> To give a Milton birth, ask'd ages more.
> Thus genius rose and set at order'd times,
> And shot a day-spring into distant climes,

Ennobling ev'ry region that he chose,
He sunk in Greece, in Italy he rose,
And tedious years of Gothic darkness pass'd,
Emerged all splendour in our isle at last.
Thus lovely Halcyons dive into the main,
Then show far off their shining plumes again.

　　　　•　　　•　　•　　•　　•　　•

In front of these came Addison.　In him
Humour in holiday and sightly trim,
Sublimity and Attic taste, combined
To polish, furnish, and delight the mind.
Then Pope, as harmony itself exact,
In verse well disciplin'd, complete, compact,
Gave virtue and morality a grace
That, quite eclipsing pleasure's painted face,
Levied a tax of wonder and applause,
Ev'n on the fools that trampled on their laws.
But he (his musical finesse was such,
So nice his ear, so delicate his touch)
Made poetry a mere mechanic art,
And ev'ry warbler has his tune by heart.
Nature imparting her satiric gift,
Her serious mirth to Arbuthnot and Swift,
With droll sobriety they raised a smile
At folly's cost, themselves unmoved the while.
That constellation set, the world in vain
Must hope to look upon their like again.
　　A. Are we then left—B. Not wholly in the dark,
Wit now and then, struck smartly, shows a spark,
Sufficient to redeem the modern race
From total night and absolute disgrace.
While servile trick and imitative knack
Confine the million in the beaten track,
Perhaps some courser, who disdains the road,
Snuffs up the wind and flings himself abroad.
　　Contemporaries all surpass'd, see one,
Short his career, indeed, but ably run.
Churchill, himself unconscious of his pow'rs,
In penury consumed his idle hours,
And, like a scatter'd seed at random sown,
Was left to spring by vigour of his own.
Lifted at length by dignity of thought,
And dint of genius to an affluent lot,

> He laid his head in luxury's soft lap,
> And took too often there his easy nap.
> If brighter beams than all he threw not forth,
> 'Twas negligence in him, not want of worth.
> Surly and slovenly and bold and coarse,
> Too proud for art, and trusting in mere force,
> Spendthrift alike of money and of wit,
> Always at speed and never drawing bit,
> He struck the lyre in such a careless mood,
> And so disdain'd the rules he understood,
> The laurel seem'd to wait on his command,
> He snatch'd it rudely from the muse's hand."

The reader will perceive that Cowper has no recollection of Shakspeare in the list of " lovely halcyons " reappearing in their shining plumes from the main : but on the other hand, that he has enough of critical discrimination to see the harm that Pope had done to poetry, leaving the " tune " which every warbler could get by heart to check all inspirations. It is a curious symptom, however, of the stagnation in which his mind had lain during his long seclusion, or of the still clinging prejudice of his schoolboy days, that all these twenty years had not modified his opinion of Churchill, or made his lineaments less heroic in the eyes of this other Westminster boy.

To see our poet calmly putting forth this little volume, so commonplace, so didactic, so entirely innocent of any prevision of the stream that was to be opened so soon in the desert, is one of the strangest things in literature. He himself was as little aware of what was coming as anybody else could be. Though he could complain of the tune that every warbler got by heart, he yet jogged on to its measure in an imperfect rendering, with an almost stolid incapacity to perceive that he too was following the hackneyed method. There was never a more remarkable instance of how little a man may know of himself and his own powers. So far as can be seen, he was not dissatisfied with his production, and it is doubtful whether he ever knew how long a distance there was between these didactic essays and the much greater work that followed. Many passages, however, in them have become the common property of the world. The story of the disciples on the road to Emmaus, the contrast between the woman who " knew, and knew no more, her Bible true," and the " brilliant Frenchman "— with several other passages, have got among the classic commonplaces of quotation; but whether this would have been the case had not their author become also the author of the " Task," it is difficult to tell. And though his first volume made little or no impression at the time, it became afterwards one of those books, perhaps the most widely popular of all books, which a religious community ventures to adopt as at once amusing and edifying. For such an audience, the cottager who was so much better than Voltaire was a matchless picture. She sits before us with her little mob-cap and her pillow, twisting her bobbins in the pretty frontispiece of an old edition : the comparison was one to dazzle and delight a whole community, to whom it was sweet to see Voltaire set down as he deserved, and the simple believer elevated. The same reason added to the popularity of the " Task." There is no such secret for making literature popular.

At this time, without expectation or warning, a new influence came into Cowper's life. The legend goes that he saw two ladies from his window shopping in the little street of Olney, one of whom was the wife of a neighbouring clergyman; and that he was so much struck by the appearance of the other, that he moved Mrs. Unwin to ask them to tea. Lady Austen " waived ceremony and paid the first visit " in any case. She was " the sister of Mrs. Jones," and the widow of some undistinguished baronet. After the invitation to tea, Cowper

took fright, and had to be coaxed and persuaded to enter
the room in which the guests were; but on making the
venture, plunged at once into that sudden fervour of
intimacy to which shy people are liable. He was not a
famous poet in those days, but a poor invalid recluse,
with a shadow of madness and misery about him, whose
story was inevitably known to all his neighbours, and
about whom there could be no delusion possible; but
though all this is against the theory that a brilliant,
lively, charming, and very likely fanciful woman, such as
Lady Austen seems to have been, meant to marry him,
it is quite enough to explain the compassionate interest
rapidly ripening into warm friendship which moved her·
at first. Men like Cowper are always interesting to
women, and there can be little doubt that, in the dull
neighbourhood of Olney, such company and conversation
as his would be a godsend to any visitor from livelier
scenes. When the new alliance went so far as to induce
her to settle in Olney in the adjoining house, with that
famous door in the wall first made to facilitate communications between Newton and Cowper, reopened, a stronger
motive is no doubt necessary. But it is a vulgar conclusion that marriage must be thought of wherever a man
and woman are concerned, and it was the age for romantic
friendships. At all events, whatever was the cause,
Lady Austen took up her abode in the deserted vicarage.
In less than three months their intimacy had sprung to
such a height, that they were Anna, Mary, and William
to each other—with still fonder additions: *my* Anna and
her William were, however, epithets which the taste of
the time, as well as the affectionateness of the religious
circle permitted, and Cowper was precisely the kind of
man with whom such relationships are practicable. He
was affectionate without a touch of passion. He was
utterly disabled by the misfortunes of his life from any

independent personal action; he was poor and dependent upon his friends; he was fifty. The mere notion of a man so circumstanced calling forth the idea of marriage at all seems inconceivable. Strange must have been the humility, wonderful the self-sacrifice of the woman who could entertain such a thought; and the gay high-spirited capricious woman who is supposed to be the second who formed designs upon the valetudinarian, shows no symptom of being either humble or self-devoted. She liked, no doubt, to have a man of unusual gifts under her influence, and was flattered by her own evident power to turn him hither and thither as she would: but that she would have made the sacrifice of her life to him, is a suggestion of which there is not the slightest evidence, and one which all the facts of the case go to disprove.

However, it is vain to attempt to throw light upon a story which has often been discussed without any conclusion, and of which we shall never know the *fin mot*, if *fin mot* there was. What is certain is that the society of this lady had the most remarkable effect upon the as yet undeveloped poet of fifty. He who had written respectable platitudes with perfect satisfaction to himself yesterday, burst forth all at once into poetry, genuine, original, and often great, emancipating his age as well as himself from all servile bonds. Moral essays of the most respectable and unexceptional kind one year, in conformity with all the canons, yet getting from the public nothing better than a respectful yawn; and in the next the " Task," with all its indifference to law and rule, its freedom and discursiveness, its unvarnished nature and truth. That the transition from Mrs. Unwin as muse to Lady Austen could have made all this difference is as wonderful as anything else in the tale. But so it would seem to have been. His Anna touched the right chord in the heart of this middle-aged man of genius. She told him the story of John Gilpin, and he, lying awake half the night laughing over it, produced next day the ballad which carries John Gilpin to posterity. She spoke to him of the Royal George, and the bell which he set tolling for the brave still sounds in all the echoes. She gave him a task, telling him that he could write on any subject, even on her sofa, and lo, the greatest poem of his generation came into being. The impulse is too distinct to be mistaken. He was a man who never did anything of his own initiative: but he who wrote "Table Talk" at Mrs. Unwin's suggestion, and was pleased with his work, does not seem the same man as he who wrote the "Task" at Lady Austen's. We can only wonder at the extraordinary difference; we cannot explain it.

Here then, after all this long preface, we have arrived at the moment when the latent forces which had been lying unknown all these years burst forth, unthought of and unsuspected; and the recluse by his chimney corner, where he wound silks for "the fair," and read the newspaper to them, and hugged himself in the snugness of domestic bliss, became the reformer of literature and the father of a new poetic age. The transition is so wonderful that it is beyond the comprehension of the spectator. He who had jogged so pleasantly in the old yoke for one stage, cast bit and bridle entirely from him in the next, renounced his old high and dry moral subjects, his classical illusions, his balanced couplets, and set out unfettered, as if he had been a new creature, upon that new yet old familiar way. We see no preparation, no gradual stirring up of poetical enthusiasm, only a little pleasant banter which made the social evening pass all the more brightly. Probably Lady Austen, who loved brightness and life, did not take any great pleasure in "Table Talk" or the "Progress of Error." Why should not he try blank

verse ? the charmed and flattered poet was very willing
to do anything to please her.   And thus all at once he
passed from the conventional to the real—to a genuine
land of inspiration.   That his poetical faith had not
changed, and that he had not received any new light
from contemporary events, is evident from the verses we
have quoted, in which Churchill still holds the palm, as
he had done in Cowper's mind twenty years before.   He
had not been brought to love better things by anything
that had happened since then.   Indeed nothing had
happened — a few ingenious gentlemen had published
poems, the names of which alone may be found in the
records, but which the world has long since forgotten.
Goldsmith indeed, who was Cowper's contemporary, had
published since Churchill's time his " Deserted Village,"
which, if not as famous as his immortal Vicar, was still
worthy of a higher place than Churchill ; but Cowper, it
is evident, was of the other faction in literature, disliked
Johnson, and took no pleasure in Goldsmith.   Thomson,
indeed, might have lent real aid in opening his eyes to
nature, but Thomson himself was not free of classic
bondage ; and Cowper had neither teachers nor models in
his generation.   But being told to take up an old system
and a forgotten measure, he did so, and made in it the
triumph of his life.

To compare the " Task " with any of the other poems
of the age would be too long a process.   Nature had not
been banished from literature ; but she appeared there
trim and dressed, her fields and her hedgerows, her halls
and cottages, all in neat and orderly lines, with here a
rustic Chloe, and there a languishing Strephon, not to
speak of the Naiads and the wood-nymphs, and soft
Ausonian breezes, and Eolus, and Boreas, and all their
crew   But when Cowper stepped forth into the rural
landscape, the whole of these attendant figures were scat-

tered to the winds. He paused in all due faithfulness
to do his best, and "sing the Sofa," for "the Fair com-
mands the song;" but scarcely has he put that piece of
furniture together, when he steps abroad into the soft
yet brisk air outside, where there is no classical torpor,
or any of those "halcyons" which he had himself celebrated, but "a ruffling wind" blowing in his face as he
stands on the top of the low hill, and sees with a pleasure
never exhausted

> "Ouse slow-winding through a level plain
> Of spacious meads, with cattle sprinkled o'er."

Nothing could be more lawless, less regular. Even
Mr. Benham, and Mr. Goldwin Smith, his last biographers,
are compelled to remark that the reflections, as a rule,
are not "naturally suggested by the preceding passage."
"From the use of a sofa by the gouty to those who,
being free from the gout, do not need sofas, and so to
country walks and country life, is hardly a natural
transition." One of the great points in the work,
indeed, is that we are made at once entirely independent
of natural transition. When he leaves the sofa, and
steps suddenly outside, all inconsequent and out of rule,
the reader is ready to applaud out of sheer satisfaction
and relief. What should detain the poet, that soft yet
cordial morning, not too still, with a "ruffling wind"
about, and "the distant plough slow - moving in the
fields"? He stands and gazes, and we with him, till
the wind rising "sweeps the skirts of some far-spreading
wood," and the branches wave in the blast, and the sound
of waters breaks into and completes the cadences of
nature. At a touch this wide and fresh landscape, where
"the sloping land recedes into the clouds," and where
the winds sweep so far and free, and the rills chime
upon their pebbles, has enlarged the world itself and

all that is therein. The rigid old pictures are like a child's sketches, all in hard lines, with no gradations of surface; but here we have at once the true artist, whose colours melt into each other, and under whose hands the depths of air and wonders of the half-seen distance come upon the canvas one cannot tell how. Perhaps it is above all this atmosphere, new to verse, which is the special charm of Cowper's landscapes; the crisp air blows about us as we read, carrying out of the depths a hundred sounds—bells from the distant towers, the voice of waters, the rhythmic rustle of the trees, and those far-off occasional notes of keener meaning, which betray a human population scattered around; or, with a still more delicate touch, the wintry landscape, frozen and still, breathes about us—

> " No noise is here, or none that hinders thought ;
> The redbreast warbles still, but is content
> With slender notes, and more than half suppress'd,
> Pleased with his solitude, and flitting light,
> From spray to spray ; where'er he rests, he shakes
> From many a twig the pendant drops of ice
> That twinkle in the withered leaves below."

In every season he has no conventional picture before him, but the scene itself in all its truth and reality, revealed by the companionship of years. None of its changing moods is lost upon him. He sees the cattle how they stand about in the torpor of the cold, and the sheep how they scatter upon the spring pastures, and the horse

> " That skims the spacious meadow at full speed,
> Then stops, and snorts, and, throwing high his heels,
> Starts to the voluntary race again,"

in the rapture of the genial season. Nothing so daring in adherence to fact, nothing so free from all consideration of what is, or is not, permitted by poetical canons,

had ever been put into verse before. After all the freedom of the following age, and the flood of realism which
has swept away so many barriers, we still wonder and
even smile at Cowper's boldness. How he could have
ventured in this first step out of the bondage of the
schools to the "stercoraceous heap" which fumes at full
length in his pages, it is impossible to tell. Had he
been a rebel born, long plotting the emancipation of his
art, he could not have gone farther, and no one since, so
far as we are aware, has ever gone so far. Perhaps as a
literary pioneer, the fugleman of the coming army, it was
well that his audacity should be beyond example as well
as beyond imitation. But it is more difficult to trace
the process in his gentle individuality, which made this
boldness practicable. Possibly his very seclusion, the
narrowness of his immediate audience, the certainty that
none of his wanderings, either in prose or verse, would be
without interest to them, gave him the necessary boldness. He followed the course of his own musings, of his
own daily routine, wayward yet regular, with no immediate
contemplation of the public, with only a pleased consciousness of the half-amusement, half-horror, of the parlour—
Mrs. Unwin, suspending her needles in consternation as
the cucumber-bed came into full view, while the livelier
Anna put down her embroidery and clapped her hands
at her poet's daring. They would laugh over it, no
doubt, as they sipped their tea, and anticipate with many
a gentle jest the confusion of the critics, and persuade
poor Mary, half-bewildered, to laugh too. And with
what delightful enthusiasm the two women would
receive the picture of that domestic blessedness which
they themselves had made, and look round upon the
originals of the picture, the close-drawn curtains, the sofa
warm in the firelight, the urn upon the table: and feel
the very needle working "patiently into the snowy lawn,"

to be made immortal.   And so it has been.   The fashion
of that blessedness has almost passed away, at least from
the imagination of England; but those who practically
love it least cannot refuse to be moved by the warmth
and repose and tender grace of that immortal parlour.
Not Adam and Eve in their paradise, not Alexander
throned and triumphant, with lovely Thais beside him,
has kept a more permanent place in the world's picture
gallery.   It is not a lofty kind of bliss perhaps, but
nothing could be more perfect within its limits.   And
the delightful union and warmth is enhanced by the
consciousness that the three people who form this happy
circle are all solitaries in the social economy, not fixed
by right in this happy routine, but giving each to each
in voluntary kindness and the delicate affinity of friendship those elements of happiness which make their shelter
so complete an emblem of the home.   Had it been a
home of the ordinary type, it would not have suited the
uses of the poet so well.   But his skill and instinct
entirely blind us to the fact that this picture, at once so
ideal and so real, is by its constitution entirely removed
from the orthodox household.   In all likelihood it never
occurred to himself that it was so.

Everybody knows this picture.   It is the one characteristic scene by which, more than anything else, the
poet is enshrined in popular opinion.   And there is no
doubt that his own generation was more grateful to him
for this sublimation of their common life, and glorification
of the fireside, than for all he did beside.   It opened to
him a thousand hearts in that great unknown mass which
says little for itself, and is no adept in criticism; but
which, when once it loves a book, carries it clear of all
comment into a fame which is beyond discussion and
above praise.   How different it was from that scene in
which Belinda's petticoat occupies so much space ! as

different as are the tiresome belle and beau with all their fripperies from the wholesome intercourse of actual life. The one, like the other, is an interior; in the one, as in the other, "the fair" is the sovereign of the domain. The very words of the Popish era still lingered on Cowper's tongue. But the whole atmosphere and every suggestion had been transformed. The "Rape of the Lock" was an innocent rape enough, but the inspiring fancy of the scene is, without intention, fundamentally impure. The encroachments of the gallant, and the half-fictitious resistance and simulated rage of the lady belong to a series of adventures older and more persistently followed than anything else in literature. That there is no harm in them is a mere accident. But Cowper changed altogether the spirit of the meeting and the meeting-place. No hot pursuit or amorous conflict, but a sweet and sober union of minds and hearts, a calm of perfect satisfaction, a mutual understanding, harmony and dependence, each upon each, are in his pages. Hazardous encounters there had been plenty; even in Richardson's virtuous novels assaults upon what is called female virtue were the invariable theme, and every women's mind was concentrated upon the determination to save her honour. But with a touch the fastidious gentle poet, fastidious in taste, pure in nature, religious in heart, made an end of all this. The honourable placid house in which men and women stood together in mutual support and sympathy and tenderness, without a suggestion of evil, was created by his hand—or say, rather, disclosed, for he was no creator. In all ages the bulk of mankind thus lives, without any fermentation of passion or illicit fancy. In the worst of times, vice is the exception. If it is rampant in high places, it is hated below. If youth is noisy and uncontrolled, the very ordinance of nature which turns men and women into fathers and mothers, teaches them that only by means of social virtue is life possible. But up to this time no one had ventured to make the fireside heroic, or set it in the front of all that is happy and beautiful. To almost all the women and a great number of the men of his age, this one achievement was enough to earn him everlasting gratitude. Cowper became the poet of the domestic circle, the apostle of the home. Even to those who did not receive with any relish the religious meditations into which his verse so easily flowed, this poetical adoption of the centre of domestic peace was almost a personal happiness.

We have said that Cowper was no creator; but when we turn to the bold and well-defined figures that cross his landscape, set down without a single wavering line or artificial grace, the force of portraiture almost reaches the height of creation. No pretty ideal figures, no Damon and Musidora, no gay Lothario or lovely Lavinia, are there. Never was a more distinct and real person than the woodman going out to his work in the morning across the snowy fields. They are all so well known that we hesitate to quote; but this picture is one which, though so simply real, can never be looked upon without a keen imaginative pleasure—

> "Forth goes the woodman, leaving unconcerned
> The cheerful haunts of man, to wield the axe
> And drive the wedge, in yonder forest drear,
> From morn to eve his solitary task.
> Shaggy and lean and shrewd, with pointed ears
> And tail cropped short, half lurcher and half cur,
> His dog attends him. Close behind his heel
> Now creeps he slow, and now with many a frisk,
> Wide-scamp'ring, snatches up the drifted snow
> With iv'ry teeth, or ploughs it with his snout;
> Then shakes his powder'd coat, and barks for joy.
> Heedless of all his pranks, the sturdy churl
> Moves right toward the mark; nor stops for aught,

> But now and then, with pressure of his thumb,
> T' adjust the fragrant charge of a short tube,
> That fumes beneath his nose ; the trailing cloud
> Streams far behind him, scenting all the air."

We repeat that scarcely any poet since, even Wordsworth in the height of his polemical determination to
employ common words and images instead of those
appropriated to the use of poetry—has put so bold a
sketch upon paper : and yet it is so entirely appropriate
and true, that not a word but of applause can be said.
Here is no wilful descent from the worthy to the mean,
as in the case of Betty Foy and Peter Bell. The poet is
as completely devoid of the affectation of a revolutionary
as it is possible to imagine. His woodman crosses the
wintry landscape, because in the first place he did so, an
excellent reason, yet not all-sufficient in art ; and secondly
because he is the very soul of the bare and wintry
season, he, and his dog, and his pipe—setting out to his
work in sturdy rural indifference, consoling himself with
such warmth as is possible, the one workman whom the
snow does not stop, whose axe supplies one of the few
familiar welcome sounds that break the spell of the
silence. The picture in all its glistening whiteness, the
sharp keen pleasure of the new-fallen snow, which goes
to the hearts of dogs and children, the man's stolid
straightforward course, satisfy our mind with a perfection
of composition which yet is pure and simple nature.   A
little while before, Cowper himself would have put a
moral lesson instead of this living group ; and Thomson,
shivering, would have painted us an ideal incident—but
poetry had now found its eyes, and its completest simple
inspiration.

And who does not remember the companion picture ?
The poet does not see it with actual eyesight—but warm
and cheerful indoors, with the firelight brightening the

winter gloaming, hears "the twanging horn on yonder bridge," and beholds the messenger in his mind's eye—as we, too, do, with a sense of elation and expectation borrowed from him, though the news that comes to us every hour or so has worn out, so far as our minds are concerned, that warm alert attention and sense of pleasure.

> "He comes, the herald of a noisy world,
>   With spattered boots, strapped waist, and frozen locks,
>   News from all nations lumbering at his back,
>   Yet careless what he brings, his one concern
>   Is to conduct it to the destined inn,
>   And having dropped th' expected bag, pass on—
>   He whistles as he goes, light-hearted wretch !
>   Cold and yet cheerful ; messenger of grief
>   Perhaps to thousands, and of joy to some,
>   To him indifferent whether grief or joy ;
>   Houses in ashes, and the fall of stocks,
>   Births, deaths, and marriages, epistles wet
>   With tears that trickled down the writer's cheek
>   Fast as the periods from his fluent quill ;
>   Or charged with amorous sigh of absent swains,
>   Or nymph responsive, equally affect
>   His horse and him, unconscious of them all."

This is one of the sights which has been entirely swept away from our experience. None of us remember that functionary as the bearer of Her Majesty's mails— but yet how true, how easy, how full of the very spirit of the night is this representation of the wayfarer, whom we hear passing from behind Cowper's curtains. In spite of ourselves we feel the thrill of gentle excitement and eagerness. Though we are deluged with newspapers, and have so many posts a day, yet we understand it all better than the things we have seen with our own eyes ; the moon reflected in the wintry flood, the dim lamps at the end of the wearisome long bridge, the little town half asleep in the slumbrous cold, but rousing with quickened pulses at the clattering hoofs and cheerful horn—and at his window the spectator, glancing out in a warm dim glow of firelight, and the little circle all expectant of the evening's reading, the imprisoned wranglers that are to be set free, and all the tumult of great London that is about to echo in the quiet, and make it still more warm, more soft and sweet.

This delightful picture, however, recalls to us the great defect in Cowper's poetry, though no doubt it was one of the qualities which gained it instant acceptance with the crowd. It is that he cannot enjoy this happy seclusion of his, nor picture forth the domestic perfection of his life without a comparison, very much to the disadvantage of all the rest of the world, who are not so happy as he. While he and those kind companions whose chief thought is how to make him happiest, " welcome peaceful evening in " in their manner, he cannot help making an invidious comparison—

> " Not such his evening, who with shining face
>   Sweats in the crowded theatre, and squeezed,
>   And bored with elbow points, through both his sides
>   Outscolds the ranting actor on the stage ;
>   Nor his who patient stands till his feet throb,
>   And his head thumps to feed upon the breath
>   Of patriots bursting with heroic rage,
>   Or placemen all tranquillity and smiles."

This runs all through his great work. He can never describe his own good fortune without joining to the picture its inevitable contrast ; as if it were a moral advantage to spend one's life in gentle idleness, and like the lilies of the field, neither to toil nor spin. He has no perception that his fireside, so sweet, so tranquil, so placid, is not the first and finest of the scenes of human life. " I crown thee king of intimate delights," he cries, addressing winter—

> " Fireside enjoyments, homeborn happiness,
> And all the comforts that the lowly roof
> Of undisturbed retirement, and the hours
> Of long uninterrupted evening know."

And then his complacency bursts forth once more.

> " No rattling wheels stop short before these gates,
> No powdered pert proficient in the art
> Of sounding an alarm, assaults these doors
> Till the street rings."

He cannot be content with being exceptionally blessed
himself; he must point his happiness with the reflection
that the greater part of the world is less happy than he;
and in doing this, every amusement passes under his lash;
the theatre especially he returns to again and again, to
point out its inferiority—and all the frivolous congre-
gations of men.

This, however, though a great drawback in point of
art, and not a small one in charity, was quite in accordance with the spirit of the religious revival which then
reigned with passionate force in England over a large
proportion of those classes to which Cowper's poetry
appealed.   Something of a natural revulsion from the
artificial pre-eminence of " society," and that atmosphere,
which, from the days of the *Spectator* to those of the
" Rape of the Lock," had infected literature, setting up
the pettiest subjects, and supposing a universal interest
in ruffles and powder, which no wholesome nation ever
was really possessed by—was no doubt in the theory that
" God made the country, but man made the town," which is
the oft-repeated principle of the poet's philosophy.   But
stronger than this and more earnest was that long-stand-
ing religious objection to all the paths of pleasure (so
called), an objection much older than Wesley, which
never fails to accompany every great religious movement.
No theory ever is so persistent, so profoundly rooted in

human nature, as to form part of movements differing in
every other respect, without having a foundation of truth
and justice which is unassailable.   The evils which
result from social excitement and pursuit of pleasure, the
vices that creep in, the feverish appetite, which grows by
what it feeds on, for more and more highly spiced diversion, the extravagance in mind, in fashion, and in purse,
into which, almost always, the tide of pleasure betrays
those who are carried away by it, are patent enough to
all beholders.   And since the day when St. Paul warned
his converts against " fleshly lusts that war against the
soul," there has never been a revival of earnest religious
feeling without this crusade against amusements, innocent
enough perhaps in themselves, yet a possible fount of
evil.   The prejudice of the Methodists and Evangelicals
was not more strong than that of their predecessors in
every reformation ; but it is nearer to ourselves and
more easily perceptible.   In the case of such a poet as
Cowper, it has a tinge of something ungenerous in it
which rouses our prejudices in their turn.   He who was
so severe upon all the pleasures of worldly life was a man
incapable of any share in them—" a stricken deer " who
had left the herd, a being unfit in body and still more in
mind for the enjoyments he decried.   His domestic
blessedness was not arrived at by a series of sacrifices
and renunciations of more brilliant happiness, but was
what he liked best, the only kind of pleasure of which
he was really capable.   And on the other hand, the
gentle audience which he addressed, which was neither
the highest nor the lowest, but the mass between, the
great middle of society, upon the vast level of which
there are neither the brilliant lights nor the tragic darkness which affect the extremes of life, was like himself
out of the way of the tide of fashion and social excitement.   It was and always must be to the bulk of any

people, rather a pleasure than a pain to be assured that high life is full of wretchedness and danger, and pleasure in all its manifestations a road to ruin. This gives a disagreeable aspect always to the fulminations of a pious recluse, and all the wide-spread and oft-repeated strictures of the retired and humble upon the gay and great. They are damning sins they have no mind to, they are dignifying their own mild and moderate possibilities with an air of noble virtue and superiority to meaner motive. But in those days people were not sufficiently at leisure to remark this. Only a generation before, Hogarth had painted those terrible discourses on canvas, which made the results of a "gay" life apparent to the dullest eyes— and Richardson and Fielding had revealed such an imbroglio of vices under the calm of ordinary life as might well have affrighted the reader. Thus Cowper's theology was scarcely to blame for the tone he took; but yet his theology gave it a deeper meaning, and pointed the shaft which all the moralists had already sharpened. To us it is the drawback, the attendant bitter to so much sweetness; to a great part of his audience, no doubt, it was the chief interest and value of his work.

But while the "Task" was in the course of writing, alas, there came into that safe, most sheltered corner, where no crevice seemed to exist through which any serpent could crawl, some of those petty miseries of which society in its turn accuses retirement and domestic life. How it was no one knows. The vulgar mind concludes easily that Lady Austen would have married the poet, and that Mrs. Unwin was jealous. Cowper himself writes a few somewhat spiteful and petty letters on the subject, putting his kind visitor, his gay and sweet companion, vaguely in the wrong; and Hayley, his biographer, with that injurious "hushing up" which conveys a worse impression than any explanations, attri-

butes the break to "a trifling feminine discord." But
the only thing certain about it, is that we shall never
know what it was. There had been a coolness shortly
after the beginning of their alliance, which was got over;
but the second breach was final; before even the book
which she had inspired was finished, Lady Austen departed.
Cowper's explanation of it to Lady Hesketh, who did not
know her, was that the habit of "paying my devoirs to
her ladyship every morning at eleven," interrupted his
work. "I was forced to neglect the 'Task' to attend
upon the Muse who had inspired the subject," he says,
with an ungenerous and petty tone in his self-defence.
"But she had ill-health, and before I had quite finished
the work, was obliged to repair to Bristol." The friendship had lasted altogether about three years. Some
soreness, it is evident, there was about the breach, which
prompts Cowper's lengthy letters on the subject; but
that is all we know. These letters ended with a forlorn
boast, that "the cause of so many interruptions" being
removed, "we have seldom any company at all." Newton
had been very doubtful as to that pleasant addition to
their life, and the "interruptions" which threatened to
give Cowper a brighter surrounding, and he was no doubt
pleased that the lively woman, who knew the world and
had kept up her relations with it, was gone.

But it is not too much to say that all that was best
in Cowper's life went with her. His work kept him up
as long as it was in hand; but the last shadows soon
began to creep up from the autumnal fields. Out of the
sudden light which had fallen upon his life, he went back
into the old monotony with a subdued, half fretful, half
proud submission. His letters, especially to Newton,
grew more and more melancholy. It is true that they
had always been of a dejected tone, and that he had
scarcely ever ceased to represent himself to the former

director of his spiritual life, as a despairing sinner shut
out from God's grace; but it is difficult to believe in the
despair of the man who spent so many cheerful days by
Lady Austen's side, who stuck in the mud with his Mary,
and wrote John Gilpin after a night sleepless with
laughter.   Fortunately the blank left by Lady Austen's
disappearance did not long continue.   His cousin, Lady
Hesketh, his correspondence with whom had been dropped
for years, one day wrote to him, moved by some sudden
impulse of kindness, and, with the eagerness of a man
who was longing for friendship and society, he flung
himself upon her.   With all his tender-heartedness,
Cowper was a man to whom one devoted ministrant was
just about as good as another, and it is evident that his
need of some one to vary the routine of existence was
greater than it had ever been.   "We are all growing
young again, and the days that I thought I should see
no more are actually returning," he cried in his pleasure.
And Lady Hesketh did not confine herself to letter-
writing; she offered help, if his circumstances required,
and he accepted the offer with a frankness and simplicity,
which no doubt made the matter easier at once to her
and to himself, but which startles the reader, who perhaps
has forgotten that all this time the poet has been dependent upon his family, receiving almost all his living from
the benevolence of his relations.   Lady Hesketh brought
him into renewed intercourse with several members of
his family, and his life seemed once more to brighten.
He wrote the poem called "Tirocinium," in order to
make out the volume, which the "Task" by itself was
too short to fill, and a few days after began his translation of Homer; which showed that his mind was in full
activity, and that neither he nor his friends had forgotten
the importance to his well-being of constant occupation.
    These two facts, however, which one would have

thought would have rejoiced all interested in him—his reunion with his relations, and his voluntary commencement of an important piece of work—seem to have alarmed and provoked the interference of Newton, who could not, it appears, consent to give up his supreme spiritual authority over his former penitent. No doubt Lady Austen had shaken it, but she had happily disappeared; and the incoming of a more permanent and legitimate influence gave to the jealous priest—for the character is one, be it Jesuit or Evangelical—a deeper alarm. It was thought that Homer, a pagan, was "greatly below the attention" of a Christian poet, and not a becoming occupation for him; and also that the society of his carnally-minded relations would do him harm. Cowper, however, is not so humble but that he takes up arms for himself at this interference. He cannot amuse himself now, he says, as he once could, with carpenters' or gardeners' tools, squirrels, or guinea-pigs. A man's mind has been restored to him, and it must be occupied accordingly. Neither has he any connections of a kind to injure his spiritual life. So unwarrantable a pretension does not make the gentle poet angry, but still he has enough of spirit to repel it. A still more unwarrantable interference was attempted a little later when Lady Hesketh, in her turn, fixed her residence temporarily at Olney, in order to be near the lonely pair. She was one of Cowper's nearest relations, warranted by family ties and superior fortune to look after him, without fear of any misinterpretation of her conduct; and she soon perceived that the "cruel solitude" of the little town was weighing heavily upon him. Accordingly she lost no time in renting for him a house in the neighbouring village of Weston, from which immediate access could be obtained to the Throckmorton grounds, which were his delight. Cowper's exultation over this new dwelling-place, its "genteel" aspect, its roominess and airiness, and manifold attractions, is like the boundless satisfaction of a child; and his letters to Newton on this subject are written with a certain deprecatory fulness, as if to disarm reproof.

But these simple wiles were unavailing. Some weeks after Newton let loose his thunderbolt; this time it was addressed to Mrs. Unwin, and it seems to have plunged them both into trouble. "The purport of it," Cowper says, "is a direct accusation of me and of her, an accusation implied that we have both diverged into forbidden paths, and led a life unbecoming the Gospel—that many of my friends in London are grieved, and the simple people of Olney astonished; that *he never so much doubted my restoration to Christian privileges*, as now that I converse too much with people of the world, and find too much pleasure in doing so." There could not be a more painful evidence that the most religious of men can be as brutal as the lowest, than this fiery arrow of Newton's "doubt" as to "the restoration of Christian privileges;" a delusion in the poet's mind which he had combated with all his might for years, which he knew had its origin in insanity, yet which in this moment of passion he suddenly adopts and sanctions, uncareful of the misery which it might produce. And this outburst was founded solely on the fact that the poor recluse had got to be on friendly terms with the Throckmortons, and that Lady Hesketh frequently drove him and his companion out! The poet condescends to go over all this ground again in another letter to his angry Pope, which is full of explanation and proof that he does not deserve the chastisement he has received. But even now he does not assert his freedom of action, or do more than defend his "consistency" against the impertinent and cruel attack. This is enough to show, however, how little safe his delicate nature and distempered soul were in the hands of a friend so masterful and remorseless.

Newton, however, was right in one point, that the translation of Homer was not the best work that Cowper could have taken up. But he was a man absolutely dependent upon others for suggestions and starting-points, and was incapable himself of striking out his further path. It is almost ludicrous to see the little stir about him of all his friends, the nurses, servants, and worshippers of the helpless poet, all tremblingly desirous of finding him something to do, and straining after a new subject, while he stands by in amiable weakness, and approves the anxious suggestions, but without any motive to set to work at them, such as Lady Austen had furnished. Lady Hesketh suggested the Mediterranean, about as strange a theme as could have been thought of. A curate in the neighbourhood thought that the Four Ages had never been adequately treated. This discussion convinces us that we are still in the eighteenth century, in the period when an abstract subject was the natural foundation of a poetical essay. But Cowper, though he listened to them all with so much docility, perhaps knew that poetical essays were not so much worth the doing now-a-days, and that he had said the most of his say in this world. Homer was good steady work, and the "mechanic exercise" of the verse was soothing to him. He got wholesome occupation, and he got a thousand pounds out of this huge task, so much bigger yet less great than the other task which had been concerned with subjects more homely than gods and heroes. It is not a work that counts for much in the story of his career. It is astonishing how like in sound and cadence a bit of this oldest and greatest of epics sounds to the "Winter Evening," or the "Walk at Noon," as we read it, though these poems are certainly not very like Homer. It was when he had completed this that the new subject was so much discussed and looked for; but by that time no new subject charmed him.   He had fallen again into the deepest depths, and Mrs. Unwin had been struck by his side with the first touch of paralysis, that most solemn of warnings.   Nothing could be more dismal than the condition of the faithful pair in this stage.   She grew exigent and selfish (as they say) who had been all devotion, demanding perpetual attention from him, and babbling in half intelligible words and frequent anger, when he was otherwise occupied ; and he strained every nerve to be of use to the invalid who had so often nursed him.   There could be no severer lesson upon the inexpediency of such alliances than the way in which kind Lady Hesketh speaks of Mrs. Unwin at this melancholy stage of existence.   The poor old lady has no right to be there among all those cousins, and though they are kind to her, yet she is out of place and bores them.   The story is dipped in the very darkest hues of domestic tragedy. "Here is a muse of seventy that I perfectly idolise," says Hayley, who in these days was half as good a poet as Cowper, and very well known through the length and breadth of the land ; but Lady Hesketh speaks of her as "Madame," and can scarcely restrain her weariness of the feeble and suffering old woman.   And thus the last days went mournfully on.

It was, however, in the last glimmering of evening light before his life sank altogether in the darkness, that Cowper wrote two of his finest productions—two of the most exquisite poems in the language—every line of which is instinct with a profound and chastened feeling to which it would be difficult to find a parallel.   These are the lines " Addressed to my Mother's Picture," and those entitled " My Mary."   Poetry has never produced any utterances more tender and true.   They are without passion, for passion does not belong to filial love; and there is not a phrase in them, not a word which could jar upon the most susceptible ear, not a touch that is extravagant or excessive. This was the one love he knew. Other affections had skimmed over him, calling forth here and there a " swallow-flight " of song: this one love alone was fully possible to him, the love half reverential, half protecting, without fear or doubt, or a possibility of delusion in it, which a son bears to his mother. The fact that he who gave forth these supreme utterances of filial affection was himself old when he produced them, brings into the relationship a tender quality which is marvellously touching. The two women whom he thus celebrates are at once greater and more lowly than he, his saints, his servants, his companions. Gratitude—in the one case visionary, in the other how real—a sense of dependence, a sense of tender superiority, mingle and blend as poetry never blended them before. Poor Mr. Hayley, Cowper's " brother-poet," with just as genuine feeling, celebrated his mother, who had preserved his life by her miraculous care from an illness which threatened mind and body.

> " 'Twas thine with constant love, through lingering years,
>   To bathe thy infant orphan in thy tears,"

says this excellent man though indifferent poet. But Cowper, though his head was all confused and astray among the gathering glooms, and his heart quivering with a thousand arrows, never errs. Any of his true lovers who was asked to supply an example of the poet at perfection, would reply with one of these two poems. They are the expression of the master-feeling of his life.

The last years of all are too sad to dwell upon. Mrs. Unwin would seem to have dropped into that imbecility of weakness which is the most tragic and humiliating

cónclusion to which this sad humanity is subject : while
he, fallen into the very depths of visionary anguish, sat
" still and silent as death," speaking to no one, asking
nothing, dwelling in a gloomy world of his own, from
which in heaven or earth there seemed no outlet. When
his Mary died he made no sign of feeling, being lost in
the stupor of his own gathering malady. He sat silent
with wild sad eyes in the Norfolk parsonage, to which he
had been removed, and had novels read to him the livelong day (Evelina for one), finding in them, heaven knows
what pitiful solace for woes that were never to be cured
in this world. Sometimes the moaning of the sea would
soothe him ; sometimes he would rouse up to make a
mechanical correction of his Homer ; sometimes even he
would write a cold and gloomy letter——for one of his
delusions was that he had ceased to be capable of affection for any one——to his cousin. All that tender care and
affection could do for him was done. He survived his
faithful companion more than three years, but they were
years of darkness, without hope or consolation. A year
before his death an incident in a book he was reading,
Anson's Voyages, caught his troubled fancy, and he wrote
the last of all his poems, and the saddest. Pacing up
and down in the failing light of the evening, the picture
of the drowning sailor, " such a destined wretch as I,"
grows before him.

> " He long survives, who lives an hour
>   In ocean, self-upheld :
> And so long he, with unspent power,
>   His destiny repelled :
> And ever, as the minutes flew,
> Entreated help, or cried——' Adieu !'
>
> " At length, his transient respite past,
>   His comrades, who before
> Had heard his voice in every blast,
>   Could catch the sound no more :

For then, by toil subdued, he drank
The stifling wave, and then he sank.

" No poet wept him ; but the page
    Of narrative sincere,
That tells his name, his worth, his age,
    Is wet with Anson's tear :
And tears by bards or heroes shed
Alike immortalise the dead.

" I therefore purpose not, or dream,
    Descanting on his fate,
To give the melancholy theme
    A more enduring date :
But misery still delights to trace
Its semblance in another's case.

" No voice divine the storm allayed,
    No light propitious shone,
When, snatched from all effectual aid,
    We perished, each alone :
But I, beneath a rougher sea,
And whelmed in deeper gulphs than he."

This is the last sound that comes to us out of the
darkness in which Cowper was fast disappearing.   Never
had a harmless life so miserable an ending.   He went
down in those deep waters without even that gleam of light
at the last, which so often gives pathetic gladness to an
ending life.   Unconsoled, he was swallowed up by those
billows.   The last words he said were, when he was
offered a cordial, "What can it signify ?"   What, indeed,
did it matter, an hour of weakness, more or less, a pain
the greater ?   By that time the gloom had reached its
blackest, the light was near.   What did it signify ?   Who
can doubt that all the ceaseless sufferings of his life,
all his miseries, some hours thereafter, had become as
dreams to him in the great and new revelation that
awaited him at the gates of heaven ?

His life had been a harmless life ; but yet it had

been full of trouble to himself, and all who were concerned in it, as unsatisfactory a human existence as ever
was. But what he failed altogether to accomplish for
himself he did for literature. He had not force enough
to break any bonds of his own; on the contrary, his
hapless feet were always getting entangled in new ones,
and at the very last, after his partial escape from the
potent sway of such a man as Newton, he made a poor
little dictator for himself out of a pompous village peda-
gogue, to whom he laid bare all the tortures of his heart.
But while he was bound in spirit he was free in his
genius, as no man else in his generation was free.
Academical rule and precedent had no sway over him;
he went out of the schools of the poets a gentle rebel,
casting all their leading strings to the winds, not saying
a word of revolt, but with a quiet obstinacy taking his
own way. He would not be bound even to logic or
sequence, but waved all those limitations lightly from
him, and did as Fancy bade, with no defiance, but only
a gentle natural waywardness. He saw, with eyes as
clear as truth itself, what was before him in the soft
fresh outside world, in which there was no intoxicating
loveliness but only a modest English landscape; and
taste and inclination at once refused to bring in any
foreign images, finding that enough, and the genuine
humanity that peopled it. He was bold to say what was
in him, and to say it his own way; he had the courage
to step back in the course of time, and bring his model
from higher sources than those of the Augustan age.
He broke the spell of Pope, and opened the way to
Wordsworth and all the singers that were being born,
while he languished and agonised. The world would
have been a different world for them if Cowper had
not been.

WILLIAM COWPER, born 1731 ; died 1800.

Published Table Talk Truths   } 1782.
    „   Progress of Error, etc. }
    „   The Task .   .   } 1784.
    „   Tirocinium   .   }
    „   Translation of Homer   1791.

CHAPTER II.

ROBERT BURNS.

WHILE Cowper was wasting his early manhood in London doing nothing, and knowing nothing either of the misery or the importance of his future life, a child was born in a clay hut among the Ayrshire wilds, in that far-distant and unknown realm of Scotland, which, though united to England by the closest bonds, was yet almost as little known to Englishmen as any foreign country. It is very difficult to realise to ourselves, indeed, what that country was before Burns and before Scott. No country in the world has owed so much to literature; and we doubt if all the enterprise and spirit of the race could ever have produced the prosperity and wealth which is now its portion, without the stimulating touch of that revelation which made Scotland enchanted ground to all Europe, and has made her sons proud, wherever they have gone, to claim her name. No two men in the world were ever more unlike than the English gentleman, gently bred and well connected, but indolent, timid, and helpless, and the impassioned peasant, full of strong desires and impulses, rash, headstrong, and daring, whose lamp of genius was infinitely more vivid, and his place in poetry greater, but whose warm flesh and blood encumbered his way even more than madness and misery did that of his contemporary. They never met, and knew little of each other; nevertheless, their work had a similar influence. The one in his blue bonnet, the other in his invalid night-cap, they stand at the great gates which had been neatly barred and bolted by the last generation, and, pushing them abroad upon their unwilling hinges, made English poetry free as she had been before.

The mind of Burns and his career launches us into an entirely changed atmosphere and new scene. He was a son of the soil, without education, without culture, without friends; all he had in the world, save a well-knit frame and arms strong to work, was genius, against which there was every possible obstacle placed, that it should not be able to do itself justice. Cowper did not begin to write till he was over fifty; Burns was done with poetry, and all things earthly, at thirty-seven. The one was a mild and feminine nature, without passion or any fleshly impulse; the other a strong and headlong being made up of them. It is strange to note how they worked together in absolute unconsciousness of their joint mission. It is difficult even to realise that the " Task " was published only two years before that volume of varied and desultory verse which raised the Ayrshire ploughman at once to the rank of poet, not in his own district or country alone, but for the world. We will not ask which of the two was the greatest wonder; though, indeed, in our own mind we have little doubt on the subject, and cannot but feel that a fresh, new, and impassioned spirit was the natural fountain from which new life might be expected to spring. Burns was free by nature of all bondage of models or rules. If any preceding poet could be said to be his master, it was such a homely and unpretending oracle as Allan Ramsay, who died the year before he was born. If the transmigration of souls were a tenable faith, it would be a pleasant superstition to believe that the

simple and genial writer of the " Gentle Shepherd " had
been permitted to come back again after his bookselling
and all his little activities, and to learn what it cost to
be a great poet, in the body—so unlike his—of that only
rustic who has ever reached the highest rank in poetry.
He and a certain foolish young Robert Ferguson, of whom
nobody would have known anything had not Burns taken
his memory into a kind of worship—and the ballads and
old songs that are in the air of every Scotch countryside
—were all the literature Burns was born to.   Afterwards,
when he struggled, with that heavenly yet not always
profitable thirst which used to be characteristic of the
Scotch peasant, into some acquaintance with general
literature, his mind had already taken its form; and
almost everything that was dictated by what his contemporaries thought to be better taste, has been condemned
by the judgment of posterity.   With a new life to eluci-
date, and all the primary passions and impulses of
humanity to furnish him with poetic themes, he was far
better off in his ignorance than the cultivated critics who
patronised him afterwards, and made allowances for his
rusticity.   He was at the fountainhead of life, and had
nothing in him to obscure that vividness of sight which
is the poet's first qualification.   That he used a form of
language which had not followed the laws of progress, and
was no longer the language of the well-bred and cultured
classes, was a more serious drawback; but that language,
again, has its felicities as well as its disadvantages, and
was infinitely better for Burns, as remaining still national,
than if he had been born in Yorkshire or Lancashire.
In short, so far as his birth and training went, Burns, we
believe, had a better beginning than, for the purpose he
was to serve in the history of his race, he could have had
elsewhere.

If it were not a necessity of civilisation that greatness

should involve social elevation, and that the poet should
be supposed to fail in life if his genius does not bring
him into the society of the higher classes, there would be
no more occasion for regretting the birth of a poet in a
labourer's cottage than there is for regretting the birth
of a statesman in a duke's castle. But it is hopeless to
think of persuading either the great writer himself, or
the world, that his rising in poetry ought not to involve
" rising in life." This was the grand curse of Burns's
existence. It was a rise in life for him when the jovial
attorneys and doctors of the little Ayrshire town invited
him to join in their booses and their controversies. It
was high advancement to gain an entrance to the houses
of the rural gentry ; and when he came the length of
Edinburgh, its professors, and its dinner-parties, what
better paradise remained for the ploughman ? But none
of these fine things were for the advantage either of his
art or of himself. His early patrons enlisted his genius
in miserable personal vulgarities of abuse which that genius
has pitifully preserved to this day, to the dismay of all
wholesome minds ; and his fine Edinburgh friends wanted
him to write a tragedy, and to abandon his familiar tongue
for the stilted traditions of the poetry of the period. These
are dangers from which, in their worst aspect, a man
is spared by being born a gentleman ; and they were far
more hard upon Burns, and more detrimental to his welfare, than any other disadvantage of his origin.

Robert Burns was born the son of two hard-working
country people; small farmers, yet not much above the
condition of farm-labourers ; very poor, proudly upright,
and independent. His father, a man of the lofty and
somewhat stern character which Scotland is credited with,
maintained a desperate conflict with poverty till the end
of his life, and never did more than keep the wolf from
the door. In external circumstances they were scarcely

better off than the villagers whose claim for Christmas coals and blankets is one of the chartered rights of English country life; but in mind they were as haughty as the Doges, holding charity as poison and debt as shame. This virtue of independence was the one only point in the family character that threatened to grow morbid. It affected the manners and ways of thinking of the poet in after years in a way which did him much harm, and embittered his feelings, at once to those who served, and those who neglected him; but this was certainly a failing which leant to virtue's side. Never was there a more attractive picture than that of this peasant household amid the ceaseless care and privations of their life. Their first little farm was sterile and profitless; the second promised better, but there, too, ill-luck overtook them in the shape of a doubtful lease and hard-hearted factor. The boys had to set to work as soon as their young strength permitted, and Robert had begun to do a man's work by the time he was fifteen. He and his brother Gilbert were sent to school as occasion served, for a few years regularly, and then, as they grew older, "week and week about," as they could be spared from the farm work. When there was no possibility of schooling, "my father," says Gilbert Burns, "undertook to teach us arithmetic in the winter evenings by candle-light; and in this way my two elder sisters received all their education." The kindly mother moved but and ben while the fireside lessons were going on, and sang them songs in the gloaming; and a certain old Jenny, brimful of ghost stories and all the ballads of the countryside, frightened and charmed the children with her endless lore. In this way, besides the breathing sweetness of the homely music, that floating literature of simple song, full of story, full of sentiment, becomes familiar to many a rustic who is penetrated by it while scarcely knowing it to be poetry. Burns had

thus the training of a complete system of rustic sentiment, philosophy, and humanity before his mind had come
in contact with printed literature at all.   The songs of
the countryside were his A B C.   In these lowly regions
there was no idea that " the words " were an unimportant
part of the performance—that they were not, indeed, the
song itself, however essential it might be to have " a
bonnie tune."   We do not know if there has been any
change in this respect among Scotch peasants ; but it
would not have been difficult to find in former days men
and women both, whose heads were full of these songs,
though they could not sing a note ; and this would seem
to have been Burns's case.   The untaught continuous
strain, mostly of love and of its woes, though with all kinds
of simple variations, from the profound pathos of " Waly-
waly "—

> " Oh Martinmas wind ! when wilt thou blaw,
>   And shake the dead leaves frae the tree ?
> Oh gentle death ! when wilt thou come,
>   And tak' a life that wearies me ?"

to the long-drawn rustic farce of " Get up and bar the
door "— was almost the only sound of gaiety in the serious house.   " Nothing could be more retired than our
manner of living (the narrative continues) ; we rarely saw
anybody but the members of our own family. . . . My
father was for some time almost the only companion we
had.   He conversed familiarly on all subjects with us,
as if we had been men, and was at great pains while we
accompanied him in the labours of the farm, to lead the
conversation to such subjects as might tend to increase
our knowledge or confirm us in virtuous habits.   He
borrowed Salmon's *Geographical Grammar* for us, and
endeavoured to make us acquainted with the situation
and history of the different countries in the world, while
from a book society in Ayr he procured for us the reading

of Durham's *Physics and Astro-theology* and Ray's *Wisdom of God in Creation,* to give us some idea of astronomy and natural history. Robert read all these books with an avidity and industry scarcely to be equalled."

Imagine the ploughboys in their winter evenings gathered about the solitary candle on the table, or smoky little oil-lamp, with those sober treatises before them, reading "with avidity," while the cheerful glow of the fire lighted up the one homely room which was kitchen and parlour and hall, and the mother's quick cheerful coming and going, and her songs, not loud enough to disturb them, gave a lively, kindly background to the little group—work over, supper preparing, warmth and rest about them. It would not have been half so picturesque, and probably there might not have been the same strain after better things, had William Burness's cottage been the laird's house; there tutors and governors would have had all the responsibility; here the serious toil-worn peasant, already growing old, helping his boys to acquire a little information on solid subjects such as commended themselves to his sober spirit, brings in an element of far higher interest. After all, one wonders whether the mother's songs did not do more for at least one of the lads than Salmon's *Geographical Grammar.* But who was to know that?

These peaceful evening scenes were often painfully interrupted. Sometimes threatening letters would come from the factor—letters threatening roup (auction) and jail, the two horrors of the poor—which "used to set us all in tears;" no separation of interests here, or division between the elder and younger, but that perfect union which made the family one. Sometimes there would be a rare visitor to interrupt the studies. On one distinct occasion, of which a record exists, the young dominie who had taught the boys spent an evening in the smoky cheerful farm-kitchen. He brought with him of all things in the world the tragedy of "Titus Andronicus," "and by way of passing the evening he began to read the play aloud. We were all attention for some time, till presently the whole party were dissolved in tears. A female in the play" (says Gilbert Burns) "had her hands chopped off (I have but a confused remembrance of it), and then was insultingly desired to call for water to wash her hands. At this, in an agony of distress, we with one voice desired he would read no more. My father observed that if we would not hear it out, it would be needless to leave it with us. Robert replied, that if it was left he would burn it." Most likely the young dominie considered the raw head and bloody bones business (which surely Shakspeare had nothing to do with) would be the right kind of excitement for the farmer's children; but the future poet was a bold critic in the indignant purity of his young imagination. Is there not something in these scenes, over which the mind lingers more tenderly than if this boy's education had been in the hands of the most learned scholars? And when the books were laid aside, and the porridge eaten, and the homely yet hospitable table cleared, came the family service, the "Let us worship God," which, in the confidential intercourse between the brothers, Robert told Gilbert had always seemed to him the most solemn of utterances. A sketch of family life more pure, more true, or more touching, was never made.

But this existence, though so beautiful to look back upon, was a very hard one. "The cheerless gloom of a hermit, with the unceasing moil of a galley-slave," the poet himself says—with an exaggeration which rarely comes into his poetry, but is scarcely ever absent from his prose—looking back upon that struggle when he seemed to have reached the heights of fame, and probably hoped to have escaped poverty for ever. His brother is more moderate, but still with a deep gravity relates the story of their laborious youth. " To the buffetings of misfortune," he says, " we could only oppose hard labour and the most rigid economy. We lived very sparingly. For several years butchers' meat was a stranger in the house, while all the members of the family exerted themselves to the utmost of their strength, and even beyond it, in the labours of the farm. My brother at the age of thirteen assisted in threshing the crops of corn, and at fifteen was the principal labourer on the farm, for we had no hired servant, male or female. The anguish of mind that we felt at our tender years under these straits and difficulties was great. To think of our father now growing old (for he was above fifty), broken down with the long-continued fatigues of his life, with a wife and five other children, and in a declining state of circumstances ——these reflections produced in my brother's mind and mine sensations of the deepest distress." But nevertheless the lads were young and capable of throwing off their " deep distress " whenever the factor's letter or some other immediate pinch of misery was a few days, or perhaps a few hours off. At fifteen Robert fell in love for the first time with " a bonnie sweet sonsie lass," who was his partner in the harvest-field, following him closely along the golden rig, as the manner was, binding as he cut the rustling poppy-mingled grain. She " sang sweetly " a song composed by a small country laird's son on one of his father's maids, with whom he was in love ——and the dark sunburnt glowing boy, with the thrill of a new emotion stirring through him, ran into song too, moved by emulation, and by all those dawning " thoughts, and passions, and delights," which are the ministers of love. " My Nelly's looks are blythe and sweet," sang the fifteen-year-old boy in his rapture in the golden autumn sunshine among the golden corn. He is not much to be pitied after all. The scene is Arcadian in its tender innocence, lit up with a sweet glow of natural light and colour, but no heat of premature or unnatural passion. The little scene in the harvest-field balances with its sweet daylight, its first love and first song, the Rembrandt interior of the farm-house kitchen and its copy-books. " Puirtith cauld," such as " wrecks the heart," and labours without ceasing—but at the same time warm, natural, hopeful life, and poetry and love : a prince could not have more.

We need not linger upon the little literature which he added after the days of the Geographical Grammar to so many better things. He read Addison and Pope in addition to the serious works chosen by his father. His boyish imagination was much stirred by the " Vision of Mirza," and his literary ambition aroused by the accidental possession of " a small collection of letters by the most eminent writers "— an unfortunate acquisition, if they had any share in forming his own style in correspondence, which was always bad, pompous, and affected. And he began the Latin " Rudiments," and acquired, by book, a little French — all very fine things for a ploughboy to aspire to, though of little advantage to him. What is much more important, however, than this, and other little attempts at self-improvement, reading-clubs, night-schools, and educational efforts of various kinds—things very fine to hear of in the case of an ordinary peasant lad, but very unfruitful when the peasant is a Burns—he lived his toilsome life in innocence, in close companionship with his excellent brother Gilbert, and in loyal devotion to his home. His early poems are full of the delightful compensations which God and poetry gave him for his premature toil. When he looked back upon his youth in after years, in prose, in the pompous retrospect of a letter

to some fine person, with whom the poet was minded to
show himself equally fine, he speaks gloomily and even
bitterly of that toil : but never in verse—never in the
happy unconscious utterances of his youth.

> " I mind it weel in early date,
>   When I was beardless, young, and blate,
>   An' first could thresh the barn ;
>   Or haud a yokin' at the pleugh,
>   An' tho' forfoughten sair enow,
>   Yet unco proud to learn."

What better representation could be given of youthful
progress than this of the " happy weary " boy, " sair for-
foughten," but proud and glad of his advance to his
heritage, a man's work ?   " He is hardly to be envied,"
says Mr. Lockhart, " who can contemplate without
emotion this exquisite picture of young nature and young
genius."   And even when he grew older and fell into
those habits of Scottish country life, which unfortunately
so often lead to mischief, there is no deterioration visible
in the young poet for some time.   He " went ower the
hills to Nannie," though the wastlin' wind blew both
rude and chill, and the day's darg had been long and
heavy; and no corrupt heart could have written words of
such honest and noble simplicity as those that tell the
story of those pilgrimages—

> " Our auld gudeman delights to view
>   His sheep an' kye thrive bonnie, O ;
> But I'm as blythe that hauds his pleugh,
>   An' has nae care but Nannie, O.

> " A country lad is my degree,
>   An' few there be that ken me, O ;
> But what care I how few they be,
>   I'm welcome aye to Nannie, O."

Never was a more manly song.   And the other love songs
of this youthful period all strike the same true note of

sentiment, refined and exquisite in their homeliness, as if
they had been the wooings of a prince——

> " Yestreen, when, to the trembling string,
>   The dance gaed thro' the lighted ha',
> To thee my fancy took its wing,
>   I sat, but neither heard nor saw :
> Tho' this was fair, and that was braw,
>   And yon the toast of a' the town,
> I sigh'd, and said amang them a',
>   Ye are na Mary Morison."

Could there be a more delicate expression of that
supremacy of one, which is too penetrating, too ethereal,
to mean merely a Judgment of Paris, a selection of the
most beautiful ?   Far beyond that ignoble conflict goes
our ploughboy ; sweet though they all are, they are not
Mary Morison—and his heart has no more to say ; an
inspiration which the most diligent study of classical
models or other means of culture could never have given.
Among the Mauchline lads and lasses, dancing wild reels
with many a snap of the fingers and rustic shout, who
taught him this highest delicacy of passion ?   Even when
the sentiment is less exquisite it is always manly and
honest.   Principal Shairp laments the country custom of
nightly meetings at doors or windows, meetings for which
the rustic lover will walk miles over hill and dale after
his day's work, and which the milkmaids and serving
lasses calculate upon as others do upon the joys of
society, as the chief relaxation of their lives.   No good
comes of these nightly trysts to many, and probably
little good came to Burns ; but as he sets forth on " the
Lammas night," when——

> " The sky was blue, the wind was still,
>   The moon was shining clearly,"

to watch the barley rigs with Annie : or when he invites
another " charmer " on a clear evening, when " thick flies

the skimming swallow," to stray with him upon his "glad-
some way," and to note the beauty of the autumn landscape——

> " The rustling corn, the fruited thorn,
>   And every happy creature,"

it is hard to think of any possible harm.   Every one of
these bursts of song reveals to us the sweet countryside
with all its woods and streams, the tender silence of
nature, the "happy living things," which the poet loves
with all the genial warmth of a nature which is in
friendship and harmony with everything God has made.
The lark which

> " 'Twixt bright and dark,
>   Blythe waukens by the daisy's side,"

is as near to him as the shepherd that "o'er the moorland whistles shrill "——and all nature is populous to his
universal sympathy.   A man with such exuberance of
tender thought and winning words was, as might be
expected, welcome everywhere to the rustic maidens, to
whom it was as sweet as to any princess to receive such
tuneful homage.   No woman at that day, in any language
(unless it were the Kätchens and Friederikas, by whom
Goethe was educating himself to all the varieties of
emotion, in the depths of Germany), had such exquisite
homage offered to her as had Mary Morison, whoever she
may have been : and it is a curious thing to realise that,
in all the English-speaking races, there was not one but
this Ayrshire rustic to whom that mystery of pure and
perfect feeling was revealed.

The medicine of this fresh and simple nature was
what sick poetry wanted to restore the noblest of the
arts.   It was obtained here at the very fountainhead.
As the great world rolls slowly one surface after another
to the shining of the sun, so when a new creator arises

a whole new earth comes gradually into sight before the
eyes of the astonished lookers on. The native sphere of
Burns was so unknown, that though his mission, like
that of Cowper's, was more to reveal than to invent, yet
the surprise of the new country discovered was to the
rest of mankind like that of a creation. A few rural
voices had indeed made the air tingle here and there,
producing upon the world around an effect not much
unlike that which might have followed had the sheep
opened their mouths to emit couplets instead of bleatings;
but rare prodigies of this kind had generally proved to
have little more to say than might have come from the
sheep. But Burns came, like Homer, from the very
fountainhead of life: nobody had taught him a note, he
had his music from nature, and he took his theme from
nature. He was as little afraid of the homeliest facts of
his landscape as Cowper was, and as observant of every
change of the atmosphere; but the principle which Cowper applied only to the external country Burns employed
for the inner man, reproducing all that was in him with
a dauntless freedom more remarkable still. And Burns
was so much the greater poet, and had in him such a
sweep and rush of inspiration, as well as such a superior
force of life, and all the added impetuosity of passion,
that his advent was far more startling and effective than
that of his gentler fellow. One wonders if they had ever
met what would have been their mutual impressions?
Would Burns have set down the mild recluse as one of
the unco good, or Cowper stigmatised his brother as a
rural rake? Nothing could be more likely; and yet in
his heart there was nothing that so touched the one as
true religion, and nothing that more attracted the other
than the life and vigour in which he was himself so
deficient. They were both equally withdrawn, though
in ways so different, from the excitements and emulations

of literary coteries.   Silence surrounded them in their
walks, though the middle-aged Englishman's was but an
invalid's stroll by the flat river side, or over the tranquil
fields—while the young ploughman "walked in glory
and in joy, following his plough along the mountain
side;" but they were equal rebels to the world and all
its conventional ways.

The poet's education was thus conducted with ideal
fitness, until he attained the age of twenty-three—an age
at which a young man in his rank is often a husband
and a father; for hard work and early independence
are very maturing influences.   And so long as he kept
in his natural rustic sphere, with all its roughnesses
and privations, its evening trysts, and miscellaneous
love-making, no fault, it would seem, could be found
with him.   He worked early and late, and had many
anxieties.   He kept free of debt (which he always held
in horror) upon £7 a year.   As they worked at the farm-
work he would communicate one poem after another to
Gilbert, who is in his way as great a wonder as the poet
himself, to those who do not understand what a poor
Scotch countryman might be.   One of the productions
thus communicated was the "Epistle to Davie," which
we may accept as the young ploughman's theory and
philosophy of life as he saw it:

> " What tho' like commoners of air,
>   We wander out, we know not where,
>   But[1] either house or hall ?
>   Yet nature's charms, the hills and woods,
>   The sweeping vales, and foaming floods
>   Are free alike to all.
>   In days when daisies deck the ground,
>   And blackbirds whistle clear,
>   With honest joy our hearts will bound
>   To see the coming year ;

----

[1] Without.

On braes, when we please, then,
 We'll sit an' sowth a tune ;
Syne rhyme till't, we'll time till't,
 And sing't when we hae done.

" Then let us cheerfu' acquiesce ;
 Nor make our scanty pleasures less,
  By pining at our state ;
And, even should misfortunes come,
I, here wha sit, hae met wi' some,
  An's thankfu' for them yet.
They gie the wit of age to youth ;
 They let us ken oursel' :
They make us see the naked truth,
 The real guid and ill.
  Tho' losses, and crosses,
   Be lessons right severe,
  There's wit there, ye'll get there,
   Ye'll find nae other where."

These verses were repeated by Robert to Gilbert in
the summer of 1784, shortly after their father's death,
when they were working together at Mossgiel, the new
farm in which each member of the family had embarked
all that he and she had, or could do, in the hope of
being able to live and toil together. It was "in the
interval of harder labour, when he and I were working
in the garden (kailyard). I believe," adds Gilbert, "the
first idea of Robert's becoming an author was started on
this occasion." As they worked among the kail, the one
said to the other that the verses were good, as good as
Allan Ramsay—sweetest praise to the author's ears ! and
that " they would bear being printed." The writer and
receiver of the rhymed epistle were both country lads,
like the critic ; and these were the sentiments which
naturally occurred to them, and the style that pleased
them. It was at Mossgiel that he first inscribed himself,
in some moment of triumph, upon the books in which he
copied out his verses, " Robert Burns, Poet," and this was

the "auld clay biggin'" where, as he sat and eyed the
smoke that filled the air with a "mottie misty" haze,
the vision of Coila, blushing "sweet like modest worth,"
with her "wildly witty rustic grace," and her eyes which
"beamed keen with honour," "stepped ben," stopping the
rash vow he was about to make to rhyme no more.

And during the two years they here laboured together, doing badly, yet by no fault of theirs, Gilbert
remembered, with proud and tender faithfulness, other
days and places in which communications of a similar
kind were made to him.   Once when the two were
"going together with carts for coal to the family (and I
could yet point out the particular spot), the author first
repeated to me the 'Address to the Deil.'"   Another
poem he heard "as I was holding the plough and he was
letting the water off the field beside me."   The "Cottar's
Saturday Night" was repeated to him on a Sunday afternoon walk, one of the few moments of leisure in their
laborious life, and Gilbert was "electrified," as well he
might be.   During these years Burns was working not
less but more hard than an ordinary ploughman, fighting
desperately to keep his position as a farmer, however
poor, rather than become another farmer's hired-servant,
which was the only alternative ; and in the midst of his
toils, unknown, with Gilbert for his audience, poured
forth a torrent of poetry as sweet and fresh and wholesome as the country breezes.   This was not a deluge of
love-songs only, as we are disposed to believe.   Among
these early productions were pictures of Scottish life such
as no man had dreamed of before, and which lit up all
Scotland with an illumination of tender light; soft outbursts of humour, genial poetic laughter—and mingled
with these such friendly rural philosophies, such pathetic
thoughtfulness, pity and charity, as go direct to the heart.
Every influence around him entered into his soul.   Its

door stood open night and day to receive everything that was weak and wanted succour, to admit everything that was lovely and noble.   In all the world there was not a created thing which he shut out from his sympathy, from the " cowering timorous beastie" in the fields to " Auld Nickieben" in " yon lowin heugh," which he was " wae to think upon," even for the sake of the father of evil. He is like a god in his tender thoughtfulness, his yearning for the welfare of all.   When he wakes by night and hears the storm shake the walls of the clay cottage, he does not hug himself in his individual warmth and comfort, or even draw close the curtains, and ·trim the fire, like the other poet, on the banks of the Ouse, but cannot get to sleep again for thinking of the creatures out-of-doors :

> " List'ning, the doors an' winnocks rattle,
> I thought me on the ourie cattle,
> Or silly sheep, wha bide this brattle
>   O' winter war ;
> And thro' the drift, deep-lairing sprattle,
>   Beneath a scaur.
>
> " Ilk happing bird, wee helpless thing,
> That, in the merry months of spring
> Delighted me to hear thee sing,
>   What comes o' thee ?
> Where wilt thou cower thy chittering wing,
>   An' close thy e'e ?"

Who could have supposed that of all places in the world a fellow-feeling so exquisite, so delicate, so tender, was waking under the roof of a clay cottage, and thinking, like heaven itself, of the humblest things—the sparrows that do not fall to the ground without our Father ? Cowper was the gentlest of men, making pets even of hares, and turning with loathing from him who would crush a worm ; but it is not to his sensitive spirit that

the darkness opens, and the silly sheep and the helpless
birds show themselves in the dreary midnight, unfortunate
brothers for whom his heart bleeds.   If it had been but
for this one revelation, that recording angel of whom we
have heard so much might have blotted out a thousand
peccadilloes.   "He prayeth best that loveth best all things,
both great and small."

But at this period there were few offences with which
to reproach the young poet.   He had taken no ill turn
as yet in his rustic career.   So far as we can see, his
country life was even marked with aspirations towards
pleasures more elevated than the ordinary round of fairs
and midnight courtships.   He and Gilbert and five others
established a club for "literary purposes" in their village.
There was no place to hold its meetings save the public-
house, but the expenditure of each member was limited
to threepence, to avoid evil consequences.   Their object
was "to relax themselves after toil, to promote sociability
and friendship, and to improve the mind."   The little
Tarbolton club debated the question whether prudence or
inclination should be most considered in marriage, and
other sentimental and social subjects.   They "found
themselves so happy" that when the club had existed a
year they gave a dance in its honour; that is, they met
together, each one with the partner of his choice, "and
spent the evening in such innocence and merriment, such
cheerfulness and good humour, that every brother will
long remember it with pleasure and delight."   If we did
not know, alas! the darker shadows that always haunt
the rural life of Scotland, this narrative would read like
Arcadia.   When the brothers removed to Mossgiel, near
Mauchline, they originated a similar club there, with
which Dr. Currie finds fault on the strange ground that
the books chosen by the little society were "less calculated to increase the knowledge than to refine the

taste." Imagine taste existing at all or any refinement in a ploughman's club in a Scotch village a hundred years ago! And we talk of progress in these days! But Burns was not destined to remain in this humble society. As his reputation grew, and his early poems became known, people much above his own condition in life began to hear of the moorland poet, and he fell into the hands of his betters, in an evil hour.

The little town of Mauchline would seem to have possessed, as most country towns did, and still do, perhaps, with a difference, a jovial society, not very scrupulous or very refined, but full of a kind of rude wit and boisterous good-fellowship, according to the fashion of the time. The high jinks of Scott's lawyers give us a sketch of this kind of wild and witty company at its best; but even that, if touched by any hand less than a master's, and dealing with any class less remarkable than the wits of the Parliament House, might easily bear a very different aspect. In a little country town, at a period when manners were coarser and license greater than at present, the jovial coterie was almost without restraint. The women were used to the absorption of the men in toddy and talk all the evening through, and the minister in many cases shared both—unless he happened to be one of those unreasonable Puritans of the New Light, who objected to everything that was comfortable, and at whom they laughed with furious jokes and merriment till the roof rang. The only leaven of this society, the salt that kept it from corruption, was its genuine humour and appreciation of everything comical, and a rude energy and boisterous fun that was in it. The heavy country wits, with snuff lying in the wrinkles of their long waistcoats, and an atmosphere of whisky breathing round them, had yet an eye for a joke, and took a grim pleasure in watching the follies of their neighbours.

They were men sometimes of good birth and connections, allied to the neighbouring gentry, and proud of their connection, though familiar, as the Scottish code of manners has always permitted, with all classes, and having their joke wherever they went. The "writer," who probably was the younger son of some neighbouring laird, the doctor, the factor of the nearest duke or marquis, any idle man with enough to live upon, belonged to this noisy coterie. Mr. Skelton, in his recent sketch of the "Year One," describes it in his little town as consisting of the provost, the lawyer, the captain of the coastguard, and the minister, the latter no less daring in jest, if a little more careful in conduct, than the others. They were ready to give a jocose patronage to religion when this was the case; but when a zealous minister, calling them to account for their peccadilloes, occupied the parish, then the very air rang with the guffaws of their defiance and ridicule.

The first social elevation that Burns obtained was, when he was admitted into the company of these choice spirits. A man who could sing a good song (especially if he had made it before singing it), or produce a lively play of hazardous jokes, or add a spice of novelty of any kind to their vigorous coarse talk, was sure of a welcome among them. Burns no doubt believed devoutly that he was being elevated to the best society when he was taken up by the Aikens and Hamiltons; and when he found nothing better than the gossip of a clique, and the cleverness of local malice, disappointment, if at all events perhaps an easier sense of familiarity, must have been in his mind. But it was no doubt a gratification to him to be made a member of the clique, and initiated into its personal hatreds and jocular malignities, till at last, in his genuine yet fictitious enthusiasm of good fellowship, he lifted the clear voice, given him for purposes so much

more noble, to sing to the confusion of his patrons'
adversaries, adding sharp darts of his own to their vulgar
gibes and coarse badinage. This is the evident reason
why it happened that the young poet, till that time the
truest new revelation of poetic genius within the limits of
Britain, nay, in the universe itself (with the exception of
young Goethe in Frankfort), opened his public career—he
who had so much fine and tender and humorous poetry
in his old scrap-books at home—with a string of verses in
which bad taste and profane meaning had not even wit
or power to justify, or the headlong race of poetic excitement to excuse them. This was what the patronage of
his betters did for him. From the "Epistle to Davie" to
the "Twa Herds," what an inconceivable downfall! the
first full of all the tranquil breadth of nature, the
sober yet ever pleasant and cheerful light of morning,
before misfortune had any bitterness, or individual passion
or anguish had disturbed the confidence of youth in its
own fate; the other a miserable local squib, requiring
pages of explanation, filled with strange names of persons
we know nothing about, bristling with allusions which
never could have possessed any zest or flavour, save to
those who were acquainted with the temporary and unlovely squabbles of the countryside. A more terrible
satire could not have been than the probably quite unconscious one which the young poet implied in the care
he took to suit his style to his audience—to rustic Davie
and Gilbert those manly views of life and labour which
would not misbecome a philosopher; to the wits of
Mauchline the servility of a rude personal attack. Burns
did not intend any such blighting comparison, but the
reader is justified in making it when he sees the debasement of this Samson making sport for the Philistines. It
could not be helped. The nearest aristocracy, such as it
was, was bound to notice the local poet. Would that

they had let him alone in the better atmosphere into which he was born! but by this time he had already begun to stumble out of that good and pure atmosphere, into dark ways—leading to those precipices from which no precautions taken by others can divert the footsteps of wayward men.

It is wonderful, however, to realise how many of Burns's finest productions were written at this period. Even in the objectionable vein thus opened, there were triumphs to be obtained. Two or three others as objectionable, and with as few redeeming qualities as the "Twa Herds"—the "Kirk's Alarm," and "The Ordination," followed—exactly the kind of verses which would naturally be produced by the coarse and clever poet of a village—the man whose personal satires are always received by his limited circle with "a roar of applause." But we think Principal Shairp and other grave critics are mistaken when they class together all Burns's attacks upon the unco good. "Holy Willie's Prayer" is a very different production from the others. It is equally, or indeed, more profane; but it is the highest kind of satire, awful in its vivid reality, a condensed and terrible picture which outdoes Tartuffe. The Hypocrite, a figure which all the poets cannot extirpate from the world, but which is their legitimate prey wherever it is found, stands out before us in a blaze of infernal light. We are not sure even that we can regret the profane suggestion which turned the poet's eye upon such a personification of evil. This tremendous sketch wants no explanatory notes, no disguise of forgotten initials; the Mauchline coterie, with many a peal of delighted laughter, might identify the victim, as the French critics did also in Molière's day; but it does not add to our terror or awe, to know that he had a living prototype and an ordinary name; and no virtuous prejudice, however natural, can be permitted to interfere with the immortality of such a poem. In all his maturer years, when his mind might be supposed to have more affinity with the tragic aspects of existence, Burns never again struck so strong and true a note.

But everything he touched in this youthful heyday of his powers was full of vigour. It would be natural to suppose that these were the days of the love songs, and that the humour and the thought came later. But this is not the case. The best of the songs came, indeed, out of the fulness of his too susceptible heart in this period ; but he had a mind also for other things. What a varied and inexhaustible storehouse must that have been, out of which, side by side with "Holy Willie," came the most perfect of homely idylls, "The Cottar's Saturday Night," and, on the other hand, the "Address to the Deil," with its ripe and humorous philosophy and tender-heartedness. Milton dignified his Satan into one of the grandest of heroes : but no man was ever "wae to think upon yon den" before this young ploughman. And what martial poet ever produced a figure more daring and splendid than that of the soldier whom this ploughman paints for us in lines of fire, in the ode which he consecrates, alas ! to Scotch Drink, the most fatal of all the ills of Scotland—

> " But bring a Scotsman frae his hill,
> Clap in his cheek a Highland gill,
> Say, such is royal George's will,
>   An' there's the foe,
> He has nae thought but how to kill
>   Twa at a blow.
>
> " Nae cauld, faint-hearted doubtings tease him ;
> Death comes, wi' fearless eyes he sees him ;
> Wi' bluidy hand a welcome gies him ;
>   An' when he fa's,
> His latest draught o' breathin' lea'es him
>   In faint huzzas."

Was there ever a more brilliant animated living

picture? The "Highland gill," after all, has very little to do with it; but he whom no faint-hearted doubtings assail—whose rush of fervid valour is limited only by the thought how best to kill "twa at a blow," who breathes out in the face of death his faint huzzas—what a vision, rapid as the lightning, plucked out of the very heart of battle!

And does not the reader see how, as these poems grew and breathed into being, the veil of the unknown was lifted, and Lowland Scotland, sweet and cheerful, came to light as when the sun rises over an undiscovered land? Some one, we forget who, has directed attention lately to the place Scotland held in the estimation of her rich and scornful yoke-fellow, before Burns and Scott were. Even Smollett, a Scotsman, dared say very little for his country. It was a land of sour fanatics, of penurious misers, of mean bowing and scraping, and servile arts of all kinds; a country which all its sons forsook as soon as possible, to fish and scrape a living out of English prodigality, and to promote their raw-boned countrymen over the honest Saxon, who was no match for their grovelling cunning. This was the best that was said for us on the other side of the Tweed. The extraordinary revolution of sentiment since (though still the old prejudice has left some unaccountable relics) is due entirely to the two poets, whose mission it was to make their country known. Burns was the first, and in some respects he was the greatest. His revelation was deeper, stronger, more original, and reached lower down—revealing almost more than a mere nationality in the warm and tender light by which he made Scotland visible: for he made the poor visible at the same time, the common people, the universal basis of society—not as objects of pity, which was the tendency of those pictures of Cowper's to which we have already referred, but as

brethren, with the same faculties, the same enjoyments
—and sometimes more beautiful and sacred enjoyments
than many of their betters. Hard must that man's heart
have been and opaque his intellect who, after reading
the "Cottar's Saturday Night," could have looked with
disdainful eyes upon any cottage : Scotland was the first
object of the revelation—but after Scotland, mankind.

All this astonishing work was done before he was
twenty-seven, while he was working early and late, living
the life of a farm labourer, though he was his own master,
and with no advantages so called, either in the shape of
general culture or acquaintance with the best models.
For our own part we are not sure that Burns's reputation would have been much lessened had he never
written another line. Critics acquainted with the best
models have given each other a sign to glorify the "Jolly
Beggars" and "Tam o' Shanter : " but no one who loves
Burns and understands him will turn, we think, by preference, or direct any new reader to these later productions. He will rather glean out of the wealth of this
marvellous youth, through which the poet passed in
many a toil and trouble, yet, "in glory and in joy," following his plough. Alas, towards the end even of this
prolific and wonderful season the glory and the joy
lessened, and shame and sorrow came the poet's way.
He began his downward career, in the manner always
too facile to his countrymen. We do not need to repeat
here the most distasteful story of the preliminary trans-
actions between him and his future wife, or the marriage
irregularly made, then broken, or supposed to be broken,
notwithstanding all our deeply rooted terror of Scotch
marriages—the father of Jean Armour preferring shame
for her to the penniless, and it is to be feared, inconstant
and unruly husband upon whom she had a legitimate
claim. Recent investigators have been so cruel as to

make it apparent that the story of " Highland Mary "
occurred in one of the lulls of the twice broken and
twice renewed connection with Jean, so that the purity
and sorrow of that tale—the well-known Sunday which
Mary and her lover spent together on the banks of Ayr,
swearing everlasting truth over the running water, with
that Bible held between them, in which Burns had written
the divine injunction to " perform thine oath ; " and the
still sadder wintry moonlight, in which he addressed his
" Mary in Heaven "—lose something of their mournful
tenderness ; and we are forced to conclude that probably
it was a good thing for Highland Mary that death stepped
in, and that all she could ever claim was that pathetic
recollection.   The poor little moorland farm was a failure,
not from any fault of the brothers, and the countryside
would seem to have turned against the rural Lothario,
who already had appeared more than once on " the stool
of repentance " and received public admonition to little
purpose.   Even his Mauchline friends were estranged
from him, one of them at least, it appears, agreeing with
Jean Armour's father that it would be rash to put a
woman's happiness in his hands.   Burns's sky, a little
while before so clear, seems all at once to have been
covered with overwhelming storm - clouds.   Nemesis
works very rapidly with the poor : in this respect there
is nothing that makes so much difference in life as
wealth.   The rich have time to sow their wild oats, but
to the poor man the process cannot last long.

The poet was altogether overwhelmed by these sudden
combinations of evil.   No doubt it was bitter beyond
expression to him to have no backing of social sympathy
and support, and the humiliation of being abandoned by
his sweetheart (who was more than a sweetheart, by this
time the mother of twin children), the bitter thought that
shame was better than himself in the estimation of her

family, and the grieved disapproval of his own—seem to have " worked like madness in his brain." He was ready to throw up the conflict altogether, to go to the West Indies and make a new beginning on a Jamaica estate, which probably, had he been any other ruined young prodigal in the country, would have been the very best thing he could do. But to make this new start money was necessary, and to get even so much money as would pay his passage was a difficult matter. In this strait, some one suggested the publication of the poetry which was kept in the drawer of a deal table, in the garret, which was his bedroom and study, at Mossgiel. Thus the greatest poetry of the age got to light, so to speak, accidentally, to assist the poet in banishing himself and retrieving his miserable fortunes far from the country he loved. A curious air of chance and caprice is thus thrown over the kindred events, happening within a couple of years, which meant so much for English literature. The " Task," the invalid's amusement, playfully undertaken to please " the fair," was printed in 1784. The date of Burns's downfall, and of the sudden necessity for money to pay his passage to Jamaica, was a little later : in 1786, out of the humble printing-press at Kilmarnock, in an edition of six hundred copies, and with a subscription of three hundred and fifty, his poetry appeared, nobody concerned thinking of much more than a local popularity, the applause of the people who spoke his own rustic language and knew every bank and brae which he had celebrated in his verse.

And for a little while this seems to have been all it attained. What should we know now, with all our additional facilities of communication, of a little volume of poems modestly published at Kilmarnock ? Natural curiosity, anxiety, and hope kept him lingering to see

what would happen before he went away. He got
twenty pounds as his share of the profits—more than
enough for his passage-money—and the fame of the
little book "spread like wildfire" in the countryside.
One or two local magnates sought his acquaintance;
among them Dugald Stewart, who was temporarily
resident in the neighbourhood, and Mrs. Dunlop of
Dunlop, one of the county aristocracy. He was pleased,
no doubt: but still took his steerage passage to Jamaica,
and sent off his chest to Greenock. It was on a gloomy
autumn night that he left the manse of Loudoun, where
he had gone to take leave of the minister, Dr. Lawrie, a
friend who was even then exerting himself busily, but
secretly, on the poet's behalf: and gloomier still were
his confused and melancholy thoughts. As he strode
over the dreary moorland in the gathering darkness, hope
forsook the young man thus " abandoned, exiled, and
forlorn." "Farewell!" he said, with all the bitterness
of the parting swelling over him—

> " Farewell ! old Coila's hills and dales,
>   Her heathy moors and winding vales,
>   The scenes where wretched fancy roves,
>   Pursuing past unhappy loves.
>   Farewell ! my friends, farewell, my foes,
>   My peace with these, my love with those—
>   The bursting tears my heart declare,
>   Farewell ! the bonnie banks of Ayr."

This was the very darkest moment before the dawn.
He had scarcely gone from Loudoun manse when a letter
arrived there from Dr. Blacklock in Edinburgh, a letter
which the kind minister had been hoping for, which seems
to have raised Burns at once from the depths of despond-
ency to immediate and brilliant hope. " It was therefore
much to be wished, for the sake of the young man," said
the blind man of letters, after much praise of the volume

his correspondent had sent to him, " that a second edition, more numerous than the former, could immediately be printed, as it appears certain that its intrinsic merits, and the exertions of the author's friends, might give it a more universal circulation than anything of the kind which has been printed within my memory." This was enough to change the aspect of heaven and earth to Burns; one of the special griefs in the combinations of distress that threatened to crush him having been the refusal of his Ayrshire publisher to run the risk of a second issue. Instead of going to Jamaica, he went to Edinburgh accordingly to push his fortune, with all the natural elation which such a change, and the prospect at last of real fame and success, naturally involved. Still, it will be perceived that it was for " the sake of the young man himself" that Blacklock counselled this step, hoping for a " more universal circulation than *anything of the kind* " had received. It would have seemed the wildest nonsense to the literary circles in Edinburgh to suppose that this young prodigy of a ploughman could one way or other affect literature, or that his second edition was of importance in any interest but his own.

We will leave to a separate chapter our sketch of the literary society of Edinburgh as then flourishing. The attitude of Burns in respect to it is very curious and interesting. Here was a young peasant, without education, without knowledge of the world, full of Scotch reserve and that *farouche* pride of the rustic which reaches the height of a passion. The pride which is supposed to accompany blue blood and great descent has justifications outside of the individual possessed by it; and in most cases it imposes a certain restraint upon that individual, and demands of him some qualities, or at least some graces, in accordance with it. But the pride of a peasant

is wildly personal, and independent of every consideration. The more he is conscious of his deficiencies even,
the more wildly bent he will be upon attentions and
observances due in society only to high social qualifica-
tions. From the moment when Burns steps into the light
in Edinburgh, this mixture of shyness, inordinate self-
opinion, and an almost polemical determination to prove
himself the equal, if not the superior of everybody round
him, appears both in his behaviour and in the private
records of his opinions. It was no doubt a very difficult
position. Uncultured, unaccustomed to the ways of
society, knowing nobody, feeling himself a kind of vague
representative, not only of genius but of man, among a
curious crowd of superiors, all more or less disposed to
infringe these rights, to patronise him, and lessen his own
sense of dignity, he appears on the defensive, always
watchful lest some affront should be intended; beguiled
indeed, into better moods in the warmth of social intercourse, but ever ready to take fire again, and to resent
not only imaginary slights to himself, but even the
civilities offered to others whom he thinks less worthy.

> "The rank is but the guinea stamp,
> A man's a man for a' that.'"

is a very fine sentiment, but it is extremely troublesome
when carried into society. It says much for the kind
impressionableness of Burns's real nature, that, strolling
about as he did, wrapped in this mantle of rustic haughti-
ness, more all-enveloping than the pride of kings, he did
after all unbend sufficiently to attract as well as to dazzle
the curious Edinburgh society, especially the ladies, whom
he " carried off their feet," according to the characteristic
Scotticism used by one of them, with his eloquence, his
old-world deference and chivalry. This was quite in
keeping with his character. Notwithstanding all his

rustic adventures, it is evident that a certain chivalrous
feeling towards women existed in him always, and the
gentle condescension of a lady not only pleases the poetic
imagination as fancifully right and becoming, but had
nothing unpalatable in it to so manly a man. He is said
to have made the remark, that whereas he had met in
his own class with men as excellent, as thoughtful, and
high-minded, as any he had encountered in these higher
circles, yet that an accomplished woman was a being
altogether new to him.

But while he owned this spell, being always too ready
to yield to feminine fascinations—which is perhaps the
most certain of all means of being liked by women—his
general aspect was not so attractive. He entered Edinburgh shy and proud, yet full of expectations, in the end
of November 1786, and instead of taking a lodging more
appropriate, went to a " close" in the Lawnmarket where
a Mauchline lad, Richmond by name, lived, and shared
his room and his bed for the greater part of his stay, thus
clinging to his friends and his natural condition, in the
midst of so many changes, with a tenacity which has at
least as much obstinate pride as tenderness in it. " I
tremble," he says in one of his letters, " lest I should be
ruined by being dragged too suddenly into the glare of
polite and learned observation." This was only a fort-
night after his arrival, but by that time he had a list of
acquaintances which shows how ready his welcome had
been. " I have been introduced to a good many of the
noblesse, but my avowed patrons and patronesses are the
Duchess of Gordon, the Countess of Glencairn, with my
Lord, and Lady Betty, the Dean of Faculty, Sir John
Whitefoord; I have likewise warm friends among the
literati, Professors Stewart, Blair, and Mr. Mackenzie, the
' Man of Feeling.' " The latter, a sort of miniature
Scotch Addison, enjoying a very great reputation in his

day, had reviewed Burns's early volume in the *Lounger*, a little periodical of the order of the *Rambler* and its many descendants, and this set him fully afloat in the knowledge of the world; for the paper is referred to by Cowper, and was widely read even in England.

Perhaps it was the fear of having his head turned by this sudden blaze of popularity which made Burns enter society with such a determination to hold his own. But granting this, there seems to have been little to find fault with in his demeanour. "In no part of his manner was there the slightest affectation," one of the bystanders tells us, "nor could a stranger have suspected from anything in his behaviour or conversation that he had been for some months the favourite of all the fashionable circles. In conversation he was powerful. His conceptions and expressions were of corresponding vigour, and on all subjects were as remote as possible from commonplaces. Though somewhat authoritative, it was in a way which gave little offence, and was readily imputed to his inexperience in those modes of smoothing dissent and softening assertion, which are important characteristics of polished manners." Dugald Stewart adds, "The attentions he received from all ranks would have turned any head but his own. I cannot say that I perceived any unfavourable effect they left upon his mind. He retained the same simplicity which had struck me so forcibly when first I saw him in the country, nor did he seem to feel any additional self-importance from the number and rank of his new acquaintance. . . . The remarks he made on the characters of men were shrewd and pointed, though frequently inclining too much to sarcasm. His praises of those he loved were sometimes indiscriminate and exaggerated. . . . His wit was ready and always impressed with the marks of a vigorous understanding, but to my taste, not often pleasing or happy."

This was the impression he made on Edinburgh—
that of a man fully aware of his own rights, and disdain-
ing to show any excitement of complacency or elation
at the notice taken of him.   When he "furnished the
greater part of the conversation," he did no more than
what he saw evidently was expected of him; and
appeared to society a wonderful phenomenon altogether,
using language as good as the best, keeping his self-
possession, setting vanity sternly at bay, upheld by the
keenest inspiration of pride.   There is nothing in his
life more remarkable or more characteristic.   His friends
seem to have written to him on all sides, warning him
against that intoxication of popular favour which has
injured so many.   To all he replies in the same tone,
" I am willing to believe that my abilities deserve some
notice. . . . I have studied myself, and know what ground
I occupy, and however a friend or the world may differ
from me in that particular, I stand for my own opinion
in silent resolve, with all the tenaciousness of property.
When," he adds with a grandiloquence not so remarkable then as now, " When proud fortune's ebbing tide
recedes, you will bear me witness that when my bubble
of fame was at the highest, I stood unintoxicated, with
the inebriating cup in my hand, looking forward with
rueful resolve to the hastening time when the blow of
Calumny shall dash it to the ground with all the eagerness of vengeful triumph !"

This anticipation recurs continually in his letters—
whether with that conscious attempt to propitiate fate by
foreseeing the worst, which is one of the expedients of
natural superstition, or in real soberness of expectation,
it is difficult to tell.   "You are dazzled by newspaper
accounts and distant reports," he says to another correspondent; "but in reality I have no great temptation to
be intoxicated with the cup of prosperity.   Novelty may

attract the attention of mankind awhile; to it I owe my present *éclat*, but I see the time not far distant when the popular tide which has borne me to a height of which I am perhaps unworthy, shall recede with silent celerity and leave me a barren waste of sand, to descend at my leisure to my former station." All this is wise to a painful degree, but it is not so altogether discouraging as the occasional outbursts of bitterness which are to be found in the still more private repository of his thoughts.

" There are few of the sore evils under the sun give me more uneasiness and chagrin than the comparison how a man of genius, nay, of avowed worth, is received everywhere, with the reception which a mere ordinary character, decorated with the trappings and futile distinctions of fortune meets. I imagine a man of abilities, his breast glowing with honest pride, conscious that men are born equal, still giving honour to whom honour is due. He meets at a great man's table a Lord Something or a Squire Somebody. He knows the noble landlord at heart gives the bard, or whatever he is, a share of his good wishes, beyond perhaps any one at table; yet how will it mortify him to see a fellow whose abilities would scarcely have made an eightpenny tailor, and whose heart is not worth three farthings, meet with attention and notice that are withheld from the sons of genius and poverty. The noble Glencairn has wounded me to the soul here, because I dearly esteem, respect, and love him. He showed so much attention, engrossing attention, one day to the only blockhead at table, that I was within half a point of throwing down my gage of contemptuous defiance."

This was the painful way in which the poet had the misfortune to contemplate that conventional standard of rank, which to more reasonable minds simplifies the regulations of society, and by making an entirely arbitrary rule, covers all the conflicts of *amour propre*, and invidious personal comparison. But, unfortunately, self-comparison was the rule of his life in this chapter of it. His peasant breeding did him no harm in his poetry, but it harmed him personally here, more than we can estimate, setting him entirely wrong in his relations to his

fellows. With an extraordinary bravado of cynical sentiment, all the more extraordinary since it is ostensibly
intended for no eye but his own, he begins a diary, in
which he promises himself to "sketch every character
that any way strikes me, to the best of my power, with
unshrinking justice." "I think," he adds, "a lock and
key security at least equal to the bosom of any friend
whatever." This was his unhappy mind in April of the
following year, after three months' experience of Edinburgh : but what his experience was in full, it is better,
perhaps, not to inquire too closely. The repression to
which he subjected himself among his fine friends, naturally demanded some outlet on the other side, and this
was not difficult to find. Men who, though inferior to
his new patrons, were yet much above his natural level
of society, men on a par, perhaps, with the Mauchline
wits who had given him his first step of social elevation
and moral debasement, held their doors open to him with
a riotous welcome. He made up to himself among these
jovial friends for the restraints of the more pretentious
circles. Two of them who survived in his regard and
became his correspondents afterwards, were masters in
the High School ; but the profession of a schoolmaster
was not a certificate of character in those days, nor has
it, strangely enough, ever been held in so much respect
north of the Tweed, in the home of popular education, as
in the other part of the island.

Burns left Edinburgh in May 1787. A letter of
thanks to Dr. Blair for his kindness and hospitality has
been preserved with the reply to it. Dr. Blair is very
kind and even approving. "Your situation, as you say,
was indeed very singular," he allows, "and in being
brought out all at once from the shades of deepest misery
to so great a share of public notice and observation, you
had to stand a severe trial. I am happy that you have

stood it so well;" but he gives the poet small encouragement to count upon his further acquaintance. "When
you return, if you come this way, I will be happy to see
you, and to know concerning your future plans of life;"
he says—not a very warm invitation. Dr. Blair, too, is
dishearteningly ready to allow that the brief day of glory
is over. "You are now, I presume, to retire to a more
private walk of life. . . . As you very properly hint yourself, you are not to be surprised if in your rural retreat
you do not find yourself surrounded with that glare of
notice and applause which has shone upon you," he says.
It was all over, the lamps extinguished, the audience
gone; he himself had settled that it would be so, and he
had no right to grumble if his friends assented; and as a
matter of fact, it is evident that they did assent.

In the midst of these painful indications of the
jangling of the chords which had been so melodious, we
may quote one or two pleasanter points in this brief
Edinburgh career. "He walked with me in spring,"
Dugald Stewart writes, "early in the morning to the
Braid Hills, when he charmed me still more by his
private conversation, than he had ever done in company;"
that is, Burns was once more himself in the free air,
among the genial influences of nature, and in the society
of one gentle spirit, not at that moment assuming the
offensive guise of a patron. "He was passionately fond
of the beauties of nature, and he once told me when I
was admiring a distant prospect, in one of our many
walks, that the sight of so many smoking cottages gave a
pleasure to his mind which none could understand, who
had not witnessed, like himself, the happiness and worth
which they contained." This comes to us with a sense
of relief and happy return to nature and truth, for which
we are truly grateful. And here is another little picture,
simple as a vignette, which shows us how the poet

appeared in the eyes of a lame shy boy seated in a corner
of one of the Edinburgh drawing-rooms, blushing yet
happy in the out-of-the-way knowledge which endless
reading had given him.   Burns had admired certain
verses attached to an engraving: " He asked whose the
lines were, and it chanced that nobody but myself remembered that they occur in a half-forgotten poem of
Langhorne's, called by the unpromising title of the
' Justice of Peace.'   I whispered my information to a
friend present, who repeated it to Burns, who rewarded
me with a look and word which, though of mere civility,
I received with great pleasure. . . . There was a strong
expression of sense and shrewdness in all his lineaments ;
the eye alone, I think, indicated the poetical character
and temperament.   It was large and of a dark cast,
which glowed (I say literally glowed) when he spoke
with feeling or interest.   I never saw such another eye
in a human head."   This is the description given by
Walter Scott, then fifteen years old, of his contemporary
of twenty-seven, which was all the age Burns had as yet
attained.

Among the many advices which were given to the
poet at this moment, which was the turning-point in his
career, there were several which suggested a closer application to poetry as the future occupation of his life.
" Your lordship," he writes, " touches the darling chord
of my heart, when you advise me to fire my muse at
Scottish story and Scottish scenes."   To Mrs. Dunlop, a
kinder and more deeply interested counsellor, he repeats
almost the same words.   " Scottish scenes and Scottish
story are the themes I could wish to sing.   I have no
dearer aim than to have it in my power, unplagued
by the routine of business, for which heaven knows I
am unfit enough, to make leisurely pilgrimages through
Caledonia ; to sit on the fields of her battles ; to wander

on the romantic banks of her rivers ; and to muse by the
stately towers or venerable ruins, over the honoured
abodes of her heroes.

"But these are all Utopian thoughts. I have dallied long
enough with life ; it is time now to be in earnest ; I have a fond,
an aged mother to care for ; and some other bosom ties perhaps
equally tender. . . . I guess that I shall clear between two and
three hundred pounds by my authorship : with that sum I intend,
so far as I may be said to have any intention, to return to my old
acquaintance, the plough, and if I can meet with a lease by which
I can live, to commence farmer. I do not intend to give up poetry ;
being bred to labour secures an independence, and the Muses are
my chief, sometimes have been my only enjoyment. If my practice
second my resolution, I shall have powerfully at heart the serious
business of life ; but while following my plough or building up my
stacks, I shall cast a leisure glance to that dear, that only feature of
my character which gave me the notice of my country."

He had been advised to write a tragedy ; to give up
his themes of common life and turn his attention towards
more elevated subjects ; to abandon his Scotch dialect,
"Why should you, by using *that,* limit the number of
your admirers to those who understand the Scottish, when
you can extend it to all persons of taste who understand
the English language ?" he is asked.

"In my opinion" (the speaker is Dr. Moore, the father of Sir
John Moore, the author of *Zeluco,* and many other books, in his day
a man of some literary reputation), " you should plan some larger
work than any you have as yet attempted. I mean, reflect upon
some proper subject, and arrange the plan of it in your mind without beginning to execute any part of it till you have studied most
of the best English poets, and read a little more of history. The
Greek and Roman stories you can read in some abridgment, and
soon become master of the most brilliant facts, which must highly
delight a poetical mind. You *should* also, and very soon *may,*
become master of the heathen mythology, to which there are everlasting allusions in all the poets, and which is in itself charmingly
fanciful. What will require to be studied with more attention is
modern history, that is, the history of France and Great Britain
from the beginning of Henry the Seventh's reign. I know very

well you have a mind capable of attaining knowledge by a shorter process than is commonly used, and I am certain you are capable of making a better use of it, when attained, than is generally done."

This was the approved recipe for making a man of letters in those days. Thus cultivated, what doubt that a tragedy, a series of didactic poems, or any other special performance that might strike the fashion of the day, could be produced at pleasure ? To Burns, who knew that he was already a poet, and had attained what none of these sage advisers could reach to, it may be supposed that this advice was by no means welcome. The authorities treated him as a beginner, one who had still his reputation to make. " Take time and leisure to improve your talents, for on any second production you give the world, your *fate as a poet will very much depend,*" says Dr. Blair—as genial critics say now to a young novelist who has produced the first three volumes, which are to be the precursors of a hundred. Burns does not seem to have returned any distinct reply. " I have the advice of some very judicious friends among the literati here, but with these I sometimes find it necessary to claim the privilege of thinking for myself," he says to Mrs. Dunlop, when he informs her that it is his intention to return to " his old acquaintance the plough." And it is to the immortal credit of Burns's good sense that he never appears to have thought of taking up poetry as a trade. To roam about the country and study Scotch scenes and historical incidents for the purpose of writing poems about them for the market, never seems to have entered into his head. He had thought for some time of the Excise, which seems to have been a service somehow attractive to men who had otherwise failed in life, or who had no opening to more lucrative work about this period. A gauger has never been a popular character, yet, for some reason or other, young Scotchmen, desirous to make a step

out of the class of artizans or small tradesmen, seem to
have regarded it with favourable eyes, perhaps because it
required little previous training, and still involved a spice
of adventure.   And Burns does not seem to have considered that there was anything derogatory in it.   That,
or a farm, perhaps both together, the one supplementing
the other—but not the struggles of a poor author, or an
artificial trade of poetical manufactures.   These were the
days of Grub Street, when young writers went up to
London with a few pounds in their pockets and a bundle
of MSS., and flung themselves on the world blindly with
the intention of living by what they called " the Muse."
This is evidently what many of his patrons expected
from Burns, and, we repeat, it is the greatest credit to
him that he never thought of adopting such an occupation.

But all these recommendations, and the moderate
friendliness which assured him, " if you are passing this
way," that " I shall be happy to see you," and the morti-
fied consciousness that this brilliant moment in his life
was over, and that nothing remained, did not tend to
increase his happiness.   He made two expeditions—one
into the Highlands, the other to the south of Scotland,
with companions of, as appears, no elevating order, and
with a bitterness in his heart that found vent in foolish
cynicism, and sometimes in reproaches addressed to the
great and rich, and anticipations of " illiberal abuse, and
perhaps contemptuous neglect."   But yet, wherever he
went, he was received with honour and enthusiasm.   A
bitter and jealous fellow-traveller, who could not understand why Burns should be better received than himself,
no doubt helped to exaggerate his uncomfortable frame
of mind.   The two dealt defiance round them, wrote rebellious verses on inn windows, and angry epigrams, and
got very little enjoyment out of their journey.   At
one house he just missed Mr. Dundas, the dispenser of

Scottish patronage at the time ; and at another, Mr.
Addington, afterwards Prime Minister, was expected, both
of whom might have been of use to the poet—but in
both cases the jealous temper of his travelling companion
hurried him away.   Mr. Addington, however, furnishes a
whimsical addition to the history at this point.   He had
been invited to meet Burns, of whose poetry he was a
great admirer, and not coming, sent a sonnet in his place,
complimenting the "pride of Scotia's favoured plains,"
and recommending to him a philosophical superiority to
fate, in lines which would be cruel if they were not so
ludicrous—

> " What though each morning sees thee rise to toil,
>   Though Plenty on thy cot no blessing showers,
>   Yet Independence cheers thee with her smile,
>   And Fancy strews thy moorland with her flowers ;
>   And dost thou blame the impartial will of heaven,
>   Untaught of life the good and ill to scan ;
>   To thee the Muse's choicest wreath is given,
>   To thee the genuine dignity of man.
>   Then to the want of worldly gear resigned,
>   Be grateful for the wealth of thy exhaustless mind."

Mr. Addington's mind was evidently not "exhaust-
less" like the poet's, whom he congratulates, in the way
of verse, and probably Burns, if put to it, would have
preferred his own estate to that of the writer of these
heartless lines.   " Depart in peace, be ye warmed and
fed," was never said with more callous cynicism.   Cowper,
who was in no special need, got a pension of three
hundred a year a little while later.   What would not
that, or the half of it, have been to Burns !   But at all
events he need not have been congratulated upon a
poverty which it was so easy to relieve.   Such compliments bear a wonderful resemblance to insults.

He returned to Edinburgh in the following autumn :
but his day was over.   Though he remained there five or

six months, he seems to have seen no more fine company.
He was perhaps more at home on the lower level, which
yet was a higher level than that upon which he was
born.   It was during this time that he indulged in the
sentimental flirtation which produced his letters to
Clarinda, a foolish episode in a not very wise life.   There
was a great deal of nonsense, no doubt, both written and
said ; but then love-letters are always nonsense to impartial lookers on, and the general style of composition was
very different then from now.   Burns was always somewhat high-flown, partly from his natural temper, partly
from his peasant breeding; but there can be little doubt
that there was genuine passion as well as a great deal of
artificial sentiment in this strange chapter of his life.
The man who wrote—

> " Had we never loved so kindly,
>   Had we never loved so blindly,
>   Never met and never parted,
>   We had ne'er been broken-hearted,"

must have meant what he said.   But then he had the
faculty, not exclusively possessed by poets, of being quite
sincere and quite impassioned in two cases at the same
time.

He left Edinburgh finally in the beginning of 1788,
having passed two winters there, one of them in the full
heyday of popularity, the other in the cold shade.   With
Burns, as with most other people, the permanent tenor
of circumstances prevailed, and after the moment of triumph he had to fall back upon his natural friends.   That
these natural friends were men of some education, ought
to have been a gain to him ; that it was not so was
probably due to the very principle that brought them
together, a love of the coarsest convivial pleasures.   He
speaks somewhere, in a moment of sober sadness, of

" that savage hospitality which kicks a man down with
strong liquors."   Still it would be hard to blame the
jovial schoolmasters for the waste of possibility and
character which his second winter in Edinburgh seems
to have involved.   In all such miserable concatenations
of circumstance we are too apt to blame the secondary
personages involved, the "bad company" which "leads
away" the individual in whom we are interested.   But
this is poor philosophy.   No man is led away whose
will is against going, and it is fit that each should bear
his own burden.   His poetry had produced him a little
fortune of about (the authorities agree in saying) £500,
of which he gave £180 to his brother Gilbert to enable
him to go on with his farm, and apparently to form a
sort of provision for their mother.   This money, "the
consolation of a few solid guineas," seems to have been
all his Edinburgh experiences brought him.   But for this
"I could almost lament," he says, "the time that a
momentary acquaintance with wealth and splendour put
me so much out of conceit with the sworn companions
of my road through life, insignificance and poverty."
There can be little doubt that a sense of failure and
downfall, and bitter perception that his social success was
momentary, and that no real change had happened in his
life, was in his mind ever after.   And he had derived no
advantage to counterbalance this from the advices and
comments of those elegant critics who were supposed to
be the dispensers of fame.   It is curious, indeed, to
observe the similarity of his experience and that of
Cowper in respect to the criticisms and emendations to
which their poetry was subject.   At one of the country
houses which Burns visited after his Edinburgh sojourn,
he was asked "whether the Edinburgh literati had
mended his poems by their criticisms."   "Sir," said he,
"these gentlemen remind me of some spinners in my

country, who spin their thread so fine that it is neither
fit for weft nor woof." The reader will be amused by
comparing with this epigrammatic summary of the criticism of the period Cowper's protest against it. It is
needless to recall to him how unlike the two men and
their works were; but in this respect they are at one.
Cowper's much more decided and lengthy expression of
indignation was called forth by an impertinence, the
alteration of a line in his "Homer," by "some accidental
reviser of the manuscript."

"I did not write the line that has been tampered with hastily
or without due attention to the construction of it, and what appeared
to me its only merit is in its present state entirely annihilated. I
know that the ears of modern verse-writers are delicate to an excess,
and their readers are troubled with the same squeamishness as
themselves, so that if a line does not run as smooth as quicksilver
they are offended. A critic of the present day serves a poem as a
cook serves a dead turkey, when she fastens the legs of it to a post
and draws out all the sinews. For this we may thank Pope ; but
unless we could imitate him in the closeness and compactness of
his expression, as well as in the smoothness of his numbers, we
had better drop the imitation, which serves no other purpose than
to emasculate and weaken all we write. Give me a manly rough
line, with a deal of meaning in it, rather than a whole poem full
of musical periods that have nothing but their oily smoothness to
recommend them.

"I have said thus much because I have just finished a much
longer poem than the last, which our common friend will receive
by the same messenger that has the charge of this letter. In that
poem there are many lines which an ear so nice as the gentleman's
who made the above-mentioned alteration would undoubtedly condemn, and yet (if I may be permitted to say it) they cannot be
made smoother without being the worse for it. There is a roughness on the plum which nobody that understands fruit would rub
off, though the plum would be much more polished without it.
But, lest I tire you, I will only add that I wish you to guard me
from all such meddling, assuring you that I always write as
smoothly as I can ; but that I never did, never will, sacrifice the
spirit or sense of a passage to the sound of it."

Thus the two great revolutionaries made their protest.

The one, with wonderful spirit and vigour for so gentle a man, in words; the other with a laugh, a *mot* only, but a sturdy disregard of all the criticisms of this kind to which he was subjected, and all the counsels founded upon these criticisms, which is more telling than verbal remonstrance. Before we quit this subject, we may note, what is a very pleasant fact to meet with, that Cowper and Burns, though they never met, had at least encountered each other in the spirit, in their poems, and with mutual understanding and appreciation. " I have read Burns's poems," Cowper writes to his friend Mr. Rose, who seems to have sent them to him, " and have read them twice; and though they be written in a language that is new to me, and many of them on subjects much inferior to the author's ability, I think them on the whole a very extraordinary production. He is, I believe, the only poet these kingdoms have produced in a low rank of life since Shakspeare (I should rather say since Prior), who need not be indebted for any part of his praise to a charitable consideration of his origin and the disadvantages under which he has laboured. It will be a pity if he should not hereafter divest himself of barbarism, and content himself with writing pure English, in which he appears perfectly qualified to excel."

This last objection was of course entirely reasonable from Cowper's point of view, though impracticable from that of Burns; but the compliment paid to him is as high as any one could desire. Burns, on the other hand, generally carried Cowper's " Task " in his pocket, and " took it out when he found himself in a lonely road, or in a brewhouse, where he had to wait sometimes to ' gauge the browst.' He enriched the margins of the copy he used with notes critical and commendatory, and from the number of the marks and the frequency of the praise, it appears that the English bard was a great favourite." "Is not the 'Task' a glorious poem?" he says to Mrs. Dunlop. "The religion of the 'Task,' bating a few scraps of Calvinistic divinity, is the religion of God and Nature, the religion that exalts, that ennobles man."

It is scarcely necessary for our purpose to dwell on the after-part of Burns's life in detail. He returned to Ayrshire after the disappointments of Edinburgh, and married his bonnie Jean—an act for which he apologised anxiously to all his correspondents, but to which he seems to have been bound in honour and also in love : for he loved her at least as well as any of the other objects of his roving affections. To speculate upon the influence that a wife of higher class and stronger principle might have had upon him is entirely vain. The instances are very few in which a good wife, or anything else, has had power enough to turn a man from dissipation when it has got full hold of him; and he was still a ploughman, full of the pride, the brag, the defiance which, far more than natural roughness of manners, disgust and repel the more delicately bred. He would probably have broken the woman's heart who had been dazzled by his poetry and eloquence, and liked his home not more but less for her superiority. There can, we think, be little doubt indeed, however injurious to a woman's pride it may be to say it, that a cultivated wife, or one who shares his intellectual interests, is by no means necessary to the happiness of a man of genius. The old-fashioned institution of a good, simple, worshipping woman, tolerant and uncritical, is perhaps better for him—or, at least, he is pretty sure to think so : an opinion in which the great mass of men who have no genius will agree. Burns, after his marriage, settled at Ellisland, near Dumfries; a beautiful situation, but, it is said, indifferent land. " You have chosen like a poet, not like a farmer," some one is reported to have said to him; yet he must, one would suppose, have been able to judge, and he carefully records the opinion of an old farmer whom he took with him to inspect the place. It turned out badly, however, whether because the land was bad, or the farmer's mind not sufficiently given to it; and he applied to be appointed to active service in the Excise, his commission for which had been given him some time before. It was an occupation which involved much moving about, and a considerable amount of adventure, and would not seem to have been unpleasing to him. One of the incidents of his life, which led to a very foolish act and some trouble, will show the exciting character of the work at this stormy period. " A suspicious-looking brig" appeared in the Solway, and Burns and his fellow-officers boarded and took her, an exploit which must have set the poet's pulses in motion. He bought the guns with which the vessel was furnished, and sent them " with a letter to the French Legislative Assembly, requesting them to accept the present as a mark of his admiration and sympathy." Robert Burns, poet, to the French nation! The braggadocio was sublime; but an occupation in which such little incidents occurred could not be altogether disagreeable to a nature craving excitement.

Of course, this foolish offering was stopped, and the sender got into trouble enough to oblige him to write an almost abject letter to Mr. Graham of Fintry, appealing to him as a husband and father to save him from dismissal. This is a very sad production; and to hear him describing the accusations against him as " the dark insinuations of hellish groundless envy," is not less sad. The wild excitement raised by the French Revolution excuses, no doubt, a great deal of this folly; and we cannot be surprised that Burns, with his bitter sense of his own failure to keep his footing among the great (strangest of all contradictions of the theory of equality——for why

should he have cared more about the society of dukes and
duchesses if they were no better than ploughmen and
milkmaids?), should have felt with double force the fire
of the excitement which turned the wisest heads.   But
there is something which wounds us in the feverish and
ostentatious folly of revolutionary sympathy, conjoined
with the equally feverish hysterical protest of " devout
attachment " to the British Constitution, when his conduct
was called in question.   No doubt it was " thae moving
things ca'd wife and weans " which prompted his alarm;
but we should be glad to have heard less of them in such
conjunctures.

Before this last stage, however, three years had passed
at the farm of Ellisland, in which much poetry was
written.   He had engaged heart and soul in the collection of songs for Johnson's *Scots Musical Museum* before
he left Edinburgh.   Some years later he took the same
warm and eager interest in a similar collection set on foot
by Thomson.   For these two publications he wrote a large
number of songs of differing degrees of merit, for which
he proudly refused all remuneration.   Two purely poetical scenes, of which his wife gives an account, instances
of the way in which his subject possessed him, as well as,
in one case, of the profound emotion out of which utterance came, are to be found in the story of this later
period.   In the beginning of the October of 1789, Burns
had been very merry.   He had written " Willie brew'd a
peck o' maut," of which Principal Shairp, with somewhat
comic gravity, says, " If bacchanalian songs are to be
written at all, this certainly must be pronounced ' the
king amang them a';' " but as the month drew near a
melancholy anniversary, the death of that Highland Mary
whom we know so little of, and who had in reality so
much less share in his life than many another, he was
observed by his wife " to grow sad about something, and

to wander solitary on the banks of the Nith, and about
his farmyard, in the extremest agitation of mind nearly
the whole night. He screened himself on the lee-side of
a corn-stack from the cutting edge of the night wind, and
lingered till approaching dawn wiped out the stars one by
one." When at last his anxious wife (who, let us hope,
was not aware what anniversary it was) persuaded him
to come in, he sat down and put upon paper his visionary
sorrow, in verses so pathetic, that no critic has ever
ventured to reckon them otherwise than among the most
beautiful that Burns ever wrote :—

> " Thou lingering star, with less'ning ray,
>   That lov'st to greet the early morn,
> Again thou usher'st in the day
>   My Mary from my soul was torn.
> O Mary ! dear departed shade !
>   Where is thy place of blissful rest ?
> Seest thou thy lover lowly laid ?
>   Hear'st thou the groans that rend his breast ? "

It is of the nature of a poet, and even had he not
been a poet, it was of the nature of Burns, to feel everything that affected him with as much fervour and force as
if nothing had ever affected him before. The other side
of his inspiration affords an equally characteristic scene.
Burns had recommended to Captain Grose, the antiquary,
to include old Alloway Kirk in the sketches he was
making for publication. The visitor suggested that Burns
should write a poem to accompany the sketch, and the
seed fell into good ground.

" The poem "—we quote from Principal Shairp, who
is the last to tell the tale —" was the work of one day,
of which Mrs. Burns retained a vivid recollection. Her
husband had spent the most part of the day by the river-
side, and in the afternoon she joined him with her two
children. He was busily engaged ' crooning to himsel' ; '

and Mrs. Burns, perceiving that her presence was an
interruption, loitered behind with her little ones among
the broom.   Her attention was presently attracted by the
strange and wild gesticulations of the bard, who was now
seen at some distance.   He was reciting very loud, and
with tears rolling down his cheeks, the animated verses
which he had just conceived :—

> ' Now, Tam, O Tam ! had thae been queans,
>   A' plump and strappin' in their teens.'

" 'I wish ye had seen him,' said his wife, ' he was in
such ecstasy that the tears were happing down his
cheeks.' . . . The poet having committed the verses to
writing on the top of his sod-dyke above the water,
came into the house and read them immediately in high
triumph at the fireside."   In this sudden heat of impulse
one of his greatest and most sustained efforts was produced.   He had neither " thrown off barbarism," nor
prepared himself for the composition of something great
by a study of all the best models, the stories of the Greek
and Latin mythology, and the events of modern history,
as his advisers had urged upon him.   But here, in a
moment, written on the top of his sod-dyke, and read hot
from his glowing mind by his fireside half-an-hour after,
came something which no critic could mend — which
critics indeed, in the exercise of a wise discretion, have
never attempted to do anything but praise.

Burns was about three years in Ellisland, and when
he gave up this last unfortunate essay in farming,
removed to Dumfries, and henceforth confined himself to
his work of Excise officer.   His whole life is recorded in
brief sums of time.   Two years here, three there, five in
Dumfries, which was the last and saddest chapter of all.
He had left all the little money his poems brought him
in the cold soil of Ellisland, and henceforward had nothing

but his small salary as an Exciseman (fifty pounds a year, he repeatedly says; seventy, we are told, when in active service) to live upon. For his songs he proudly refused to take any payment, and he appears to have been taken at his word by everybody concerned. No other edition of his collected works seems to have been called for, notwithstanding the universal enthusiasm they had called forth; so that the five hundred pounds which he brought from Edinburgh represented all that his genius did for him in this way. And of that he got little good. Many a hard word has been said about the inferior post in which Scotland permitted her greatest poet to earn his children's bread and to die: but had his friends been steadfast enough to push him onward to a better grade, there was less harm than has been supposed in the Excise. This seems to have been his own ambition, and would have contented him fully; but perhaps his foolish exuberances in the way of politics, his toasts instead of Pitt " to a better man George Washington," his present of guns to the French Convention, and other such un- necessary and undignified demonstrations of wounded pride and revolt, made his advancement impossible. There is little doubt that he was, as he says, " devoutly attached to the British Constitution," and as loyal as there was need to be. But he was an injured (he thought) and disappointed man, injured by being poor and a poet, and by the received fictions of social life, which made dukes and earls more great than he. It is impossible to doubt that he meant no more than this—and probably he would have said much less, but for the excitement of all those wild assemblies in which the rude wits of the countryside drew the poet out for their own entertain- ment, and led him by their applauses and incitements to wilder and wilder rashness of speech. The foolish epi- grams and broken verses which were born of this period

(as well as many most beautiful and touching poems)
are the mere poetic froth of a harassed and perturbed
mind, and as such should be swept altogether out of
recollection.   It is not thus that we desire to take leave
of Burns.

Fortunately he never attempted any tragedy, as his
cultivated advisers had suggested : but it is said that he
had thought of a subject for a drama, to be called " Rob
M'Quechan's Elshin."   This was to be founded upon a
popular legend of Robert Bruce.   That hero, according to
the story, when defeated on the water of Cairn, had the
heel of his boot loosened in his flight, and appealed to
Robert M'Quechan to fix it—who to make sure ran his
awl (or elshin) nine inches up the king's heel.   This
does not seem a very promising subject for a dramatic
poem, and Burns fortunately never went farther than to
mention the notion to his friends.   His only attempt at
dramatic composition was the " Jolly Beggars," about
which a great many critics have expressed unbounded
enthusiasm.   We [1] are unable to join in these universal
plaudits, and we believe that now-a-days few enthusiasts
for Burns care to do more than repeat the conventional
praises of this wild fragment.   Its vigour is unquestionable, but there is little constructive power, and only the
most primitive daubs of character.   M. Taine considers
it the *chef-d'œuvre* of the poet, and devotes several pages
to the discussion of its sentiments and personages.
" J'espère que voilà du style franc, et que le poete n'est
pas petite bouche," he says; but these qualities by themselves, however valuable, do not make poetical merit.

[1] There must always be, we presume, however age and experience may
modify nature, a certain inability on the part of a woman to appreciate
the more riotous forms of mirth, and that robust freedom in morals which
bolder minds admire.   It is a disability which nothing can abolish, and
we hasten to forestal criticism by avowing it.   In such matters the reader
will judge for himself how much our opinion is worth.

In this particular, vicious sentiment need not tell more than virtuous, in our opinion, and the confined atmosphere of " Poosie Nansie's," is to ourselves as much inferior in art as it is in wholesomeness to the country freshness which is Burns's true atmosphere.   His great effort in narrative poetry, " Tam o' Shanter," is more worthy, we think, of the universal praise bestowed upon it, though we agree to a large extent in Mr. Carlyle's less elevated estimate.   In neither of these poems is the heart appealed to at all, nor any but the lower faculties of the imagination.   Tam indeed, lingering in the alehouse, putting off as long as possible his severance from its delights, but when once fairly started, retaining enough of the warmth within him to present a courageous, muddled, humorous front to fate, afraid of nothing,—

> " Whiles holding fast his gude blue bonnet,
>   Whiles crooning ower some auld Scots sonnet,"

is as luminous a picture as could be of the Scottish peasant as distinguished from others of his kind, with his touch of rude poetic possibility, and the lurking fun which is never altogether absent from his musings. Sancho Panza would have seen no vision in Alloway Kirk, though he would have been as reluctant to leave his inn, and would have carried as many bottles under his belt as any man.   But we cannot pretend to be impressed by the witches' dance, even though Sir Walter Scott answers for it that " it is at once ludicrous and horrible."   The horrible is the merest artifice, and we do not in reality care a straw for accessories so manifestly theatrical as the " coffins " standing " round like open presses," and the dissecting-room furniture on the tables ; a comparison, for instance, with Goethe's weird assembly of the same kind will show at once the inferiority of the picture.   Faust's backward retreat of terror and disgust

when he sees " a little red mouse " leap from the mouth
of his pretty partner is such a touch of diabolical genius
as Burns has no pretension to equal.   But, on the other
hand, Tam is entirely out of the possibilities of the great
German.   His round-eyed wonder, the warmth of the
whisky in him, the humour of his muddle-headed spectatorship, not in the least impressed by this " horror,"
which the critics have discovered, is in its way unapproach-
able.   We can imagine him laughing under his breath as
he spurs the faithful Meg along the darkling road with all
that wild train at his heels.   In his tipsiness and pawky
simplicity and sense of the real underneath the imaginative, he is never a bit afraid, nor does the poet represent
him as being so.   " Tam kend what was what fu' brawly,"
and cared no more for " Auld Nick in shape of beast " than
Cuvier did.   This we think entirely deprives the poem of
that hold upon the imagination which the supernatural,
seriously intended, ought always to possess.   But Burns,
who wrote it with tears of mirth " happing down his
cheeks," meant nothing but fun, or we are greatly mistaken, and fully attained all the effect he aimed at.

Several of his most beautiful songs were the product
of these last years, along with a great many others which
were little worthy of his great name, and which it seems
a pity to preserve at all.   "John Anderson, my jo " is,
however, fine enough for the severest critic.   Many a
glowing image of youthful love he has left us, the best
of them as delicate and pure in their passion as ever
lyrics were; and here the circle of fervid verse is completed by the most perfect utterance of old and faithful
affection.

> " John Anderson, my jo, John,
>   We clamb the hill thegither ;
> And mony a canty day, John,
>   We've had wi' ane anither :

Now we maun totter down, John,
    But hand in hand we'll go,
And sleep thegither at the foot,
    John Anderson, my jo."

The end of most lives is sad : either the speed of the
current as it approaches the fall conveys a sense of tragic
haste and desperation such as are inseparable from our
ideas of a sudden ending, or the stagnation of old age
waiting for its release, appals and chills our hearts.   In
either sense the concluding chapter is sad.   In Burns's
case it was doubly so : for the miserable feeling of a life
thrown away and wasted, adds to the almost intolerable
pang with which we see a man in the fulness of his
powers swept along, dissatisfied, embittered, disappointed,
out of the world, which he still might have been so capable of serving.   Everything in those last years suggests
the image of a wild torrent, flowing quicker every moment
towards the precipice over which it must disappear in
clouds of angry foam.   He vindicated his better nature
only by the wretchedness which overwhelmed him at
every moment of thought, a wretchedness from which he
was glad to escape into the continual excitement of dissipations quite unworthy of him.   He had many excuses
—his life of constant movement, riding over ten parishes,
with now and then an encounter with smugglers, or such
an adventure as that which made him master of the guns
of the smugglers' brig—and the popularity he had attained among all the jovial spirits of the district—offered
a hundred temptations.   " From the castle to the cottage,
every door flew open at his approach ; and the old system
of hospitality then flourishing, rendered it difficult for the
most soberly-inclined guest to rise from any man's board
in the same trim that he sat down to it.   The farmer, if
Burns was seen passing, left his reapers and trotted by
the side of Jenny Geddes (his mare) until he could per-

suade the bard that the day was hot enough to demand
an extra libation. If he entered an inn at midnight,
after all the inmates were in bed, the news of his arrival
circulated from the cellar to the garret ; and ere ten
minutes had elapsed the landlord and all his guests were
assembled round the ingle, the largest punch-bowl was
produced, and

'Be ours to-night—who knows what comes to-morrow ?'

was the language of every eye in the circle that welcomed
him. The highest gentry of the neighbourhood, when
bent on special merriment, did not think the occasion
complete unless the wit and eloquence of Burns were
called in to enliven their carousals."

This latter class failed him, however, at the end.
We do not pretend to believe that there were any qualities in the Dumfriesshire gentry which would have made
their notice an instrument of salvation to the poet ; but
so far as they were of use in keeping him to decorum
they failed him at his greatest need. Not that this was
to be wondered at. A man who, after dinner, was capable of insulting rudeness to a lady in her own drawing-
room, was a dangerous acquaintance, and even his best
friends shrank from the risk. And a man who openly
committed himself by approval of revolutionary sentiments, by sympathy with rebels against the English crown,
and adversaries to it, could scarcely hope for advancement
in the Government service. Thus the clouds closed in
around him, and there seemed no opening from whence
succour would come.

He died at thirty-seven. Had he died ten years earlier
his reputation would scarcely have been less, and he would
have escaped a great deal of misery ; but it is not for us
to reckon with Providence. Even if we hesitate to accept
Mr. Carlyle's conclusion that he was the greatest man of

his generation, the one most fit to rule and command, we may nevertheless allow that he was by far the greatest poet. Cowper is placed beside him in the bead-roll because, so distant as they were from each other, they both helped — or rather, they wrought between them — the permanent enfranchisement of poetry, her right to see things as they were, and to express herself as she pleased, in whatsoever manner liked her, reserving her power to touch the innermost soul, whether she went back to lift the mantle of Milton, or picked up a homely medium of utterance on the roadside. No harp, no lute was longer necessary. We got rid of the antique attendance of " the Muse." A new life and a new freedom came into the language, and the bondage of Pope, and precedent, and the best models, was loosed from the soul. Burns died in 1796—Cowper not till 1800. It would be hard to say which life was most tried, most unfortunate, most sad. Had either man—he who stormed his life out in mid-career, or he who drank out all the dregs of mournful age—known how to rule his own spirit, how different might have been the record! But Cowper had the excuse of mental disease : whereas no apology can be made for Burns, except that which pity makes for the victim of a defective will in all circumstances. This fatal deficiency equalises all human qualities, and makes the man of genius, alas ! only a little more luckless, not better, than the veriest fool.

ROBERT BURNS, born 1759 ; died 1796.

Poems published in Kilmarnock, 1786.
2d Edition in Edinburgh, with additions, 1787.
3d Edition, with Tam o' Shanter, etc., 1793.
4th   „   „   „   1794.
Edition published after his death by Dr. Currie, with letters, 1800.

CHAPTER III.

LITERATURE IN SCOTLAND BEFORE BURNS.

THE Edinburgh of Burns's day is a somewhat difficult
study for the inquirer. It is represented by a number
of notable persons, of whom there are, however, pictures
so different that we scarcely know which to adopt. All
the biographers of Burns represent him as seduced from
the calm delights of a refined society, into the jovial
undercurrent of tavern life, where third-rate men and
vulgar joys swept him away out of a better career. And
when we turn on one hand to the books and periodicals
of the time, to the languishing periods of the "Man of
Feeling," and the weak Addison-and-water of the *Mirror*
and the *Lounger*, this view of the situation has a certain
support. But on the other hand Sir Walter Scott, and
later, Lord Cockburn in his *Recollections*, unfold before
us a society so outspoken and so homely, so tolerant of
the easier vices, so ready to forgive everything that had
fun and spirit involved in it, that we are bewildered and
cannot tell what to think. Could Nicol and Carmichael
and the Crochallan Club, to which several of Burns's
biographers attribute all his dissipations, have been more
riotous and merry than that assembly, periodical and un-
changing, in which Counsellor Pleydell was found at high
jinks by Colonel Mannering? But then the "Man of
Feeling" would have been as much out of place in such

an assembly as the grave English soldier himself, who did
not know what to make of it. Henry Mackenzie, the
author of this book, was the representative of Edinburgh
at that moment in the field of *belles lettres*. He was a
poet after his kind; he had written tragedies, he was the
author of the sentimental romance of the period, and he
was also its favourite critic and essayist. Most curious
is the picture he presents to us. Never was Edinburgh
more individual, never perhaps was she so jovial. The
town was full of remarkable men, whose names were
known all over the world—and of scarcely less remarkable women, whose *bon mots*, and whose daring opinions
and ways, were known at least over all Edinburgh. Lord
Cockburn affords half-a-dozen sketches of old ladies, old
in his time, who must have been in full bloom in the days
of Burns, whose strong and racy individuality it would
be hard to match anywhere. A more racy or less mim-
mouthed society could scarcely be.

Perhaps the circles into which Burns fell, among men
upon whom the gravity of age had stolen, the Robertsons
and Blairs, the gentle blind poet Blacklock, so fluent in
verse, with his little band of pupils—and even Dugald
Stewart himself, the most suave of professors, a man who
was good and gentle by temperament, and in whose presence we feel sure no riot could have been possible—had
more seriousness, if not more culture than belonged to
the strong and gay, and somewhat reckless and cynical
humour of the Scotch capital. The latter indeed is the
least Scotch of all his learned contemporaries. It is
evident that he held an imposing position in Edinburgh.
To enter his class was, as Lord Cockburn tells us, " the
great era in the progress of young men's minds." Lat-
terly his house was filled with pupils from more courtly
circles; English youths with great names and a great
future, gazing with keen eyes and all the interest of

novelty at the wonderful little metropolis, where intellectual interests were the chief occupation of men.
Dugald Stewart, however, is far more like the ideal of an
Oxford tutor than a Scotch professor, and good Scotsman
as he was, has little of the characteristic national flavour
of the time.   But Henry Mackenzie has no national
character at all—and the impression of Edinburgh which
he leaves upon the reader's mind is curiously false and
artificial.   It would answer for "the Bath" or "the
Wells," or any centre of provincial fashion and self-
exhibition.   The *Mirror* and the *Lounger* afford us no
glimpses either of those alarming old ladies who spoke
out their minds with such daring frankness and such
broad Scotch, like that fine moralist, a clergyman's widow,
who. at eighty, hearing how a lady's good fame had
suffered from a prince's indiscretion, shook her shrivelled
fist and cried out, "The damned villain! does he kiss and
tell?"—or of the witty lawyers, so little scrupulous in
words, so keen and sharp of wit, respectful of no shams
nor of much else—or even of the historians and philosophers who gave the town its seal of distinction.   Those
quaint and venerable figures in their old dining-rooms, or
perambulating their favourite walk in the Meadows, under
the shadow of old George Heriot's Hospital, never make
the slightest appearance in the supposed accounts of contemporary manners, by which the *Lounger* hoped to claim
a place beside the more famous weekly records of English
society.   All that we get from it is a misty glimpse of
fashions and dissipations, like, though at a long distance,
the society sketches of the *Spectator*, petty and provincial,
and many times watered.   Mackenzie was the first to
give a really generous and discerning criticism of Burns,
putting him at once in his right place as a poet, which
is infinitely to his credit; but though he was the recognised exponent of literature and society at the time, he

gives us not a single indication of any society into which
it could have been worth the ploughman's while to
appear at all.

This curious deficiency is scarcely comprehensible,
unless from the ambition Mackenzie had to spread his
Lounger beyond Edinburgh, and the sense that Scotland
was still a barbarous and unknown country to the larger
minds of English readers. When we remember that he
actually adds a *glossary* to the "Address to a Mouse,"
quoted in his article on Burns, as if that "good broad
Scotch" which was spoken by so many of the best people
in Edinburgh was unknown to the delicate ears of his
hearers, we feel that elegant fiction can go no farther; it is
as odd as any other affectation of the "*Precieuse*" period.
"Even in Scotland the provincial dialect which Ramsay
and he (Burns) have used is now read with a difficulty
which greatly damps the pleasure of the reader," he says.
The natural result from this is that Mackenzie's sketches,
professedly of Scotland, are as little like Scotland as they
are like Germany. They are of no country under the
sun. They are of that vague typical region invented by
Addison, which is filled by examples of all the virtues
and vices, and where a perpetual crusade against the
fashion and its vagaries is the chief spur of existence.
Marjory Mushroom comes to town; she has her head
turned with new dresses and high *têtes* and feathers, is
persuaded to paint, and meets a great many tempters to
folly in the shape of fine ladies and fine gentlemen—
and coming home again is wretched, and fills the heads
of all the Misses Homespun with illegitimate longings.
Or Mrs. Careful describes how, occupied like Virtue's
self in teaching her little girls, she is interrupted by innumerable callers, who spoil her morning. Or it is the
story of Eudocius and Clitander which edifies the reader;
or Colonel Caustic, who is a weak imitation of Sir Roger

de Coverley, represents chivalry and all the Graces, with
a great many indignant and sarcastic remarks upon the
inferiority of everything in the present to everything in
the past. An Addison of Tunbridge Wells, doing all he
can to ignore the fact that his assemblies and plays are
not the real resorts of fashion, but yet with no more difference in his tone than the heavier atmosphere of Kent
necessitated, might have written just such moralities.
Here and there, with a breath of regret, he owns, indeed,
that Edinburgh as a fashionable centre is not the chief
of cities. "There is a sort of classic privilege in the
very names of the places in London which does not extend to those of Edinburgh," he says. "The Canongate
is almost as long as the Strand, but it will not bear the
comparison upon paper; and Blackfriars Wynd can never
vie with Drury Lane." The Canongate is one of the
grandest old streets in Europe, and was still at that
period, whatever its sanitary conditions may have been,
the abode of the remnants of those great people for whom
its stately houses were built, and it is amusing to hear
that it is not to be compared to the Strand. This is
very like Mrs. Hardcastle's speech in the play, when she
asks, with regretful humility yet pride, How can any one
have a manner who has never seen "the Pantheon, the
Grotto Gardens, the Borough, and such places, where the
nobility chiefly resort?"

Just so the Edinburgh critic sighs yet smiles, with
an underlying consciousness that, after all, he is almost
as fine a gentleman as those who flourished their canes
in the Mall, or frequented the most classic of coffee-
rooms. Yet those featureless and uncharacteristic fables
were produced by Mackenzie and his coadjutors in the
very heart of that merry, noisy, somewhat rough, profane,
and convivial Edinburgh, which was, perhaps, the most
individual of all local societies. They had their head-

quarters in Creech's shop, in the house once inhabited
by Allan Ramsay, upon the brow of the hill, close to the
spot once occupied by the old town cross, where in the
afternoons all the town came out, to walk about the open
space and listen to the bell-ringing, for want of a better
entertainment; or rather to enjoy their jokes, which
were more funny than refined, and their gossip, which
was full of audacious freedom. To think that the "Man
of Feeling" could have looked out daily upon this jovial
crowd, and perhaps gone afterwards for his dish of tea to
the close on the Castle Hill, where Mrs. Cockburn received Burns with enthusiasm, and where there were
dances and junketings "nine couples on the floor" of the
small drawing-room, and "the bairns vastly happy;"
and many an old Scotch song and new anonymous ditty,
in cunning imitation of the old, was made and sung—
and yet have nothing but Mushrooms and Homespuns to
talk about in his commentary on society! Perhaps he
shook hands, on his way, with John Clerk of Eldin or
Henry Erskine, broad Scots and broad jokers both, or
rubbed shoulders with old Miss Suph Johnstone, the
amazon of the day, whose song, "Eh! quo' the tod, it's a
braw licht nicht," proves what her dialect was. He
could not move a step, indeed, this elegant disciple of
Addison and Rousseau, without having his ears offended
with the vigorous vowels and gutturals, the daring wit,
and audacious talk, of a community as strong as unre-
strained, as profane and as convivial as ever made a town
merry; and yet he gives us a glossary of Burns, and sets
before us a gallery of pastels, swains, and nymphs, and
conventional rustics and fine ladies, as his contribution to
the satirical and sentimental history of his time.

This is all the more curious that Henry Mackenzie was
no impostor, but really knew society, and was himself an
important figure, none better known in Edinburgh, where

he lived to our own days, a highly respectable and respected townsman, bearing the romantic title of his principal work to his grave. " The Man of Feeling," which is a very mild dilution of the sentimentalism of the time, with a good deal of Sterne in it, and a good deal of Rousseau, is not without some prettiness of composition, and even occasional just remark. Perhaps it was a certain pride in the thought that Scotland had here produced an elegant moralist of her own to rival her richer and greater neighbour, who up to this time had been unquestionably in advance of her in this as in most other departments of literature, which gave to the work its unusual popularity. However it may pique our patriotism to say so, it is no doubt true that Scotland, like every junior partner in a great historical union, has always had a most lively jealousy of her wealthy sister, and delighted in nothing so much as in the ability to hold her own in all peaceful contests of arts or letters. While neither Burns nor Scott existed, Henry Mackenzie was always something : and perhaps it pleased the jocund little capital all the better that he stood up to the adversary on his own ground, giving her a Lounger of her own in emulation of all the Spectators and Ramblers, than if he had struck out the fresh vein of her own humours and oddities, which was happily reserved for a more potent magician. There is nothing of what in these modern days of slang we call " bumptiousness " in the " Man of Feeling." He is too well-bred to throw down his glove to the potentates over the Border. He prefers, with plausible elegance, to prove that there is no manner of difference between them. In early youth, indeed, he was seduced into one or two attempts to copy the old Scotch ballad, that effort of industry being popular at the time. But his ballads had never been battled over, like Hardyknute and Sir Patrick Spens, and are very inferior

productions—while the didactic verse, into which he
flowed inevitably afterwards, is as full of reference to the
ordinary subjects of "town," as if the poet had never
issued from within the sound of Bow Bells. When he
describes the houses of the great, it is a town mansion
which is his model, with "giant knocker" and powdered
footman; when he rhymes his harmless fable about
Truth and Business, it is a cockney in "a neat-built
country box"—

> "So near, that with an easy ride,
>   A man may breakfast in Cheapside"—

who is his model of the latter quality. The fashionable
auction where "Sir Lappet" hurries in his "papillots,"
chattering politics and bric-a-brac—

> "The Queen of Denmark—there's a figured bowl,
>   The marquis writes me that the Tuesday's poll—
>   What gewgaw things! your glass, my lord: are these,
>   Oh miserably vulgar! not Chinese!"

and all the Laelios and Lamias, the city turtle, the dissipations of the great, are all imitations and antiquated
imitations, the fashion taking some time to travel from
London to Edinburgh. The "Man of Feeling" has to
deal with peasants of romantic nature and the finest
sentiments, and with unfortunates upon the streets
who are as delicate and refined as any princess, and
whose betrayal into vice has every machination of vil-
lainy to excuse it; who are, indeed, only the more
immaculate and interesting from having sinned. The
benefactor and hero is a gentle youth, who lives but to
do good, and be loved, and who, after an unfortunate
interval of doubt as to the affections of the matchless
maiden whom he has chosen, dies of the joy of hearing
that she loves him! This is indeed a superfine hero,
and everything he says and does is equally delicate and

irreproachable. The " Man of the World " which followed, and which is equally fine, but much more objectionable, has a mixture of Richardson in his worst
peculiarities, the hairbreadth escapes of Pamela, over and
over repeated—and not always escapes : with an absence
both of wit and nature which takes all possible right of
existing from such detestable complications. Julia de
Roubigné is a poor little shadow from the other Julia
of the Nouvelle Heloise. So sapless, imitative, and artificial were the productions which held the palm of
literary achievement in the capital of Scotland, when
Burns, eager, yet proud, distrustful, and suspicious, holding himself on his guard like some herald, or bearer of a
flag of truce in an enemy's country, appeared to the
wonder and admiration, yet doubt and alarm, of the old
sovereigns of literature. The honour that remains to the
" Man of Feeling " is that he had discrimination and
sense enough to give his word of praise, and that with
no stinted hand, to the ploughman poet.

The other correct and regular poet of the time was
Dr. Blacklock, who also, to his great credit, at once
recognised and applauded the new light. His poetry is
of the same smooth and characterless description, but his
story is a touching one ; he was blind from his infancy,
but was so kindly guarded and served both by relations
and friends that, though without means of his own, he
acquired a classical education, or at least enough of it to
qualify him for the Church of Scotland, not much more
exacting then than was the Church of England when she
received Crabbe with nothing but a little Latin into her
bosom. He got a living, but his parishioners were not
satisfied with their blind pastor, and after an interval of
discomfort he left them in the hands of a substitute,
reserving some portion of the stipend to live upon, and
with this came to Edinburgh, where he received into his

house young men attending the University, and was himself received into the genial society of the place.   He got a good and tender wife notwithstanding his blindness, and a great deal of that respect mingled with compassion, which a man, so heavily burdened in the way of life, almost invariably inspires, but which perhaps is always a half-humiliating sympathy.   Poems with such titles as " Ode to Aurora on Melusa's Birthday," " Ode to a Young Gentleman bound for Guinea," etc., sufficiently indicate the character of his verses.   In the short memoir which we have of him, written by Mackenzie, there are a great many special quotations made, and lines selected, to show that, notwithstanding his blindness, he was capable of describing nature.   This, of course, must have been simply in imitation of the lavish colours, the purple evenings and rosy mornings of the poets : but there is a pathetic correctness in his enumeration of the yellow crocuses and purple hyacinths, which touches the heart.   He was a good man, and, considering his infirmity, prosperous and fortunate.   But the consciousness of this disability appears to have kept him somewhat sad, and his later life seems to have been touched with melancholy from a very natural cause.   " Some of his later poems express a chagrin, though not of an ungentle sort, at the supposed failure of his imaginative powers ; or," " the Man of Feeling" adds, " at the fastidiousness of modern times, which he despaired to please."   Poor gentle poet !—his " Muse," his gift of " Song," had been the sole ground upon which he had risen into local reputation ; and there are few more moving occasions for at least a sentimental sympathy.   We feel with him, even if we smile at the hot but weak indignation with which he stigmatises the new standards—standards, alas ! which he could never come up to, and which settled his fate.

> " Such were his efforts, such his cold reward,
> Whom once thy partial tongue pronounced a bard.
> Excursive on the gentle gales of spring
> He rov'd, while favour imp'd his timid wing,
> Exhausted genius now no more inspires ;
> But mourns abortive hopes and faded fires.
> The short-lived wreath, which once his temples graced,
> Fades at the sickly breath of squeamish taste,
> Whilst darker days his fainting flames immure
> In cheerless gloom, and winter premature."

Again we say poor poet ! He had as much right to call the new influences which condemned his old-fashioned rigid verse, " a squeamish taste," as they had to break up the foundations and scatter the waning honours of that lingering, feeble superstructure, which had been elongated like a house of cards upon the system of. Pope. He showed his insight above any of the other tuneful brethren by recognising that his day was over, and his laurels incapable of supporting that "sickly breath." These discontented verses are the swansong of the ending age. " The Man of Feeling " was conscious, for his own part, of no such failure.

At the same time there existed in Old Edinburgh, in the very region where flourished the *Mirror* and the *Lounger*, and all their far-fetched conventionalisms, a true and generous little concert of songs rising from various quarters, which handed on a better tradition, from Allan Ramsay, whose pastoral strain, if not without affectation, had rung true and clear, down to Burns. They were chiefly women, ladies of the best blood and breeding, who performed this genial office, with little parade, and more enjoyment than fame. " The grand old ballad of Sir Patrick Spens," as Coleridge calls it, was, all authorities are now agreed in saying, an innocent forgery, and written by Lady Wardlaw, who was the author of several other mock-antique ballads, which, however, were not

mock poetry, but worthy the place they attained. Miss
Jean Elliot produced one of the versions of the " Flowers
of the Forest," Mrs. Cockburn another : while Lady Anne
Lindsay gave us the exquisite and pathetic little romance
of " Auld Robin Gray," a ballad so true to the soil, so
pure and tender in sentiment, that its genuine truth and
nature make all the artificial features of the surrounding
literature look more false than ever—

> " Oh, lady nursed in pomp and pleasure,
> Where gat ye that heroic measure ? "

How was it that art, so true yet so simple, could exist
in so many obscure corners, while the false and bedizened
artifice which took her place sat in the high places, and
was constituted the judge of everything ? This is one of
the curious circumstances in literary history which it is
difficult to explain, except from the fact that the frost
stiffens with a kind of desperation the moment before the
south winds begin to blow, and the ice chains to melt
away. Behind backs, out of the reach of the critics,
Edinburgh no doubt laughed in her sleeve at the " Man
of Feeling." But Scotland has always cherished such
songs as these in her heart. They breathed about the
country far and wide, and were known and sung long
before they were printed, the national genius for song
having survived everything ; and it was appropriate that
through this homely channel the revival should come.
What does Mr. Carlyle say: " The smallest cranny through
which a great soul ever shone " ? But when he said
this, he forgot what we do not doubt he very well knows,[1]
all that song has been to Scotland since that speech was
made about the making of laws and the making of
ballads. Song, or rather Songs : the word in the plural

---

[1] These words were written before the loss of Scotland's last great
writer, which we have now to lament.

has perhaps a somewhat different meaning, not that of a melody only, which might please the hearers almost as much if Do-re-mi were the syllables employed to give it utterance, but an art which was poetry, at least as much as music, and into which thousands entered with enjoyment for the sake chiefly of the beautiful " words." This distinction is perhaps worth the consideration of the student. Ballads like " Auld Robin Gray," songs like the " Flowers of the Forest," were a great deal more than music ; the simple old tune " set " to each was little more than the breath which carried the poetry into many a melting heart. This mingled faculty, half one art, half the other, was never extinguished, and always independent of the verse-maker's elaborate rules. It was the breath of life in old Scotland. When the " Man of Feeling " reigned in artificial and tottering state, these collections of songs, unnoted messengers, flew about the country to which they were indigenous, keeping up in it a soul of fresh and natural sentiment when there was little else to do so—a fact which made it more appropriate than any one has cared to acknowledge that the new power in literature in the north, the new poet, should take by nature to this national medium, the art his country has always loved.

HENRY MACKENZIE, the Man of Feeling, born 1745 ; died 1831 ; published his chief work 1771.

THOMAS BLACKLOCK, born 1721 ; died 1791 ; published volume of poems 1746.

CHAPTER IV.

GEORGE CRABBE.

AT the very time when the two unconscious revolutionaries who have occupied our time so long were loosing
the bands and opening the prison gates of poetry, and,
with her, of literature in general, there was happening at
the same moment one of those curious returns upon old
customs, which so often give a whimsical variety to a
great movement.   It would be amiss to say that Crabbe
had no part in the new revolution.   He whose themes
are so severely chosen from annals unknown to the
Graces, and whose stern submission to fact deepened and
strengthened what we may call the imaginative realism
of his great contemporaries, had his full part in the
destruction of those attenuated canons of literary art,
which were no longer capable of restraining the impulse
of the new life; but nothing could be more entirely in
accordance with all the conventional laws of a poet's
struggle, and final acceptance by the world, than the early
facts of his history.   All that was ever written of Grub
Street comes true in his tale of misery and aspiration.
He is at his outset the very poet of Hogarth, the
philosophical vagabond of Goldsmith, the poor author
whose image it is so hard to dissociate even from the
hard-working and well-to-do literature of to-day.   While
Cowper was roaming gently and legitimately, yet, so far

as contemporary opinion went, wildly enough by all the
windings af the Ouse, patronless, and indifferent to everything but the diversion of his own distracted spirit; and
Burns bringing out through a local printer, and for local
gratification, his first modest volume—Crabbe was starv-
ing in London, writing letter after letter to one magnate
after another, in hopes of being picked up out of his
garret, and on the strength of approbation from some
acknowledged authority, finding himself at last on the
way to fame.   There could not be a more curious difference—all the more as Johnson and his supporters had
thrown cold water on Grub Street, and all but pulled
down the great Dagon of patronage.   New ideas, however, travel slowly, and perhaps the son of the rough
Suffolk " Saltmaster," half-official, half-fisherman, was not
aware that the patron, as a literary institution, had got
his deathblow.   To him London was still a place where
the streets were paved with gold—where genius was
understood, and poetry a sort of " Open Sesame " to every
noble door.   The contrast is extraordinary — and it
becomes all the more marked from the fact that Crabbe
was one of the few with whom the obsolete institution of
literary patronage was entirely successful.   He found the
man, noble and generous, and open-hearted—noble, that
is in heart and spirit, though not in rank—who is the
ideal patron of whom every poet dreams : and whose
image has always made it possible for visionary men to
believe in and struggle after the favour of the great,
hoping always to find under the graceful drapery of a
title, that all-feeling, all-comprehending being, whose
patronage will be an honour, and his help something like
the help of an angel—" Is not a patron, my lord, one who
looks with unconcern on a man struggling for life in the
water, and when he has reached ground encumbers him
with help ? "   Johnson had asked so long before as the

period of Crabbe's birth; but the country lad who came to London with his poems a hundred years ago, half educated, and completely inexperienced, retained the old notions that belonged to a previous generation, and never seems to have doubted that he would find some one to stand between him and want—nay, to open the way for him to success and fame. And the wonderful thing was that he succeeded and found what he sought.

George Crabbe was born in the seafaring village of Aldborough, on the Suffolk coast, in the year 1754. He was thus five years older than Burns. Except that he was an English villager with a touch of the sea in everything about him, his breeding was not much dissimilar from that of Burns, with the great difference, however, that the Scots parents' profound piety and anxious appreciation of education were wanting in the probably much more plentiful and comfortable home of the revenue officer. These were the days when salt was taxed, and Crabbe's father was the collector of the duties,—with a charge of warehouses it would appear,—probably custom-house warehouses, in which he made his sons fill up their idle time; but he was a man of violent temper and not of exemplary habits. Crabbe's education was of the smallest. When he was fourteen his professional training as a doctor, the trade (for it would be absurd to call it a profession) selected for him, began, and he entered upon life as an apprentice to a country surgeon. It is a curious illustration of the loose training of those days, that Crabbe set up for himself as a doctor in Aldborough at the age of two or three and twenty, with scarcely any further training in his profession than that he had received from the country surgeon, whose apprentice he had been. He was in London for a few months professedly attending the hospitals, and he was for some time assistant to an apothecary—but this was all his

education came to. Probably in that sharp sea air among
those salt-marshes, and in days so much less occupied with
sanitary considerations than our own, disease was more
straightforward and simple than now—otherwise there is
something appalling in the idea that the lives of a village
might be committed to the charge of a youth so imper-
fectly trained.

He did not like his profession, however, nor did it
like him—and he was in love, and a poet. No doubt,
though he was always a modest and somewhat matter-of-
fact man, he felt in himself many faculties to which the
dreary village life afforded no development—and dreams
of some one who would appreciate and understand him,
and of a larger existence in which his higher qualities
would have scope, stirred within him. His home was
mean and uncongenial, his Sarah hopelessly removed from
him so long as he was without the means of maintaining
her, and nothing but the angry sea, the oozing marshes,
the dull peat bog and stubbly common, and low sky
hanging over the flat country, composed his surroundings.
" With the best verses he could write, and with very
little more, he quitted the place of his birth, not without
the most serious apprehensions of the consequences of
such a step—apprehensions which were conquered, and
barely conquered, by the more certain evil of the prospect
before him, should he remain where he was."   When we
add that the " very little more " which enabled the poor
young surgeon to make this prodigious venture, was five
pounds borrowed from, or rather given by, a local
magnate, Mr. Dudley North, the desperation of the project will be all the more apparent. He obtained this by
writing to Mr. North, with whom he does not seem to
have had any prior acquaintance. His passage to London,
though only in a sloop sailing from a neighbouring little
seaport, in which he lived with the sailors, cost him a

considerable part of the sum—and he arrived in London with a "box of clothes, a small case of surgical instruments, and three pounds"—no friends nor any resource by which he could help himself, and nothing but the poems in his pocket upon which to build his forlorn hope. He lived at first in a hairdresser's shop, was kindly patronised by a linen-draper in Cornhill, and spent his evenings at "a small coffee-house near the Exchange," where he was so fortunate as to meet respectable and intelligent companions. But even such humble delights were not long to be kept up upon nothing. The first thing he did was to offer his poems for publication. "Sylvanus Urban" rejected them with good-humoured contempt. Then he began to write letters, which, had he not been a poet, could be called nothing but begging-letters, to one great personage after another. Lord North, the Prime Minister, took no notice of his application, neither did Lord Shelburne. Thurlow, to whom he enclosed some of his verses, returned a cold note, regretting that he had no time to read poetry. We do not know whether Prime Ministers and Lord Chancellors now-a-days have similar applications made to them; but the impartial reader will feel almost an equal pity for the high functionaries who were thus at the mercy of every rhymester. Crabbe was received graciously at their tables in after years, and made the inevitable reflections on the subject—but our wonder at the boldness of the young poet is greater, we fear, than our indignation with the great men who did not take him up. Granting, however, that his possession of the poetic gift gave him a claim upon the rulers of the country, the bitterness of his repeated disappointment is very real. To Lord Shelburne he sends a letter, half in verse, half in prose, "Ah, Shelburne, blest with all that's good or great," cries the poor poet:

> " Oh hear the Virtue thou reverest plead ;
>   She'll swell thy breast, and there applaud the deed.
>   She bids thy thoughts one hour from greatness stray,
>   And leads thee on to fame a shorter way ;
>   Where, if no withering laurel's thy reward
>   There's shouting Conscience, and a grateful Bard ;
>   A Bard untrained in all but misery's school,
>   Who never bribed a knave or praised a fool ;—
>   'Tis Glory prompts, and as thou read'st attend,
>   She dictates pity, and becomes my friend ;
>   She bids each cold and dull reflection flee,
>   And yields her Shelburne to distress and me ! "

"My lord," he adds, "I now turn to your lordship, and entreat to be heard. I am ignorant what to ask, but feel forcibly my wants—patronage and bread. I know no other claim on your lordship than my necessities, unless my Muse, and she has, I am afraid, as few charms."

In the depths of private life it happens to us all to receive letters scarcely less touching, and quite as un-authorised ; but it is to be feared that we show very little respect for their eloquence. To meet with the model of such productions in the writing of a poet who has since found a place in the records of fame, is curious enough. The fashion was dying down to a low level even then, but had not quite gone. Lord Shelburne took no notice of this effusion, but Crabbe, when years after he was the guest of the statesman whose favour he had sought in vain, recalled, not unkindly, the different conditions in which he waited at those same doors with his heart beating, looking for a reply that never came. His journal of this anxious period of his life is wonderfully natural and affecting. It is addressed to Mira, which was the poetical of plain Sarah, his betrothed ; but when disappointment and trouble overwhelm him, when he has " but sixpence farthing in the world," and so many melancholy appeals flying about which the great people will take no notice of, it is with a touching return to fact and nature that he cries, "Oh, Sally, how I want you!" from the bottom of his heart.

The London in which Crabbe thus starved and struggled was a more picturesque, if not so comfortable, London than the one we are familiar with. He gives his Mira a description of the Gordon riots which took place during the summer. "In my way I met a resolute band of vile-looking fellows, ragged, dirty, and insolent, armed with clubs, going to join their companions." He stands and looks on while Newgate is pulled to pieces, and "never saw anything so dreadful." When the governor's house was reduced to "a mere shell of brick-work, they kept a store of flame there for other purposes; it became red-hot, and the doors and windows appeared like the entrances to so many volcanoes. But I must not omit" (he adds) "what struck me most. About ten or twelve of the mob getting to the top of the debtors' prison, whilst it was burning, to halloo, they appeared rolled in black smoke mixed with sudden bursts of fire, like Milton's infernals." Through these lurid gleams he sees the prisoners "conducted through the streets in their chains." Pleasanter are the records of his Sunday experiences, when he goes to church, and sends the sermon to refresh his reader. "As I'm afraid my ever dearest Mira has not a preacher so affecting as my worthy rector, I shall not scruple to give his morning discourse in the way I have abstracted those before." Thus the anxious maiden in Suffolk has a share in all he says or does; and though the absolute dependence of the young man upon hopes so chimerical as the patronage of statesmen for his "Muse" is very strange to us now-a-days, yet his confidence, and tenderness, and piety, make a very pleasant picture—not too sad, since success comes at the end.

Dr. Johnson was still living, and the greatest author-

ity in letters ; but it does not seem to have occurred to
Crabbe to appeal to the great autocrat. It is somewhat
curious, indeed, to find in Cowper, whose career began
during the early reign of Johnson, and in Crabbe, who
crossed that reign towards its end, so little recognition of
the great Pope of Literature, who to our eyes dominates
his age. Nothing can be more remarkable, however,
than the blindness of contemporaries, and perhaps Johnson was too alarming for the new generation, never much
disposed to acknowledge the masters of a former cycle.
When he had exhausted all other resources young Crabbe
addressed himself in his despair to Burke. He sent him
a long letter, giving a narrative of his distressed condition and the disappointment of all his hopes, in which
several of his poems were enclosed. His situation was
almost hopeless when he took his little packet to Burke's
door. " I appeal to you, sir, as a good, and, let me add,
a great man. I have no other pretensions to your favour
but that I am an unhappy one," said the poor young
adventurer. " Mr. Burke," says Crabbe's son and
biographer, " was at this period (1781) engaged in the
hottest turmoil of parliamentary opposition, and his own
pecuniary circumstances were by no means very affluent ;
yet he gave instant attention to this letter and the verses
it enclosed. He immediately appointed an hour for my
father to call upon him at his house in London, and the
short interview that ensued entirely and for ever changed
the nature of his worldly fortunes. He was in the
common phrase ' a made man ' from that hour. He
went into Mr. Burke's rooms a poor young adventurer,
spurned by the opulent and rejected by the publishers,
his last shilling gone, and all but his last hope with it ;
he came out virtually secure of almost all the good fortune
that by successive steps fell to his lot ; his genius acknowledged by one whose verdict could not be questioned ; his

character and manners approved by a noble and generous heart, whose benevolence knew no limits but its power."

The relations between patron and dependant cannot be called either wholesome or pleasant, and literature has little occasion to regret the change of system; still, there is something in this sudden deliverance which touches the heart more than any mere bookselling. To go, poor and quivering with the keen shafts of anxiety, seeing no light around you, and no way of escape from your trouble, into some gracious presence, and in a moment—in the gleam of genial eyes, in the very tone of a voice—to feel yourself saved from all that wretchedness, and the doors of life softly rolled open before you; and in addition to all, a friend gained for life and for death, what sudden happiness could be like it? The young applicant had his poems and a stainless character; but, except these, scarce anything else—a little Latin, a very little medicine; no money, no friends, no connections; and Sally in the country (who is Mira on fine days when the sun is shining), gazing wistfully over the gloomy sea and the flat barren waste, for every post that came in and every sad letter. What a letter he must have written to her that evening! How he must have lingered on every feature of the noble patron, and every word he had uttered! To the country lad it was a great thing to have seen Burke at all; but to have won his smile and his favour, to have heard him say, "He has the mind and feelings of a gentleman," to have received the promise of his help, the immediate recognition of his friendship, what blessedness was this!

Crabbe was of the virtuous kind. He must have borne his evidences of modesty, honour, and manliness, and of a character which never would bring shame upon any one who befriended him, in his countenance. He was little more educated than Burns, and not half so

eloquent or entrancing; yet how great is the difference!
Partly, no doubt, this difference was in the warm-hearted
Irishman whose generosity was so ready and so kind.
But Burke did not take his countryman Goldsmith in
hand as he took Crabbe; there must be, on the other
hand, a something in the protected which will respond to
the efforts of the protector. Burns going off from the
midst of the lords and ladies to a tavern in the wynds,
where, in the wild talk and encounter of wags and wits,
these lords and ladies were sometimes the subjects of the
laughter—was a very different sort of being to protect
and push forward from this gentle and good young
fellow, who never was less than respectable and orderly,
whatever he did — a man full of natural duty and submission, sure to do his patron credit. Why is it that
every man of genius could not be as Crabbe was? Burke
seems to have taken the young fellow from his city
garret, from the lowliness of his sea-side village, into his
own house, "domesticated him under his own roof, and
treated him like a son." Alas! if Burns had got such a
chance it is most likely some cloud of offence, some
dropt decorum, or sharp touch of sarcasm, would have
broken the bond within a week. In Crabbe's case the
adoption of the poet and his interests by this generous
protector, who had never seen him twenty-four hours
before, was complete. Much has been said about literary
jealousies and quarrels, but little about the helpful hand
which many a man of letters has held out to his brother.
Burke was more than a mere man of letters; but he
could not be left out in any literary history, and we do
not know where to find another instance of such complete and powerful help to the ignorant and inexperienced. He went over the poems with the young author,
pointing out to him certain apparent faults, which the
young man amended with ready compliance. "When

all was done that his abilities permitted, and when Mr.
Burke had patiently waited the progress of improvement
in the man whom he conceived to be capable of it, he
himself took 'The Library' to Mr. Dodsley, then of
Pall Mall, and gave many lines the advantage of his own
reading and comments.   Mr. Dodsley listened with all
the respect due to the reader of the verses, and all the
apparent desire to be pleased that could be wished by the
writer; and he was as obliging in his reply as in the
very nature of things a bookseller can be supposed to be
towards a young candidate for poetical reputation."   This
is somewhat enigmatical; but its meaning seems to be
that Dodsley, who had before rejected the MS. summarily,
published it now at the poet's risk, and, with a generosity
not common, "gave to the author his profits as a publisher
and vendor of the pamphlet."

The success of 'The Library' gave some reputation
to the author, and was the occasion of his second poem,
'The Village,' which was corrected and a considerable
portion of it written in the house of his excellent friend,
whose own activity and energy of mind would not permit
a young man under his protection to cease from labour,
and whose judgment directed that labour to its most useful attainments."   The exertions of this "excellent friend"
were not confined to one mode of affording assistance.
"Mr. Crabbe was encouraged to lay open his views past
and present; to display whatever reading and acquirements he possessed; to explain the causes of his disappointments and the cloudiness of his prospects, in short, to
conceal nothing from a friend so able to guide inexperience and so willing to pardon inadvertency."   "It was
in the course of one of their walks" (adds the son who
has quoted the above from an autobiographical sketch
which his father left behind him) "that Burke, after some
conversation on general literature, suggested by a passage

in the Georgics which he had happened to quote, on observing something that was going on in his favourite farm, passed to a more minute inquiry into my father's early days in Suffolk than he had before made, and drew from him the avowal that with respect to future affairs he had a strong partiality for the church. 'It is most fortunate,' said Mr. Burke, 'that your father exerted himself to send you to that second school : without a little Latin we should have made nothing of you ; now I think we shall succeed.' "

Here was true patronage ; and it is impossible to have a better view of the advantages and disadvantages of that happy system. Upon the score of this " little Latin," and a few inquiries made into Crabbe's character in his native place as a matter of form, the statesman and orator, backed by other influences, got the Bishop of Norwich to ordain right away, apparently without study or preparation of any kind, the fortunate object of his kindness. In this particular case, as no doubt in many others, no harm, but a great deal of good came of it, and probably neither Oxford nor Cambridge, nor all the theological faculties in existence, could have created a better country parson than the poor surgeon's apprentice out of Suffolk, the half-trained doctor whom an indulgent bishop accepted on Burke's word, backed by the favourable representations of Mr. Dudley North (the original lender of the five pounds) and Mr. Charles Long. But to make Sancho Panza a governor was scarcely a more arbitrary exercise of patronage. Every day such arrangements were becoming less possible, and Burke belonged to the advancing side, if not actually to anything that could be called the party of progress, when he thus gave, at the end of the system, the most triumphant evidence of its power. This power extended into every quarter from which advantage could come to the young poet. " When

' The Library ' was published, the opinion of Burke had
its effect upon the conductors of the various periodical
works of the time.　The poet received complimentary
critiques from the very gentlemen who had hitherto
treated him with such contemptuous coldness."　And in
still higher regions the same all-prevailing influence told.
" His kind patron had spoken of him in favourable terms
to the stern and formidable Thurlow, and his lordship was
now anxious to atone for his former neglect.　He received
Mr. Crabbe (having invited him to breakfast) with more
than courtesy, and most condescendingly said, ' The first
poem you sent me, sir, I ought to have noticed ; and I
heartily forgive the second.'　They breakfasted together,
and at parting his lordship put a sealed paper into my
father's hand, saying, ' Accept this trifle, sir, in the meantime, and rely on my embracing an early opportunity to
serve you more substantially when I hear that you are in
orders.'　As soon as he left the house he opened the
letter, expecting to find a present of ten or perhaps
twenty pounds ; it contained a bank-note for a hundred !"
Could any incident show more clearly the extraordinary
change which a century has made ?　A young poet of our
days would be as much confounded by the generosity of
" Accept this trifle, sir," as if his noble entertainer had
kicked him downstairs, however much the hundred
pounds might be wanted.　We seem to have fallen back
fifty years at least, even from the day of Cowper and of
Burns—notwithstanding that the system of publishing
by subscription must always have a certain eleemosynary
aspect.　Thurlow's promise, however, does not seem to
have borne very much fruit, and Crabbe had no objection
to the bird in hand, which was worth more than any in
the bush.

　　" The Library " was as slight a foundation as could
be imagined for " complimentary *critiques* " and poetical

fame. To conceive of it, indeed, as appearing an independent publication, among other books, and attracting
any notice at all, makes the reader's head go round. It
is shorter than any of the individual poems which formed
Cowper's first volume, and is so completely of the old
order of manufactured verses, ground out by the "mere
mechanic art," which was Pope's legacy to the world,
that we can but look back astonished at the possibility of
finding, in such a production, the foundation of a lasting
fame. Here, as in the sudden transition of the author
from the wretchedness of destitution to all the comfortable certainties which his friends provided for him, we
feel ourselves in an earlier age, a different world. Other
"singers" were twittering at the time in various corners,
gentle Hayley, whom we love for his kindness to Cowper,
learned Darwin among the fantastic sentimentalities of
his garden, whom his greater grandson has restored to the
recollection of the world, and many more. So far as this
earliest production of Crabbe's "Muse" goes, there would
seem to have been little reason to separate him from
the mildly-tuneful crowd; but the same Review which
characterised Cowper as "a man of a sober and religious
turn of mind, with a benevolent heart, and a serious wish
to inculcate the precepts of morality," but "not possessed
of any superior abilities or power of genius," described
Crabbe's little composition as "the production of no
common pen"—so strangely uncertain are the guides of
popular opinion.

The halcyon moment, however, which the young man
spent under Burke's roof as a member of his family,
meeting all the great people of the day, and presented
with little billets such as the above, could not last for
ever. And after his ordination he seems to have had an
immediate experience of the other side of life, which was
not encouraging. His first occupation was as curate of

Aldborough, and it can scarcely be supposed that his
native place, where every rough fellow about the little
pier had known him familiarly in a position very different
from that which he now occupied, would afford a comfortable beginning in his new profession.   He was " unkindly received," and saw so many " unfriendly counte-
nances about me," that " I am sorry to say," he continues,
" I had too much indignation, though mingled, I hope,
with better feelings, to care what they thought of me or
my sermon."   This was not a very promising way of
beginning a clergyman's life; and though we are all
aware that a prophet has no honour in his own country,
it is painful to hear of unfriendly faces on the one side,
and to see on the other what a gloomy aspect the place,
and everything in it, bore to Crabbe's eye.   No glamour
of kindly association is in the picture he gives of this
native village.   The very landscape becomes blighted and
barren under his hands—

> " Rank weeds that every art and care defy,
>   Reign o'er the land, and rob the blighted rye ;
> There thistles stretch their prickly arms afar,
>   And to the ragged infant threaten war.
>
>   *   *   *   *   *
>
> Here joyless roam a wild amphibious race,
>   With sullen woe display'd in every face,
> Who far from civil arts and social fly,
>   And scowl at strangers with suspicious eye.
>
>   *   *   *   *   *
>
> As on the neighbouring beach yon swallows stand,
>   And wait for favouring winds to leave the land ;
> While still for flight the ready wing is spread,
>   So waited I the favouring hour, and fled—
> Fled from those shores where guilt and famine reign,
>   And cried, ah, hapless, those who still remain !"

It is very unusual to find a poet thus gloomily re-
vengeful of early unkindness, giving up his native village
to the horror of his readers.   Burns had fewer comforts

to look back upon than those possessed by Crabbe, yet
" Coila" was to him the queen of countries, and his
dearest hope was

> " For puir auld Scotia's sake,
>   Some useful plan or buik to make,
>   Or sing a sang at least."

But these distinctions will always remain both in life
and poetry, and some souls receive with enthusiasm of
kindness what others take as cause for endless complaint
and hostility.   Perhaps, indeed, his almost invariable
preference for the darker side, and sense of the matter-of-
fact misery lying underneath every sentimental surface of
country life, is more than anything else the cause of
Crabbe's fame.   From time immemorial every poet had
celebrated the charms of that rural existence in which
men were supposed to cultivate their own fields, to be
made glad by the plentiful harvest, and consoled by the
tranquillity around.   But Crabbe saw " the knees tremble
and the temples beat " of the reaper under "the dogstar's
raging heat;" he saw the labourer return home, not for-
getting all his cares like Burns's Cottar, but " imbibing
the evening dew " through his " warm pores," and hoard-
ing up " aches and anguish for his age."   And it was
scarcely possible that there could be much sympathy
between him and his townsfolk, whom he describes so
bitterly, " the artful, surly, savage race," who had not
cared for his ministrations to their bodies, and were little
likely to be more disposed to receive his ministrations to
their souls.

He remained here, accordingly, but a few months, and
it seems evident, from all his after-experiences, that he
never was popular as a clergyman.   Perhaps a certain
mixture of genial optimism and belief in the good
qualities of the human race is necessary to the holder of

a cure of souls. And Burke, always his friend, was as unwilling as Crabbe could be, to let his *protégé* languish in a poor curacy, in that uncongenial salt-water atmosphere. He procured for him the position of domestic chaplain to the Duke of Rutland, " a station such as has in numerous instances led to the first dignities of the church." This happy result, however, did not happen in Crabbe's case. He was not more than two years at Belvoir, during which time he was presented by Thurlow —with an assurance that, " by God, he was as like Parson Adams as twelve to a dozen "—with two small livings in Dorsetshire—livings which he does not seem so much as to have visited for several years. Afterwards, by the interest of the Duchess of Rutland, he was permitted to exchange them for two of superior value in the vale of Belvoir; and this, until a late period of his life, was all the preferment he obtained.

It was while he was in Belvoir, entirely separated from the life to which he has given such forcible and gloomy expression, that " The Village," the first of Crabbe's works which indicated his true power in poetry and his real place in his generation, was published. It had been written some time before, and it is said that the stern vigour of the lines in which he expressed his satisfaction in escaping from his native place was the special part of his poetry which moved Burke to so high an estimate of him. The poem was of a very different order from the artificial commonplace of " The Library." It not only chimed in with the sweeter contemporary voices so soon to be raised in the interests of nature, by directing " the Muse " out of all the conventional scenery sacred to her, to the homes and common life of the poor —but it outdid both Burns and Cowper in this particular by showing these homes in the naked prose of their most matter-of-fact aspect, neither lovely, nor happy, nor contented, but full of squalor, misery, and pain. This was the last touch in the picture, the discord that was needed for the perfection of the music. Fictitious pictures of peasant felicity have been common enough in all ages. When the luxurious have been sated with luxury, and the splendid with splendour, it has not been an unusual device to ape the simplicity of rustics, and make an elegant travesty of the life of the cottage to refresh the palace. In this way Marie Antoinette, when society was sickest, played at being a milkmaid in Trianon. And as in life, so in literature. Rousseau had set up the rural life as the only one that approached perfection, and with all the force of conventionality, had declared the conventional to be the bane of mankind. It was a poetical commonplace that Corydon and Phillis were blessed above all the emperors and kings. This has always stood first among the voluntary delusions which have pleased the over-civilised. It was Crabbe's special gift to dig his axe down to the very root of this last refuge of artificial sentiment—

> " . . . The Muses sing of happy swains,
>   Because the Muses never knew their pains,"

he says ; and with all the fervour of indignant truth, and something of the sternness of a controversialist, places before us the bare and sober truth of that form of existence which all these pastoral pipes had celebrated in fictitious strains—

> " I grant indeed that fields and flocks have charms
>   For him that grazes or for him that farms ;
>   But when amid such pleasing scenes I trace
>   The poor laborious natives of the place,
>   And see the midday sun, with fervid ray,
>   On their bare heads and dewy temples play ;
>   While some, with feebler heads and fainter hearts,
>   Deplore their fortune, yet sustain their parts—

> Then shall I dare these real ills to hide,
> In tinsel trappings of poetic pride?
>   No; cast by Fortune on a frowning coast,
> Which neither groves nor happy valleys boast;
> Where other cares than those the Muse relates,
> And other shepherds dwell with other mates;
> By such examples taught, I paint the Cot,
> As Truth will paint it, and as Bards will not:
> Nor you, ye Poor, of letter'd scorn complain,
> To you the smoothest song is smooth in vain;
> O'ercome by labour, and bow'd down by time,
> Feel you the barren flattery of a rhyme?
> Can poets soothe you, when you pine for bread,
> By winding myrtles round your ruin'd shed?"

This was Crabbe's mission in the new age. Cowper took England back to the spontaneity and ease of Nature, and showed her how much more beautiful and perfect was the real landscape even of her plains and undistinguished fields, and how much nearer the heart the incidents and accidents of daily life, than any inverted antithesis of savage mountains and smiling valleys, of Rapture and Despair. And Burns brought out the very sweetness of the natural heart, its tender musings, its love, its mirth, its compassion, the great thoughts, the sorrows, and joys that dwell in all human houses, as in his dwellings of the poor. These were the apostles of an equality such as needed no blood or tears to establish its beneficent law, which bound together the highest and the lowest, not by casting down one or raising up another, but by revealing each to each, where each was most real, and showing how love and grief, and all the inner consciousness of humanity, were among all true lovers, fathers, mothers, children, in all conditions the same. Crabbe's work was the completion of all this, though the more painful part. It was to dispel a false light which had separated the peasant, artificially, just as much as pride of place had separated the peer, from the general

sympathy—to prove the Arcadian fields to be regions of
labour, hard and bitter, as any on earth, and the happy
peasant to demand all the pity, all the succour, that the
wretched need.   Crabbe forged the last link in the chain
—overthrew the last delusion.   He led the student of
Belinda's curls back to human life as Cowper did, and
Burns; but he taught him a sterner lesson—a lesson
equally essential to the clearing and opening up of the
new world.   "The Village" is entirely occupied with
this task.   The description of the dreary heath, and flat
unfertile sands, the weeds that paint the country with
vain splendour, "like the nymphs whom wretched arts
adorn," the inhabitants, full of "sullen woe," strikes a
key-note, which is carried out from page to page with
bitterer force—

> " Where are the swains, who, daily labour done,
>   With rural games play'd down the setting sun ?"

they are occupied in the arts of the smuggler or the
wrecker—

> " Or will you deem them amply paid in health,
>   Labour's fair child that languishes with wealth ?"

the poet asks, and draws us that picture of the labourer,
to which we have already referred, strained to his utmost
through the day, infected with all the miasmas of the
damp air at night—the weak striving to keep up with
the strong " till long-contending nature drops at last."

> " Or will ye praise that homely, healthy fare,
>   Plenteous and plain, that happy peasants share ?"

he cries: and shows them crushed by " the missing of a
stinted meal."   Then comes a picture of the old man
who once drew the straightest furrow, and was " chief in
all the rustic trade," now driven from one petty occupation to another, and with no refuge but the workhouse,

of which such a picture follows as makes the reader
shudder—

> " Theirs is yon House that holds the parish poor,
>   Whose walls of mud scarce bear the broken door ;
>   There, where the putrid vapours, flagging, play,
>   And the dull wheel hums doleful through the day ;—
>   There children dwell, who know no parent's care—
>   Parents, who know no children's love, dwell there !
>   Dejected widows with unheeded tears,
>   And crippled age with more than childhood's fears ;
>   The lame, the blind, and, far the happiest they !
>   The moping idiot, and the madman gay."

Nor does the poet leave the poor man, whom he
traces remorselessly through all these miseries till he has
deposited him, without even the burial ceremonies of
religion—for

> " The busy priest, detain'd by weightier care,
>   Defers his duty till the day of prayer "—

among the " mingled relics of the parish poor."

Thus Crabbe fulfils his part without flinching in the
great work that had to be done. To disclose the poor
man, that he is as good as yourself, with as many sweet-
enings of affection, as many sublime thoughts in his
lowliness, was the mission of one poet ; to disclose him
sternly as so much worse than yourself, though your own
flesh and blood, is the harsher errand of the other : but
both of them were wanted, and without the one the
other would not have been complete. Not one more
than another of these poets was conscious of his mission.
No burden of prophecy weighed upon the heart of the
gentle pluralist, the good parson who retained an inclination towards dukes and great folks all his life, and was
never very popular among the class from which he
sprang, and whose sufferings impressed him with all the
more horror that he had but just escaped them in his

own person—any more than there was in Burns a consciousness of the gaping wondering world looking on,
while his plough disturbed the mouse and crushed the
daisy, and asking, with a gasp of incredulous amazement,
where he got those thoughts so much above his place?
That the sublimest thoughts were not above that place,
nor yet the most squalid misery below the enduring of
these heirs of heaven, was what the two had to tell.   It
was of more worth to the world than the fiery doctrines
which were being proclaimed in blood and flame across
the Channel—of more worth because going below the
outsides of things, and preaching no arbitrary equality
and fraternity, but a brotherhood and a common standing-
ground which was fundamental.   Burns "rhymed for
fun," that is for the relief of his own spirit, to find a
natural outlet for that which was in him—and Cowper
for health, for distraction, to find in the company of the
poet's unknown friends, those who had ears and could
hear, deliverance from himself.   Crabbe was less spontaneous than either of them ; he had the mark of the old
régime upon him : he wrote his poems in the way of
honest daily work, and with a distinct object : not knowing much more about the deeper scope of what he said
than that the bias of his nature inclined him to such and
such subjects.   But all three, nevertheless, unconsciously
worked together and helped each other out.

To show how differently these poems got into being
from the others we have already treated, we may follow
the course of "The Village" into the world.   It was sent
by the author to Burke, who transmitted it in his turn
to Johnson.   The autocrat received it very graciously.
"It is original, vigorous, and elegant," he writes.   "The
alterations which I have made I do not require him to
adopt, *for my lines are perhaps not often better than his
own.*"   Boswell too refers to the incident with great

pride in the benignity of his idol. " The sentiments of
Mr. Crabbe's admirable poem as to the false notions of
rustic happiness and rustic virtue, were quite congenial
with Dr. Johnson's own, and he took the trouble not only
to suggest slight corrections and variations, but to furnish
some lines *where he thought he could give the writer's
meaning better than in the words of the manuscript.*"
Crabbe does not seem to have found fault either with
this exercise of autocratic criticism, or the benign humility
of the admission, that " perhaps my lines are not often
better than his own "—and adopted the six lines which
Johnson supplied apparently without a murmur ; while
Boswell adds, with smiling complacency yet candour, " I
must, however, observe that the aids he gave to this
poem, as to the ' Traveller ' and the ' Deserted Village '
of Goldsmith, were so small, as by no means to impair
the distinguished merit of the author." But when the
poem had gone through this wonderful ordeal more
remained. It was again revised by Burke, who " proposed one or two trivial alterations, which my father's
grateful feelings induced him to adopt, although they did
not appear to himself improvements." " There were not
wanting, I have heard," adds Crabbe's son and biographer,
with natural indignation, " friends in Suffolk, who, when
' The Village ' came out, whispered that the manuscript
had been so cobbled by Burke and Johnson, that Crabbe
did not know it again when it was returned to him."
Perhaps these good-natured friends were not without
some excuse for their mistake—being ignorant, as such
critics are, that neither Burke nor Johnson could have
written " The Village " with all their united genius, to
save their lives.

Crabbe married shortly after, and his career had but
few vicissitudes — a removal from one parsonage to
another, the births and deaths that fill to overflowing the

hearts of those most immediately concerned, yet count for
so little in the outward history; a married life not quite
so blissful as the faithful love before it had promised;
and yet no tragic troubles of any kind, nothing but the
mingled thread in which there is generally so much more
of the dark than bright, of common life.   Notwithstanding the wonderful good fortune of his beginning, no
special advantage came to him afterwards in his career,
which, so far as his profession was concerned, was a very
ordinary course of small promotions and indifferent content.
He was benevolent and kind, but not generally popular
—worshipped by his children, but greatly restrained in
his social instincts by the delicate health of his wife, and
not very happy at home.   He was a great botanist, a
mathematician, and an industrious student, making up
the deficiencies of his preliminary education both in
classics and the modern languages, reading a great deal,
and thus occupying himself with many of those aids to
existence, which help a man, not too busy or too happy,
to get through the lingering years.   " The Village " was
published in 1783.   In 1785 an insignificant and un-
meaning production called " The Newspaper " appeared,
dedicated to Thurlow; and it was not till the year 1806,
twenty-two years after, that the " Parish Register," the
author's next work, was completed.   Between these two
dates so much had happened that it was nothing less
than a new world, into which the poet, with the same
message on his lips, enlarged and rounded with superior
art, yet perhaps in its diffuseness less impressive than
the terse solemnity of " The Village," now reappeared.
Such a gap breaks any life in two: but it did so still
more at a period when the whole face of English literature was being remodelled, and one of the greatest waves
of poetical genius which the world has known had swept
over the country.   Crabbe lived long enough to take his

part, after the share he had in the opening of this poetical era, amidst the full concert of younger voices, all sweeter, tenderer, more sympathetic than his own, yet wanting his harsh note to give them musical perfection.

In point of religious feeling Crabbe was at the opposite extreme of sentiment from Cowper.   The private journals of his youth show him devout and pious—but in all the expressions of his maturer life it is evident that the staid ideal of a composed and moderate religiousness, which seems to belong to a dignified establishment and settled irrevocable system, was his highest model of Christianity —and that all undue zeal or fervour appeared enthusiasm or fanaticism to his sober eyes.   He was greatly annoyed when he went to Muston, one of the livings which he had held for years without ever visiting it, to find dissent flourishing within the fold.

> " True to his Church he came ; no Sunday-shower
>   Kept him at home in that important hour ;
>   Nor his firm feet could one persuading sect,
>   By the strong glare of their new light direct,"

is the description he gives of the " noble peasant Isaac Ashford," one of the few ideal sketches in his repository. He has no sympathy with the painful strain of religious anxiety, or any vehement attempt to ameliorate the lives of others, or purify the general stream of existence.   He is not oppressed or disturbed in his own soul by the evils round him, but accepts and describes them methodically as the natural drawbacks of humanity.   Of the parsons whom he brings in review before us in the " Parish Register," through the reminiscences of the old sexton Dibble, it is difficult to guess which he sympathises with most.   They are all treated with the same matter-of-fact, semi-satirical, and quite impartial touch.   The good sleepy soul who slumbers even in the pulpit; the wit who grinds the parish and takes tithe even from the sexton ;

the " golden times " of the wealthy and liberal parson, at whose " plenteous board " even " cool Dissenters fed," and who spread his gifts right and left; the author rector (presumably Crabbe himself), whose delight was all in books, who shunned men and women alike, " and hurried homewards when his tasks were done "— all these incumbents are kindly drawn : but the last of all, the " Youth from Cambridge,"

> " Who did much his sober hearers vex,
> Confound the simple and the sad perplex,"

is the only portrait in which he touches his usual jarring and painful string. This latest holder of the cure of souls is the impersonation of that type of religion which inspired Cowper, which, in the early fervour of Wesley and his coadjutors, had regenerated the country, stirring up and quickening religious life even among those most opposed to the new spirit, but which by this time had fallen into the fashion of the Evangelical party.

> " ' Conviction comes like lightning, he would cry ;
> In vain you seek it, and in vain you fly ;
> 'Tis like the rushing of the mighty wind,
> Unseen its progress but its power you find ;
> It strikes the child ere yet its reason wakes ;
> His reason fled, the ancient sire it shakes ;
> The proud, learn'd man, and him who loves to know
> How and from whence those gusts of grace will blow,
> It shuns,—but sinners in their way impedes,
> And sots and harlots visits in their deeds :
> Of faith and penance it supplies the place ;
> Assures the vilest that they live by grace,
> And, without running, makes them win the race.'
> Such was the doctine our young prophet taught."

The conclusion of this sketch, in which the fervid preacher on his death-bed is smitten by compunctions as to " the good I've wrought," and the defilement of " his

moral rags," and alms-deeds, with the sexton's consolatory
assurance—

> " Your faith's your prop, nor have you pass'd such time
> In life's good-works as swell them to a crime,"

shows the calm ecclesiastic's disapproval of all highly
wrought spiritual influence, as well as Crabbe's strong
dislike to the Evangelicals, of whose teaching he gives
so cruel a version.　In the accompanying tale of " Sir
Eustace Grey," an effort in a new direction and not a
happy one, the climax of the madman's story is his conversion, which by the narrator of the tale is evidently
intended to appear as mad as any of the delusions that
have gone before.　Crabbe was thus a world apart in
religious feeling from the gentle recluse of Olney ; as
different as the self-commanded and thoroughly respectable parson was from the rustic rake and self-tormented
penitent of Ayr and Dumfries.　Good man ! he had so
much the better part of life, that he need not grudge the
very different movement of the heart with which we turn
to these two unfortunates, the favourites and the victims
of life, whose miseries he escaped, though he shared in
some degree their consecration.

GEORGE CRABBE, born 1754 ; died 1832.

Published The Library, 1781.
　　　　　 The Village, 1783.
　　　　　 Parish Register, 1807.
　　　　　 The Borough, 1810.
　　　　　 Tales in Verse, 1812.
　　　　　 Tales of the Hall, 1819.

CHAPTER V.

THE COTERIES BEFORE WORDSWORTH——THE SWAN OF
LICHFIELD.

WHILE these new and altered voices gained day by day a
wider hearing, it must not be forgotten that a great many
relics of the former epoch were still surviving about the
country, and that careful couplets were still being elabo-
rated, and all the scaffolding of criticism which had been
put up for the perfection and polishing of every monu-
ment of the Augustan age, still obscured the smaller erec-
tions, the Temples of the Muses, which adorned here and
there an ambitious poet's garden or nobleman's park.   If
the coteries were dying out in London, where the old
lion's roar grew feebler, and Bozzy had been led away
into matrimony and Scotland, and the genial house of the
Thrales was broken up, and all the society that waited
upon Johnson's nod was dispersed or dispersing, the spirit
which had animated them was still surviving in various
favoured spots in the country where the learned and the
witty congregated together, and a little centre of intellectual amusement and ambition, giving occupation and happiness to a great many gentle lives, was set up.   One of
these, of which we have the most admirable details, was
established in Lichfield under the shadow of the palace.
The gentle historian who has set it forth before our eyes
is Anna Seward, herself a poet, according to all the estab-

lished requirements of the day, the correspondent of many
of the most distinguished persons of the time, a delightful feminine pedant, with all the graces of the ending
century.   Her letters, and her life of Dr. Darwin, admit
us with all due ceremony, yet friendliness, into the
charmed circles round the Close of Lichfield, to all the
tea-parties and the rural expeditions, the literary discussions and love-makings of the time.

Erasmus Darwin was the physician of this favoured
circle.   He was a man of boundless personal energy, a
big, clumsy, stammering, witty and genial personage, with
an "extreme scepticism as to human truth," great powers
of sarcasm—but, withal, that largeness and impetuosity
of character which so often insures popularity, and especially pleases women, to whom its vigour, and sweep, and
speed, are delightful by contrast.   It was not, however,
only to the refined and critical ladies of the Close, but
to the whole country round, that this lumbering doctor
commended himself.   He was very skilful in his profession, very benevolent and charitable, and apparently
full, in deeds, of that regard for others which his words
did not disclose.   There is something in the description
of him which recalls the other great native of Lichfield,
who was by no means a favourite in his own country.
Darwin, like Johnson, was ungainly, "his limbs too heavy
for exact proportion : the traces of a severe small-pox :
features and countenance which, when they were not
animated by social pleasure, were rather saturnine than
sprightly, a form inclined to corpulence, a stoop in the
shoulders, and the then professional appendage, a full-
bottomed wig," bring a figure before us very like that of
the more memorable man, who satisfied his own extraordinary nature, so made up of nobleness and weakness,
by the fine superstition of his penance in Lichfield market-
place, where, as everybody knows, he stood bareheaded in

the rain, amid the staring spectators, to expiate a boyish disobedience. Perhaps just then the pretty young ladies from the Bishop's palace tripped by in their airy muslins, and wondered much to see the strange spectacle; or the other busy doctor, elbowing the crowd, pushed the gazers out of his way as he went on to his patients, and stammered scorn at the unlikely sentiment. "Mutual and strong dislike," Miss Seward tells us, "existed between them." In all Dr. Johnson's letters, dated from Lichfield, the name of Darwin is never mentioned, "nor indeed," the historian adds with dignified surprise, any of the ingenious and *lettered* people who lived there—while of its more common-life characters there is frequent mention, with many hints of Lichfield's intellectual barrenness— while it could boast a Darwin and other men of classical learning, poetic talents, and liberal information!" One of these was the writer's father, a canon of the cathedral, who had edited the plays of Beaumont and Fletcher, besides writing verses, of which little record has been kept; but this was quite enough to make him a member of the literary class, and deeply sensitive to the fact of being passed over. "By people of literary taste and judgment," Miss Seward says, her father's work "is allowed to be the best commentary on those dramatic works which has appeared;" and "Shakspeare had few more spirited eulogists than Mr. Seward." Another of the Lichfield literati overlooked by the arrogant Johnson was Archdeacon Vyse, who was "not only a man of learning, but of Prioric talents in the metrical impromptu." "Gentle reader, behold an instance!" cries Miss Seward, and thereupon quotes a poem of nine long stanzas made upon a certain "fair Charlotte Lynes" at a convivial meeting of Lichfield gentlemen, *most of whom could make agreeable verses.* But though the flowers of poetry flourished there, thorns grew among them. These verses were

much read, admired, and copied. Mr. Vyse thought his
fair Charlotte growing too vain in consequence, and once,
when she was complimented on the subject, in a large
company, he said smilingly—

> " Charlotte the power of song can tell,
>   For 'twas the ballad made the belle,"

which was not very chivalrous, nor even gentlemanly.
" *These*," adds Miss Seward, " were the men whose intellectual existence passed unnoticed by Dr. Johnson in his
depreciating estimate of Lichfield talents. But Johnson
liked only *worshippers*."

Anna herself was the flower and climax of all these
wits. She was a beautiful girl, with a classical education,
and the greatest " taste," according to the tenets which
still held fast hold of literary coteries, at once an accomplished writer of verses and the keenest of critics. Whenever she quotes, as she is fond of doing, a set of verses,
her instinct of analysis is at once at work. As an example of the literary atmosphere before the winds blew
away all these gentle mists of verbal play, we may quote
Miss Seward's comment upon one of her hero's productions
—an elegy of which we give only the verses discussed—

> " Dread dream that, hovering in the midnight air,
>   Clasped with thy dusky wing my aching head,
> While to imagination's startled ear
>   Toll'd the slow bell for bright Eliza, dead.
>
> " Stretched on her sable bier the grave beside,
>   A snow-white shroud her breathless bosom bound,
> On her wan brow the mimic lace was tied ;
>   And Love and Virtue hung their garlands round."

" The second verse " (says Miss Seward) " of this charming elegy
affords an instance of Dr. Darwin's too exclusive devotion to distinct picture in poetry : that it sometimes betrayed him into bringing objects so precisely to the eye, as to lose in such precision their
power of striking forcibly upon the heart. The pathos in the second

verse is injured by the words 'mimic lace,' which allude to the
perforated borders of the shroud.   The expression is too minute
for the solemnity of the subject.   Certainly it cannot be proper for
a shocked or agitated mind to observe or to describe with such petty
accuracy.   Besides, the allusion is not sufficiently obvious.   The
reader pauses to consider what the poet means by 'mimic lace.'
Such pauses deaden sensation and break the course of attention.   A
friend of the doctor's pleaded strongly that the line might run thus—

> "'On her wan brow the *shadowy crape* was tied,'

but the alteration was rejected.   Inattention to the rules of grammar in the first verse was also pointed out to him at the same time.
The dream is addressed—

> "'Dread dream that clasped my aching head,'

but nothing is said to it, and therefore the sense is left unfinished,
while the elegy proceeds to give a picture of the lifeless beauty.
The same friend suggested a change which would have remedied
the defect thus—

> "'Dread was the dream that in the midnight air
>   Clasped with its dusky wing my aching head,
>   While to,' etc.

"Hence not only the grammatic error would have been done
away, but the grating sound produced by the near alliteration of the
harsh *dr* in 'dread dream' removed, by placing those words at a
greater distance from each other.   This alteration was for the same
reason rejected.   The doctor would not spare the word *hovering*,
which he said strengthened the picture ; but surely the image ought
not to be elaborately precise, by which a dream is transformed into
an animal with black wings."

This will afford an example of the process going on
over those verses, which now win here and there the
attention of the student, but are carefully avoided by the
general reader, who no longer is in the mood to be
interested in " bright Eliza's " problematical shroud.   Thus
they talked while the tea-kettle simmered, and " Miss
Pussy Po " purred at her mistress's feet.   The beautiful
old rooms in the palace were the home of taste and poetry
and friendship ; most of the gentle company there " could

make agreeable verses." Young Mr. Edgeworth, "a young and gay philosopher," and his eccentric friend Mr. Day, were drawn to Lichfield by the reputation of Dr. Darwin. Here also came "the Rev. Mr. Michell. He was skilled in astronomic science, modest and wise;" "The ingenious Mr. Kerr of West Bromwich; Mr. Boulton, known and respected wherever mechanic philosophy is understood; Mr. Watt, the celebrated improver of the steam-engine; and above all others . . . the accomplished Dr. Small of Birmingham."

Such was the doctor's private circle which Johnson scorned. Mr. Edgeworth and Mr. Day were the only ones specially honoured with notice from the palace. Of the former, we are told that "his address was gracefully spirited and his conversation eloquent; he danced, he fenced, and winged his arrows with more than philosophic skill." Besides these qualities he is known to fame as the father of "the great Maria," and to Lichfield as the husband of several wives, drawn from among her fairest : but Mr. Day was still more interesting. "He published in later years two noble poems, ' The Dying Negro ' and ' The Devoted Legions ': also ' Sandford and Merton,' which by wise parents is put into every youthful hand." A number of charming young women made up the company—all lovely, to judge from the enthusiastic descriptions of the historian, and herself and her pretty sister among the loveliest there. Sir Walter Scott, who saw Miss Seward only in old age, gives his testimony that she must have been "exquisitely beautiful." The Vale of Stowe lay at their feet, visible from the palace windows ; and coming home from their walks and rides, the young people worshipped, whenever they came in sight of them, the three beautiful towers, called by one enthusiastic girl "the Ladies of the Valley," under shelter of which Anna the Muse, and pretty Sarah, who died at eighteen, and Honora

the adopted child, had grown into beauty and fascination.
Young Major André, one of the most lamented victims of
the American War, was a member of one of those cheerful groups, and many a poetic youth paid his homage.
None of them, however, had so romantic a story as Day,
whose adventures Miss Seward tells at length, and all his
philosophical failures in life. Her description of him is
worthy of quotation, if only to show the kind of pen-
and-ink painting which was popular in these days.

"Powder and fine clothes were at that time the appendages of
gentlemen. Mr. Day wore neither. He was tall, and stooped in
his shoulders ; full made, but not corpulent ; and in his meditative
and melancholy air a degree of awkwardness and dignity were
blended. We found his features interesting and agreeable, through
the traces of a severe small-pox. There was a sort of weight upon
the lids of his large hazel eyes ; yet when he declaimed

"'Of good and evil
Passion and apathy, and glory and shame,'

very expressive were the energies gleaming from them beneath the
shade of sable hair, which, Adam-like, curled about his brows. . . .
In the course of the year 1770 Mr. Day stood for a full-length
picture to Mr. Wright of Derby. A strong likeness and a dignified
portrait were the result. He stands, leaning his arm on a column
inscribed to Hampden. Mr. Day looks upwards, as enthusiastically
meditating on the contents of a book held in his dropped right
hand. The open leaf is the oration of that virtuous patriot in the
Senate against the grant of ship-money demanded by King Charles
the First. A flash of lightning plays in Mr. Day's hair, and illu-
minates the contents of the volume. . . . Dr. Darwin sat to Mr.
Wright about the same period. *That* was a simply contemplative
portrait of the most perfect resemblance."

Dr. Darwin was not so attractive as this unlucky
philosopher, whose freak of training a perfect wife for
himself is so well known, and was so unsuccessful. Miss
Seward gives the whole story of it, and describes "the
beauteous Sabrina," a foundling girl whom he brought to
Lichfield, in order to train her into an epitome of all the

virtues, as an object of great interest to the ladies in the palace. When his experiment failed, he discovered that Honora Sneyd, the beautiful girl who was the adopted child of Canon Seward, and the darling of his house, was everything his fancy had painted. But Honora, whom André had adored, would have nothing to say to the philosopher, nor would her sister, to whom he afterwards transferred his affections. Even before the episode of the beauteous Sabrina, this original had been jilted, and had written "a beautiful elegy," in half-a-hundred verses, upon his evil fate. Thus, finding in every event an occasion for more stanzas, or for a flood of carefully polished couplets, to be subjected to all the criticisms of the coterie, these poetical people went through life consoling themselves with literature amid all its harsher realities. No doubt the Muse helped Mr. Day through the many vicissitudes of his sentimental career. Nor were these the only poets of the society. Mr. John Gisborne, who wrote "The Vales of Weaver;" Mr. Munday, whose poem upon "Needwood Forest," printed for private circulation only, "one of the most beautiful *local* poems that has been written," as the enthusiastic historian informs us, she presented to Sir Walter Scott at the very end of her life as a distinguished token of friendship; Sir Brooke Boothby, whose claims do not seem to be founded upon any special production, and many more, fluttered round the two central figures, those of clumsy Dr. Darwin and the beautiful Muse of the Close. She has a great enthusiasm for all those now unknown sons of genius. The effusions of Mr. John Gisborne are such, she thinks, that it "would disgrace the national taste if they should be suffered to pass away without their fame;" and in order to ensure them some share of it, she quotes at great length from this "efflorescence of a rich imagination" such verses as the following :—

> " As the sonorous North assails
>   Weaver's bleak hills and leafless vales,
> With awful majesty of might,
> He bursts the billowy clouds of night ;
> Booms the resounding glens among,
> And, roaring, rolls his snows along."

Miss Seward puts a footnote to the word " booms."
" A word," she cries, " admirably expressing the noise of
winds, and applied to it here for the first time in poetry."
What a delightful fund of occupation for a gentle unem-
ployed life must have been given by those prolonged
commentaries ! Better even than those labours of the
needle—

> " The well-depicted flower
> Wrought patiently into the snowy lawn,"

for which " the Swan of Lichfield" (which was this
charming young woman's poetical title) was equally distinguished.

Miss Seward's own poetical efforts were begun very
early ; she played with the muse from her childhood.
" At first," she says in one of her letters, " my father
encouraged it." He was himself a poet, as well as the
editor and critic of the old dramatists.   " But my mother
threw cold water on the rising fires," she adds ; " and even
my father ceased to smile encouragement upon these
attempts after my sixteenth birthday, in which Dr. Darwin unluckily told him that his daughter's verses were
better than his—a piece of arch injustice to my father's
muse which disgusted him with mine."   These little
minstrels, it is evident, were very touchy and jealous of
their respective degrees of excellence.   After this early
suppression, however—but how long after we are not in-
formed—the famous rites at Batheaston, where another
poetical coterie existed under the auspices of a certain
Lady Miller, developed and introduced to " the world,"

such as that world was, the elegant strains of the jealous
canon's daughter. The Batheaston celebration was held
periodically (once a week, we think, while the season
lasted), and all the elegant visitors of the Bath who had
the honour of Lady Miller's acquaintance drove over to
this highly superior kind of garden party. Miss Austen,
we presume, was not old enough to have taken part in it,
or certainly Catherine Morland, with her wide-open eyes,
would have had an invitation, and gazed at all the poets
and poetesses. When the fine company had assembled,
the competing poems, which had been put into an
" Etruscan vase," were drawn forth in succession by the
judges, and read aloud, to the delight of all those persons
of taste. Among Miss Seward's collected works there are
a great many elegies and monodies headed " Prize poem
at Batheaston ;" and Miss Burney gives a lively account
of the ceremonial in her diary. These celebrations
emancipated Anna from the cold shade of domestic
repression, and by this time, no doubt, the Swan of
Lichfield had grown old enough to have her own way.
There is a very pathetic story of the death of her sister
Sarah at nineteen, on the eve of her marriage, which no
doubt made the will and wishes of Anna of double importance in the bereaved house. Pretty glimpses of a
generous and impulsive young woman appear even through
the antiquated graces of her narrative. Lady Northesk,
an interesting stranger dying of consumption, stopped at
Lichfield on her way to the north to consult the doctor,
whose fame was great in all the country round ; and it
occurred to Dr. Darwin that hers was a case in which
that romantic remedy transfusion of blood, so seldom
heard of except in novels, might be efficacious. Miss
Seward immediately offered her own lily-white arm as the
fountain of new life to the new friend whom she had
taken up with romantic fervour. " My health is perfect,

neither am I conscious of any lurking disease, hereditary
or accidental.   I have no dread of the lancet, and will
gladly spare from time to [time such a portion from my
veins to Lady Northesk as Dr. Darwin shall think
proper."   When things had come so far as this, however,
the poetical doctor drew back, alarmed by the risk,
alleging the difficulty of " the construction of a proper
machine " for the injection.   But Lady Northesk never
forgot the generous offer ; and it gives us a pleasant
picture of the enthusiastic girl, to whom Friendship,
celebrated in a thousand verses, was the most sacred of
ties.

Here, however, we see the two poets, the doctor and
the maiden, in a still more poetical combination.

" About the year 1777, Dr. Darwin purchased a little wild
umbrageous valley, a mile from Lichfield, amongst the only rocks
which border that city so nearly.   It was irriguous from various
springs, and swampy from their plenitude.   One of its native
features had long excited the attention of the curious—a rock, which
in the central depths of the glen drops perpetually about three
times in a minute.   Aquatic plants border its top and branch from
its fissures ; no length of summer drouth abates, no rains increase,
its humidity ; no frost congeals its droppings.   The doctor cultivated
this spot, ' and paradise was opened in the wild.'   Not only with
trees of various growth did he adorn the borders of the fountain, the
brook, and the lakes, but with various classes of plants, uniting the
Linnæan science with the charm of landscape.   For the Naiad of
the fountain he wrote the following inscription :—

SPEECH OF A WATER NYMPH.

" ' If the meek flower, of bashful dye,
        Attract not thy incurious eye—
    If the soft murmuring rill to rest
        Enchain not thy tumultuous breast—
    Go where ambition lures the vain,
        Or avarice barters peace for gain !'

" Dr. Darwin restrained his friend Miss Seward's steps to this
her always favourite scene, till it had assumed its new beauties from

cultivation. He purposed accompanying her on her first visit to his
botanic garden, but a medical summons from the country deprived
her of that pleasure. She took her tablets and pencil, and, seated
on a flower-bank in the midst of that luxuriant retreat, wrote the
following lines while the sun was gilding the glen, and while birds
of every plume poured their song from the boughs."

The reader would like to see the verses thus poetically
composed ; but he is not very likely, save with some
research and trouble, to find them in the three long
volumes of poetry which Miss Seward left behind her,
or even in their illegitimate place where they stand at the
head of the " Botanic Garden," which is Dr. Darwin's
chief title to poetic fame—so we may be excused if we
quote from them here.   After an address to " ye proud,"
whom the gentle poet adjures to " come not here," the
true favourite of the muses is thus invited :—

" But thou, whose mind the well-attempered ray
    Of Taste and Virtue lights with purer day,
    Whose finer sense each soft vibration owns
    Mute and unfeeling to discorded tones ;
    Like the fair flower that spreads its lucid form
    To meet the sun, but shuts it to the storm :
    For thee my borders nurse the glowing wreath,
    My fountains murmur, and my zephyrs breathe,
    My painted birds their vivid plumes unfold,
    And insect armies wave their wings of gold.

" And if with thee some hapless maid should stray,
    Disastrous love companion of her way,
    O ! lead her timid step to yonder glade,
    Whose weeping rock recumbent alders shade,
    There as meek Evening wakes the temperate breeze,
    And moonbeams glimmer through the trembling trees,
    The rills that gurgle round shall soothe her ear,
    The weeping rock shall number tear for tear ;
    And as sad Philomel, alike forlorn,
    Sings to the night reclining on her thorn,
    While at sweet intervals each falling note
    Sighs in the gale and whispers round the grot,

The sister-woe shall calm her aching breast,
And softest slumbers steal her cares to rest.

" Thus spoke the Genius as he stept along,
And bade these lawns to Peace and Truth belong."

"By the genius of the place is meant its first culti-
vator, Dr. Darwin," Miss Seward adds in a footnote.
When she gave her poem to the doctor, he "seemed
pleased with it," and suggested the "Linnæan System"
as "a happy subject for the Muse." "I will write the
notes, which must be scientific," he said, "and you shall
write the verse." Miss Seward, however, demurred.
She did not think that the plan was "strictly proper for
a female pen," probably because of those loves of the
plants which bore so large a share in it; but "she felt
how eminently it was adapted to the efflorescence of his
own fancy."

This was how the "Botanic Garden," that "magnificent poem," a work which, according to Miss Seward,
"forms a new class in poetry, and by so doing gives to
the British Parnassus a wider extent than it possessed in
Greece or in ancient or modern Rome;" a poem that, "if
poetic taste is not much degenerated, will live as long as
the Metamorphosis;" which "must endure so long as the
English language shall exist; nay, should that perish,
translation would preserve the 'Botanic Garden' as one
of its gems"—came into being. Few readers of the
present day will have so much as seen this lengthy and
elaborate production. It was published (or at least part
of it) in 1781, just about the time when Crabbe was
making his first essay. The second part, however, was
not given to the world till after the three great new poets
whom we have already treated had fully occupied the ear
of the world. And yet with that contrast in 'existence,
and the new life coming in so strongly, the "Botanic
Garden" was a successful and popular work. Darwin

was paid £900 for it, which is one test of its excellence.
The doctor, however, though so fine a poet, was not a
very scrupulous man. He took those elegant lines which
Miss Seward, seated on a bank of flowers, and taking out
her tablets and pencil, had written for him, and made.
them, without any acknowledgment, the introduction to
his poem. They are quoted as a specimen of his poetical
style in Chambers's excellent *Cyclopædia of Literature*.
The gentle Muse of Lichfield is very moderate and very
dignified in all she says on the subject—nevertheless there
is a touch of indignation in the tone with which she re-
claims her property.

Such an appropriation is not much in keeping with
the big and rude and burly image, in itself very unlike
that of a poet, which is developed with no small power
in Miss Seward's memoir. It is a pity she had not left
poetry alone, and given us more of those graphic if high-
flown descriptions—but the sentimental flood of her letters
is too washy to be waded through in search of other gems
of this kind. She was complimented in her turn by
Darwin, who owed her so many compliments, as the
inventress of epic elegy—and by Hayley, the biographer
of Cowper, himself a songster of the same order, and cul-
tivating poetry and taste among his neighbours in a
similar way. He describes " the Muse of Elegy " in a
poetical tribute addressed to her.

> " Speaking to earth the kind enthusiast came,
>   And veil'd her heavenly power with SEWARD's name,"

while all that listen to her strains

> " Bless the enchanting lyre by glory strung,
>   Envying the dead who are so sweetly sung."

Miss Seward, however, does not claim any unrivalled
power for herself even in this special vein. " Many excel

me in writing verse," she says with dignified modesty, "perhaps scarcely one in the vivid and strong sensibility of its excellence, or in the ability to estimate its claims." It is her strong sense of this "ability to estimate" the claims of genius which makes her criticisms so bold and gives her praise such a triumphant certainty. An amusing proof of her confidence in her own powers is given in one of her letters, in which she takes it upon herself to improve the prose style of (of all people in the world) Addison, informing a correspondent that "you will find the words in italics which strike me as forming the inelegance of Addison's style, and you will perceive that words within hooks constitute its redundance." Her discrimination is more perceptible when she upholds the cause of a new poet against the old. "When," she says, "with avowed delight in the poetic powers of Cowper's ' Task,' the writer of these strictures, in conversation with Dr. Darwin and Sir Brooke Boothby, asked their opinion of that poem, each declared they could not read it through; each taxed it with egotism, with prosaicism, with a rough and slovenly style, and with utter want of regular design."

Such were the ways of judging and the methods of criticism current among the old school. Miss Seward thinks that it was "the jealous spirit of authorism" which "darkened the candour" of her doctor. But as she tells us shortly after that he "had ever maintained a preference of Akenside's blank verse to Milton's ; declared that it was of higher polish, of more chaste purity, and more dignified construction," we may be permitted to doubt his critical judgment, without even her charitable supposition that his " taste " was somewhat enervated by too much refinement. Refinement, indeed, except in verse, does not seem to have been Dr. Darwin's quality, and the velvet pile of his poetry sits oddly enough upon the homespun of his character, to use a congenial simile.

The curious link of connection between the opinions which this scientific manufacturer of rhymes had begun to hold and express in the end of last century, and those which have made his descendant remarkable in this, is very interesting to the imagination; and we wish Erasmus Darwin had been a little more heroic. One or two incidents, however, of an interesting kind, are related of the energetic doctor. The elegy to " bright Eliza," which we find criticised so closely, was conceived if not written while Dr. Darwin was in attendance upon the lady, who afterwards became his wife. She was at the moment the wife of another man, but that had not hindered some passionate expressions of poetical devotion. The lady had been seized with violent fever, and the doctor was sent for. " Not being requested to continue in the house through the ensuing night, which he apprehended might prove critical, he passed the remaining hours till day-dawn beneath a tree opposite her apartment, watching the passing and repassing lights in the chamber. During the period in which a life he so passionately valued was in danger, he paraphrased Petrarch's celebrated sonnet, narrating a dream whose prophecy was accomplished by the death of Laura." The idea of this he afterwards extended into the elegy. However, that *nuit blanche* under the tree, of the stout, stammering, hard-headed, unbelieving doctor, a middle-aged widower, under the windows of another man's wife, has a sort of grotesque romance, all unlike his artificial and elaborate strains, which touches the heart a little, though it is difficult at the same time to refrain from a smile. We feel that Miss Seward, knowing the circumstances, should not have been so hard on the *dr*ead *dr*eam; but then perhaps she did not think the lady worth all that trouble; and certainly it was very improper on the part of the doctor.

To balance the romance we have a semi-heroic narrative of a certain occasion on which Dr. Darwin, who, as a rule, eschewed all intoxicating liquors, was persuaded to drink more wine than was good for him. It was while on a boating expedition, and in the middle of a hot midsummer day. To the horror and astonishment of his friends, the half-intoxicated doctor suddenly plunged out of the boat into the river, when they were close to Nottingham, and rushing in his wet clothes across the fields, reached the market-place before they could overtake him. Here they found him mounted on a tub, making an oration to the gaping multitude around. " Ye men of Nottingham, listen to me," he said. " You are ingenious and industrious mechanics. By your industry, life's comforts are procured for yourselves and families. If you lose your health, the power of being industrious will forsake you, *that* you know : but you may not know that to breathe fresh and changed air constantly is not less necessary to procure health than sobriety itself. Air becomes unwholesome in a few hours if the windows are shut. . . . I have no *interest* in giving you this advice. Remember what I, your countryman and a physician, tell you. If you would not bring infection and disease upon yourselves, and to your wives and little ones, change the air you breathe ; change it many times a day by opening your windows."

After which abrupt address he got down from his tub, and went back with his friends to their boat. The dripping philosopher on his homely platform, the gaping crowd about him, an eager apothecary of his acquaintance vainly endeavouring to persuade him to come home with him and change his wet clothes, and the astounded excursionists standing by not knowing what to make of their friend's vagary, form an amusing picture. He was before his age so far as regards sanitary conditions, it is evident : poetry is a different matter.

But the Lichfield coterie altogether gives us a quaint and amusing picture of the little literary societies spread over the face of the country, where Taste was set up as the tutelary spirit, and Criticism of the minutest carefulness, serious as if the fate of empires hung upon her decisions, pondered every line, and "most of the gentlemen," not to say the ladies also, "could make agreeable verses." Lady Miller at Batheaston was, as has been said, the presiding genius of another of these refined circles. And there was Hayley in Sussex, in that landscape which Cowper found too mountainous and exciting, with Mrs. Charlotte Smith in her cottage near, who would come and read them her romances till the little circle thrilled with interest, and counted the hours from evening to evening, that they might trace a little further the history of Celestina or Louisa. They were all devoted to Nature, these clever people, and never tired of describing her. She was to them a benevolent and lovely old princess, clothed in embroideries and ornamented with countless jewels. They patronised her, and went to her for consolation as they would have gone to any other old queen of society who was benignant as well as splendid. Their intercourse with her was a sort of continuous *fête champêtre*, at which she was hostess, giving them tea and smiles, patting them on the shoulders when they were melancholy. She had little to say to the common herd, but for her favourites was there ever so amiable, so tender a dowager? They could not sufficiently exclaim to themselves and each other how delightful she was, how sweet and kind. Miss Seward was, so to speak, a maid of honour, or Lady High Chamberlain to this beautiful old queen: and Dr. Darwin, if not a court physician, was at least so scientifically devoted to her court robes and the handsome appearance and value of her surroundings, that he too was entitled to her most bewitching smile.

But all this is very different from the atmosphere
which now fills our heavens and earth. It is the prettiest
possible side of the old *régime* which was ending. Except that now and then some one died or was crossed in
love, there seems little sign of earthly ills or passions in
that flowery city, surrounded by such soft distances, and
crowned by the " Ladies of the Valley," the three towers
where old art and heavenly music and religion had their
mysterious throne. Art, it is true, as represented by a
Gothic cathedral was held in but little store, and religion,
save in sentiment, was kept carefully in her right place ;
but yet the towers were dear from association, and enhanced the attractions of that sweet old goddess who
dwelt outside the town, growing innumerable banks of
flowers, and ready at any moment to have all her minstrels and all their admirers out to tea.

ANNA SEWARD, born 1747 ; died 1809.

————

ERASMUS DARWIN, born 1731 ; died 1802.

Published Botanic Garden in 1781.
Loves of the Plants in 1789.

CHAPTER VI.

THE NEW BROTHERHOOD.

WHEN the face of English literature had been thus changed, the old follies put to flight and the new life brought in, with a tremulous ecstasy and universal quiver of emotion and movement, the time came for that new flood of genius which is the distinction of our own day.   It is true that at least two generations have come and gone over the earth since Wordsworth and his brother poets were first revealed.   But they all lived well into our own century, and they belong to a condition of things entirely altered from those which influenced the former epoch.   Our living poets are their legitimate and unquestioned descendants, and the Age which they have made illustrious is as yet scarcely completed; so that we are justified in calling this last great era of poetical history our own time. Wordsworth, Southey, and Coleridge in one group; Byron, Shelley, and Keats in another; Scott—an army in himself; and various smaller but still remarkable figures, came all together, as splendid a band as has ever breathed the same air—rivals, coadjutors, fellow-workmen, perfecting a new system and establishing a new reign. Into these mingled voices Crabbe lived long to add his harsh yet effective tone.   But the other Precursors had disappeared in the wilderness through which they had hewed out for their successors so wonderful a path.

Burns remained a power and inspiration among the new race, affecting even the sober and dignified mind of Wordsworth as one of the most living of influences; but Cowper, who is so much less forcible and commanding a figure, and in whom there was no energy of passion to keep hold of the imagination of his heirs and successors, would seem to have passed away from their recollection altogether. So far as the new school of poets was concerned his mission was little acknowledged, notwithstanding that his poetical inheritance fell, like so much else that was rich and rare, into the hands of the immortal Dalesman, the poet of those wide atmospheres and silent skies, which in so different a form had breathed life into the invalid upon the banks of the fat and languid Ouse.

It is difficult to understand by what quaint and arbitrary link of association the three friends, who were to forge between them the next links in the poetical chain, got to be called the Lake poets—or rather got to be joined in so close a fellowship that their names cling together inevitably like a line in a beadroll. There was so little real affinity between the serious, almost solemn, manhood and musing genius of Wordsworth, the mystical and wayward spirit of Coleridge, and the virtuous precision and hard-working faculty of Southey, that they might have founded three different schools, instead of, by obstinate fiction, being held to represent but one. However, it is too late now to attempt to disturb the classification which lasted all their lives, notwithstanding that even their appreciation of each other, so enthusiastic and generous in youth, waned with the progress of the years.

The first appearance of this new group to mortal view is in the brisk and somewhat impertinent pages of Mr. Joseph Cottle, a bookseller in Bristol, himself one of the old race of local versemakers, and in his way a homely

Mæcenas, always ready with a good deal of enthusiasm and a small sum of money, both of which things were greatly in request among the penniless but ardent youths. Bristol, too, was one of the centres of lively and artificial literary life, so many of which were at that time in existence. The presiding genius, however, was of a sterner kind than the Swan of Lichfield. Hannah More, surrounded by her admiring sisters, was the ornament and pride of the neighbouring country, and though it would not seem that Southey, a native of Bristol, had attracted her notice, yet Mr. Cottle had permission to conduct any friend of his to an audience of the great woman of letters, whom all the fine personages in the country came to worship, and who had recently evolved a poet out of her milkwoman—though this is scarcely respectful to Anne Yearsley, who, though a prodigy and subject to the fate of such, had considerable power of versification and much poetical feeling, and was worthy of a better fate. Mr. Cottle himself was a poet, and so was his brother Amos,[1] who died young, and whose portrait the good man published along with those of the great Three whom he was instrumental in introducing to the world. His complacent and confused gossip is not to be compared with the more dignified narratives of the lives of the poets, but it is not without some power of portraiture, and it brings the young men before us in a group, a sort of rude fresco-painting, such as is sometimes more effective than a finer work of art. Southey and Coleridge were introduced to him by Robert Lovell, their friend and associate, " a young Quaker," who was also a kind of a poet (indeed in Bristol, as in Lichfield, most of the gentlemen seem to have made agreeable verses), and

[1] " Oh Amos Cottle ! Phœbus, what a name
     To fill the speaking trump of future fame !"
          BYRON'S *English Bards and Scotch Reviewers.*

who communicated to the mind of Cottle something of
his own admiration for his gifted friends, one of whom
came from Cambridge, and the other from Oxford, in
itself an argument for respect. They had both, however,
broken off their college career abruptly, leaving their
Universities without degrees, and the lives of each had
already been tinged with adventure. Southey, the most
perfectly well conducted of young men, had been expelled
from Westminster school for overbold speech in a schoolboy newspaper. Coleridge, for some purely fantastic
motive, had enlisted in a cavalry regiment, and spent
some months under that curious discipline, not without
enjoyment. Now, the two had got a fancy in their
heads, struck out somehow between the dreamy but inexhaustible invention of the one and the romantico-
practical imagination of the other, of emigrating to
America with a few chosen friends, and setting up a
new Utopia——a dream-colony of Apostolic freedom and
equality, where every worldly possession should be in
common, and idyllic peace and plenty and love should
reign. Lovell, the young Quaker, was one of the brethren
vowed to this enterprise, looking forward to it with eager
excitement; and, mad as the scheme appears to us, it
would seem to have had some air of possibility at the
moment, since Southey's mother and her family intended
to join the expedition, and for some time the minds of
an anxious circle of people were occupied with it. They
met in Bristol apparently with some remote intention of
sailing from that place, if Providence would but send
them a little money with which to buy agricultural
implements and pay their passage-money. And there
were other inducements. Lovell was already married to
a Miss Fricker of Bristol, to one of whose sisters Southey
was engaged; and Coleridge lost no time in falling in
love with a third. The Pantisocracy, which was to be

the name of their society, exacted marriage, and this was
about the only practical step the brethren took to carry
its requirements ont.

Such was the group which suddenly gathered in the
path of the excellent Mr. Cottle, surprising him into such
mingled emotions of complacency and reverence as fill
his gossiping book with their reflection still. He had
the discrimination to perceive that these were poets far
exceeding any faculty of his, but he felt at the same time
the benign superiority of money, giving him an advantage
over them, which he was generously willing to use for
their good.   They were penniless, though their plans
were so magnificent, and their little stock-in-trade was
an unsaleable article, which the ordinary merchants in
literary commodities would not buy. Indeed, it was only
one of them who had any stock-in-trade at all; Coleridge's few poems were not half important enough for
publication, and Mr. Cottle was somewhat of a wizard to
detect the genius of which there was as yet so little
proof.   But what an importation of life and hope this
little band brought into the old Bristol streets ! Young
Southey holding his handsome head high ; young Coleridge with all the mystic future in his big dreamy eyes,
and his mouth full of endless projects, one rising out of
another like flowers from a stem ; the first a refined and
chivalrous gentleman at all times ; the other an enchanter
whose eloquence no man could withstand. To hear them
talk of the new world that lay before them, the visionary
society they were to form, the " undivided vale " by the
side of the Susquehannah—soft-syllabled stream, which
no doubt must flow like its name, and was chosen for
that exquisite reason—in which their home was to rise,
the conditions of the paradisiacal life they were to lead
there—could any poem be more delightful ?   By the
gravest calculations, they had made out that two hours a

day would suffice to get their daily bread out of that
fertile poetical soil, and the rest of the time would be for
poetry, for love, for endless talk, for books and the contemplation of nature : what matter that in the meantime,
but for Mr. Cottle, it would have been difficult to pay
their lodgings ?   All such sordid troubles would be over
if once they could but reach that Land of Promise.
Southey had Joan of Arc almost ready, which, "should the
publication be anyways successful," would be enough, he
thought, "to carry me over, and get me some few acres, a
spade, and a plough."   Coleridge had not even so much
as that to trust to, but expected the spade, the plough,
and the passage-money to drop down upon him from the
genial skies.

In this strait Cottle came to the rescue nobly.   He
offered Coleridge thirty guineas for a volume of poetry
yet to be written, and the same to Southey ; while he
undertook, at the same time, to give fifty pounds for
" Joan of Arc "— altogether a romantic liberality which
no sane publisher, who had not been at the same time a
poet-worshipper and possessed of the gift of divination,
could have ventured on.   And the young men helped
themselves on by delivering lectures, of which some, we
cannot help suspecting, never came further than the
prospectus ; for it is difficult to imagine how Coleridge,
at such a moment, could lecture upon the French Revolution, at that period in full and feverish career, contrasting
it with the great Rebellion, without raising more excitement than was tolerable among the people of Bristol.
For the subject was not one which either side took calmly,
and the two young poets, it need scarcely be said, were
wildly enthusiastic on the side of Freedom and the
French, and lost no opportunity, poetical or otherwise, of
denouncing all action on the part of England against
them, and cursing, in good round oaths, all the demon-

powers who were uniting together to crush France and the new-born liberty which from her they hoped was to extend to all mankind. Southey turned out in later days the best of High Tories; and Coleridge, though he made so many fierce onslaughts upon Mr. Pitt in his belligerent days, was not of a spirit adapted for political partisanship. But at this early period they were all aflame for the great cause of Freedom—their enthusiasm unquenched even by the blood and carnage of the Reign of Terror. It was their opinion that all existing governments, and that of England above all, were rotten at the core; and their Pantisocracy, their ideal city, was not only a refuge for their own souls from the evil of the times, but intended to be a tremendous protest against England, in which her philosophical sons no longer found it possible to live.

The earlier career of these two visionaries (of whom the elder was but twenty-two) had been simple enough. Southey's progenitors and relations were people with some pretensions to gentility; and his own life, his parents being poor, had been spent under the protection of an eccentric aunt, whose house was his home, and of a benevolent absent uncle, who had undertaken the expense of his education. The aunt, Miss Tyler, had been kept as long as possible in ignorance of the two great anticipations of her nephew's life, his intended emigration and marriage, and when she made the discovery her indignation and resentment were so great that Southey had to quit her house in the midst of a storm of rain, and to walk from Bristol to Bath, where his mother was: nor did he ever see the protector of his childhood again. This sudden abandonment threw him with double fervour into the brotherhood, already so close and intimate: he describes his condition as follows, with youthful grandiloquence, to the faithful friend, Grosvenor Bedford, who was

the constant confidant of his troubles and joys, both now
and during all his life :—

"There is the strangest mixture of cloud and sunshine. An
outcast in the world, an adventurer living by his wits, yet happy
in the full conviction of rectitude, in integrity, and in the affection
of a mild and lovely woman ; at once the object of hatred and
admiration, wondered at by all, hated by the aristocrats—the very
oracle of my own party ! . . . Do not grieve that circumstances have
made me thus ; you ought to rejoice that your friend acts up to his
principles, though you think them wrong. Coleridge is writing at
this same table ; our names are written in the book of destiny, on
the same page."

One of the joint projects of the two youths, thus
united by fate, was the publication of a magazine, " which
we can undoubtedly make the best thing of the kind ever
published ;" but this did not at the moment come to anything. They had, indeed, a hundred plans ; and that part
of their time which was not devoted to schemes of intellectual advancement was devoted to love - making and
projects of another kind. " If Coleridge and I can get
£150 *between us*, we propose marrying and retiring into
the country, as our literary business can be carried on
there, and practising agriculture, till we can raise the
money for America, still the grand object in view,"
Southey says. It was the fashion of this age of friendships that the young poets should publish their productions jointly, two or three in one volume ; and Coleridge
went even farther than this, actually writing a portion of
the " Joan of Arc," which was his friend's mainstay.
Nevertheless clouds soon began to arise between them ;
the Pantisocracy grew doubtful to Southey very soon after
he had spoken of it as " still the grand object in view."
But it was the return of his uncle, Mr. Hill, the consular
chaplain at Lisbon, which finally removed him from the
agitated but delightful little society in Bristol. This
kind relative had maintained him at school and college in

the hope that his education would terminate decorously in orders and a good living. His after life proved that no career could have suited him better; but at this tumultuous period, when all the world was still seething with, the strong excitement of the great Revolution, and all kinds of volcanic impulses were agitating young minds, he had no toleration for such an idea. Perhaps it is unjust to say, though Southey's son does not hesitate to say it, that his political views were such as "rarely fail to produce lax and dangerous views in religion;" but at least it is true enough that the tremendous innovations in politics which were being worked out in France, and which had startled all Europe and stirred up every lingering doubt and question everywhere, gave double force to those instinctive rebellions and resistances which seem to be inherent in youth; and that the mere idea of authority, and of a settled and long-established order, was enough to turn aside the excited minds of the generation, which hoped for nothing less than new heavens and a new earth. Southey felt in this moment of ebullition,— he, the predestined churchman, the man of duty and obligation, born to re-adopt and cling to all the loyal prejudices of a conservative race,—that to take the vows of the Church upon him would be "perjury." Before leaving Oxford he had tried medicine, but shrank from the special studies of that grand but terrible profession with the sickening horror of an extremely sensitive mind and nature. The only profession that remained was the law, which he hated scarcely less; but he was reasonable even in the wildness of his youth, and felt that when it became necessary to meet his uncle some feasible way of turning his education to account must be settled upon. Mr. Hill came to England in the autumn of 1795. He was the only member of his family, now that his aunt was entirely alienated from him, who could be of any

use to the young man, and his coming seems to have been
looked for with natural anxiety and alarm. "Suspense
shall be the subject of my tragedy," Southey cries on one
occasion; "indeed I have often the heartache." But
when the uncle came the youthful rebel was met with no
reproaches. Mr. Hill was kind and judicious, and never
seems to have abandoned the blameless youth, whose very
vagaries were virtuous. The only thing he insisted upon
was that his nephew should go back with him to Lisbon
for several months—one of those most natural and
common domestic artifices by which imprudent attach-
ments and objectionable associates are to be got rid of,
as it is always hoped. No doubt the excellent chaplain,
skilled in the fickle mind of youth, believed that all this
effervescence of early folly would blow off (as it did, but
not so easily), and that the change and novelty would
soon empty his nephew's heart of the ineligible Edith and
the unlucky "Muse."

It is curiously characteristic of Southey, who is the
embodiment of the romantic-practical amid the vaguer
poetical spirits of his brethren, that he should have taken
a step which balked the good uncle's incipient plans
before they had begun to be carried into execution. On
the very day of his departure he married Edith Fricker.
They parted at the church door—the bridegroom going
off upon his travels, the bride, with her wedding-ring
suspended by a ribbon round her neck, to the house of
Cottle, always kind. "Never did man stand at the altar
with such strange feelings," Southey says. "She returned
the pressure of my hand, and we parted in silence." It
was the maddest imprudence, for even the marriage-fees
and ring were paid with Cottle's money; yet there was
the ring of the true mettle, the energy and life of a manly
mind even in its folly—and of something better still, of
the noble instincts of that supporting and protecting love

of which he was an embodiment all his life. It is evident that the Frickers were very poor. By marrying Edith, Southey made a provision for her instantly possible. When he had anything himself, he could share it with her according to the rights given him by that hurried ceremony; and " should I perish by shipwreck, or any other casualty," he says, " I have relations whose prejudices would then yield to the anguish of affection, and who would love and cherish and yield all possible consolation to my widow." This gives to the high-flown folly of the secret wedding a consecration and an excuse. Not only to Edith, the mild and lovely, but to all her family, the wives of the other Pantisocrats and poets, Southey was henceforth the fountain of succour and life.

" Joan of Arc " was published just as he sailed away, dull and wretched, hating the voyage, and not without a certain nervous apprehension of its physical risks. He had got fifty guineas for the poem from good Cottle, and indeed we think this was quite as much as it was worth. The mission of the peasant prophetess—revolt made into duty by religion and a commission from heaven—was the kind of subject above all others to suit his mind and creed; for, whatever wild ideas might possess him, his imagination was fundamentally religious, and the romantic traditions of the past had not ceased to affect his fancy, though his mind was penetrated by the brilliant hopes and fallacies of the moment. It suited Southey, therefore, to show how redemption came from the poor, the ignorant, and lowly, how the heart of genius was stirred by the sight of the oppressed and slaughtered peasants, the young bridegroom, the father of little children, the widow's son, all sacrificed in odious war, while kings and nobles trifled and quarrelled, and let the humble masses pay for it with their blood. And the noble, pure, unworldly, Shepherd-Maiden, what poet is there who has not felt the fascination of her appearance amid all the dismal records of the wars ? But Joan has not brought luck to her poets. The painful length of the tale, the long discourses put in, with a mistake which is so common in narrative poetry, just at the moment when action and not discourse is imperative, the turgid heaviness of these long-winded discourses themselves, the mingled and disordered romantic machinery which twists in two or three episodes of ordinary love-making with the course of the grander history, make the poem almost unreadable now. We do not know, indeed, who but a student would attempt it. " Wat Tyler," the curious little revolutionary sketch which Southey had written at a still earlier age, and which he was compelled to publish by the malice of ungenial critics, when he had altogether changed his opinions, has much more spirit and nature in it.

Coleridge had been trained in a harder school. Though he spoke with great tenderness of his family, he seems to have been singularly abandoned by them from his boyhood up. He was brought up at Christ's Hospital, working his way through hardships and miseries which it is painful to contemplate, and was sent to Cambridge afterwards, against his will, the visionary boy with his multitudinous thoughts being too lawless and too individual to estimate the advantages of scholarship and classical education, though no scholar ever loved better the lore itself. At the University he had begun by gaining distinctions of the usual academic kind ; but tiring suddenly of this adoption of other men's ways, or moved by pure waywardness and a desire to try a new order of unknown conditions, he went off in the midst of his career to London and enlisted in a cavalry regiment, calling himself Silas Titus Comberback, with boyish humour, yet loyal adherence to the " Es-tee-se " which had been his baby nickname. In his regiment, if we may trust

Mr. Cottle, he entered with all the large sympathy that belonged to him into the new life so ill suited to his nature, and bewitched the troopers, as he did every company into which he ever drifted afterwards, with his golden mouth, his boundless interest in life, his power of interesting others, and his marvellous wealth of words. This strangest of freaks did not last very long, though authorities are divided as to how he got out of it : whether by the aid of his officers after an involuntary exhibition of learning, or in a still simpler way by the interference of his family, to whom his whereabouts was revealed by an acquaintance who met him accidentally. Of one thing we may be quite sure, that if this extraordinary sentry did hear an officer make an erroneous quotation, he would correct him without more ado, and probably discourse to him on the meaning of the passage, and all Euripides intended to put into it, with illustrations from the entire range of the Greek drama. The existence of a couple of young subalterns likely to quote Euripides to each other is, however, more unlikely.

After this escapade Coleridge returned for a time to Cambridge, then bethought him of Pantisocracy as a cure for all the ills of life, and wonderful provision for its future blessedness ; and having the idea confirmed and strengthened in his mind by the faith and zeal of his disciples, expatiated upon it and enlarged it, till the liquid flowing Susquehannah became something real to him, and the colony in Bristol was as if it had already gotten to the other side. It was much the same to him, nay, perhaps better, to have it there in glowing theory,— theory far more perfect than any execution,—than to take the actual steps necessary for its transportation. But to Southey this was not equally satisfactory. The way in which these two appear in Mr. Cottle's book is very curious. Though he cannot help having a certain

contempt for them, yet he had the greatest reverence for
them.   Coleridge, in particular, was a kind of inspired
idiot to the bookseller.   Southey's absurdity was not
much more than was inevitable to youth; but Coleridge
was the very type of that wonderful fool yet sage, that
lamentable yet ineffable being with whom genius, and
especially poetical genius, has always been identified.
It was sufficient occupation for a bystander to listen to
his magnificent plans, and to see their vanity; to note,
half with anger, half with amusement, all his wiles and
devices to elude actual work; and at the same time to
admire and applaud what, when " much enforced," he
would produce at a venture, flashing forth with no
trouble at all verses such as nobody else could invent of
all the tuneful throng, and talk such as man had never
talked before.

Coleridge would seem to have been entirely without
friends, or any succour or help, or even communication
with his family at this time.   They had freed him from
his soldiering; and perhaps this freak had disgusted the
good people, for there is not the smallest further appearance of kindred in his life.   And he was in all ways so
much poorer than his friend Southey, that not only had
he no kind uncle to make openings for him, but no " Joan
of Arc " to prove at least his power of work.   He had
not even, like so many penniless sons of fame, the talis-
man in his pocket, the manuscript with which fate might
be defied.   He had neither money nor money's worth.
A few fugitive poems, a few courses of lectures, some of
them only in intention, a million of plans, one as good as
the other, equally and impartially regarded by their in-
ventor, who was ready to take up or lay down any of
them at a moment's notice, and with no one but Cottle
to whom he could look for aid, his prospect was sufficiently blank.   And thereupon he married to mend mat-

ters !   The foundation upon which he established a household is about the slightest that ever supported any such superstructure.   "Aware of his narrow circumstances," Cottle says, " and to make his mind as easy in pecuniary affairs as the extreme case would permit, I thought it would afford a small relief to tell him that I would give him a guinea and a half (after his volume was completed) for every hundred lines he might present to me, whether rhyme or blank verse.   This offer appeared of more consequence in the estimation of Mr. Coleridge than it did in his who made it, for when a common friend asked him when married " How he was to keep the pot boiling ?" he very promptly answered that " Mr. Cottle had made him such an offer that he felt no solicitude on the subject." He was but twenty-three, in all the chaos of youthful fancies, but confident and eloquent as always, full of novel ideas on every subject, and dazzling everybody with his genius, though he had done absolutely nothing to prove the possession of that indescribable inspiration which seems to have rayed out of him like light through a lantern.   For one thing, the wants and requirements of the young couple were modest, if their temerity was great. Southey had considered the attainment of a hundred and fifty, or even a hundred, certain pounds a year between his friend and himself, enough to warrant the two marriages : and a guinea and a half for every hundred lines may have appeared an inexhaustible fortune to Coleridge. We feel almost disposed to utter a thanksgiving even now, that this liberal offer was not made to Southey before he set out upon his voyage, else how many hundreds, nay, hundreds of thousands, of meritorious, carefully-polished lines might we not have seen !

Coleridge took a cottage at Clevedon, on the muddy shore of the Bristol Channel, and here for a short time he seems to have been as happy as ever imprudent lover

was.   The descriptions of the "pretty cot" and the
"pensive Sara" who shared it are sweet and tranquil, as
the sober certainty of bliss ought to be.   Probably it was
his first experience since his childhood of a home, and the
unaccustomed charm held him happily captive.   But the
home was not very stationary ; they went back to Bristol
when the first enchantment was over, then to Nether
Stowey, another village in Somersetshire.   In the meantime, Coleridge started a little paper or weekly magazine,
which was to be "undoubtedly the best thing of the kind
ever published," as Southey had said.   It was to contain
the sublimest speculation and poetry, along with a weekly
summary of news and debates ; and Coleridge went about
the country from town to town getting subscribers, varying
his other occupations at the same time with that of a
preacher.   It was chiefly in Unitarian chapels that he
preached, that vague and always intellectual sect having
somehow attracted him during this misty period ; and he
appeared in the pulpit in coloured clothes, and occasion-
ally discoursed upon such subjects as the Hair-powder
Tax, to the consternation of his audience.   Notwithstanding this curious choice of subject, his eloquence must have
strongly affected the good provincial people whom he
addressed, for it became some time after a question to be
gravely debated in his life whether he should not settle
down at Chursbury as a Socinian minister, a conclusion
chiefly prevented by the Wedgewoods, Josiah and his
brother, who offered him an annuity of a hundred and
fifty pounds a year that he might relinquish the project,
and be able to devote himself to literary work.   A second
edition of his volume of poetry had likewise been called for,
which by Cottle's liberality added a little more to his funds.
But the *Watchman* proved an entire failure, two numbers
only appearing, and these not paying their expenses—fatal
drawback, for which no amount of genius can make up.

Before this timely succour arrived, however, it is worth while quoting his own account both of the state of mind in which he was, and his intentions for the future :—

"I verily believe no poor fellow's idea-pot ever bubbled up so vehemently with fears, doubts, and difficulties, as mine does at present. Heaven grant it may not boil over and put out the fire. I am almost heartless.[1] My past life seems to me as a dream, a feverish dream, all one gloomy huddle of strange actions and dim-discovered motives, friendship lost by indolence, and happiness murdered by mismanaged sensibility. The present hour I seem in a quickset hedge of embarrassments. For shame ! I ought not to mistrust God ; but, indeed, to hope is far more difficult than to fear. . . . A sort of calm hopelessness diffuses itself over my heart. Indeed, every mode of life which has promised me bread and cheese has been one after another torn away from me, but God remains. . . . There are some poets who write too much at their ease from the facility with which they please themselves. They do not often enough

> "'Feel their burdened breast
>   Heaving beneath incumbent Deity.'

So that to posterity their wreaths will look miserably, here perhaps, an everlasting Amaranth, and close by its side some weed of an hour, sere, yellow, and shapeless. They rely too much on story and event, to the neglect of these lofty imaginings that are peculiar to, and definite of the poet. The story of Milton might be told in two pages. It is this which distinguishes an epic poem from a romance in metre. Observe the march of Milton, his severe application, his laborious polish, his deep metaphysical researches, his prayer to God before he began his great work : all that could lift and swell his intellect became his daily food. I should not think of devoting less than twenty years to an epic poem. Ten years to collect materials and to warm my mind with universal science. I would be a tolerable mathematician. I would thoroughly understand mechanics, hydrostatics, optics, and astronomy, botany, metallurgy, chemistry, geology, anatomy, medicine ; then the mind of man ; then the minds of men ; in all travels, voyages, and histories. So I would spend ten years ; the next five in the composition of

---

[1] This word seems to be used by both Southey and Coleridge in the sense of without heart, discouraged, disheartened, as we should say.

the poem, and the five last in the correction of it. So would I
write, haply not unhearing of that divine and nightly whispering
voice which speaks to mighty minds of predestinated garlands, starry
and unwithering."

It is fine to see the desponding poet forget himself
and those little troubles about the bread and cheese, and
rise to this great climax. No one yet, so far as we are
aware, has ever prepared a great epic after this prescrip-
tion ; even Wordsworth, who has approached it most
nearly, can scarcely be said to "have warmed his mind
with universal science." But such a flash of purpose,
lofty and ideal, comes, perhaps, more easily to those who
make little attempt to carry their theories out, than to
those who are seriously affected by them. We doubt,
indeed, whether an epic which took twenty years' incu-
bation would be worth the trouble ; but not less fine was
the vision of something great that some day might be
attained, or, at least, any day might be dreamt of, dilating
the dreamy eyes, and expanding the full lips.

About this time another and a greater figure suddenly
comes upon the scene. A young pair from the north
country, brother and sister, he a young man of serious
mind and aspect, she a delicate spirit, a sort of poetical
Ariel; both of them overflowing with poetry and enthusiasm, had come to the neighbourhood some time
before. They were orphans, and had been long separated ;
and the pleasure of setting up a sort of home together,
enhanced by the still greater pleasure of the discovery
that each was to each the most congenial companion,
filled their lives. Their means were as humble as those
of the other young poets with whom they had not as yet
been brought in contact, but more certain. Wordsworth
had produced scarcely anything and earned nothing : but
he had inherited from a friend a little fortune, £900,
upon the interest of which he felt himself passing rich,

And Dorothy had a hundred pounds of her own. What was wanted more to be happy ? Why they left their native dales which they loved so faithfully, for that tamer coast, we are not told ; but here they were, established near the sea, spending their poetic leisure in the open air, in their garden, in endless walks and talks, while the young fortunes of the Coleridges and Southeys were being decided on the other side of the county. Wordsworth, like the others, had no great heart for the academical life or learning. He had taken his degree, which neither of the others did, but he had brought no distinctions with him from the University, a reflection which ought to teach these great bodies a certain humility. Wordsworth, however, had completed his education in a way which comparatively few men had attained to. In the long vacation of 1790, in the full fervour of the early revolution, he went to France, and saw with his own eyes the events which fired all Europe. Everybody now knows the lines in which he described the sentiment of the time.

> " Bliss was it in that dawn to be alive,
>   But to be young was very heaven, oh, times
>   In which the meagre stale forbidding ways
>   Of custom, law, and statute, took at once
>   The attraction of a country in romance."

Nothing could be farther from the nature of this serious youth than the noise and din of revolution ; but to him, as to so many others, the outburst of new principles and new life in France was like a new gospel. It is hard now, knowing all that followed, to appreciate rightly the wonderful and entrancing novelty of that revelation. It sounded like the sublimest lesson of Christianity made into a national code, and about to actuate all the movements of political life in which so different a principle had reigned in spite of Christianity.

That all men were brothers had been feebly breathed in
sermons for near two thousand years, but to hear it proclaimed from the throat of a whole people, a " unanimous
hero nation," with no parable in it but a claim of irre-
sistible and undoubted right, electrified every generous
heart.   Wordsworth landed in France on the eve of the
day when Louis XVI. took the oath of fidelity to the
Constitution.   He was not old enough or wise enough to
see what dark and fatal forces were lurking underneath
the popular joy.   He accepted the code of freedom and
brotherhood as he would have accepted the proclamation
of a new and noble king whose right to the throne all
acknowledged with acclamations, and whose reign was to
bring in the golden age.   Few, perhaps, of the hot
politicians who were kindled by the news, received it
with such profound belief, with such intense satisfaction,
as this grave young observer, to whom all noble principles
were kindred.   France, to him, took in a moment that
curious representative position among the nations which
it has been her strange fate to occupy ever since.   Political changes were the least of the great things which the
vast assembly of visionary souls throughout Europe,
who then fixed their attention upon her words and ways,
and this young Englishman in particular, expected from
her.   She was the champion of humanity.   She was the
spiritual Quixote, the last and greatest of the knight-
errants.   The Bastille was not only one actual stronghold
of tyrannical power, but the palpable image of all oppres-
sion overthrown.   The poor prisoners who crept out
dazzled to the eye of day were emblems of human faculties
enslaved, and human hearts broken by tyranny, but now
gloriously emancipated and restored for the use and
service of the world.   What was going on in Paris was
for the instruction, for the warning and guidance of mankind, the first step of a new and happier history ; and

that great town itself was but a stage on which the greatest of dramas was set forth in its first scene.

Wordsworth did not break out into revolutionary verse, nor did it occur to him to attempt to rouse his own country by any celebration of the old heroes of virtuous rebellion, as Southey did, whose mind was so much less moved than his. But after his first view of the riotous joy of France in her emancipation, he went back, at the earliest opportunity, drawn by an increasing fascination of interest in the great tragedy as it worked itself out, and inspired by an earnest and lofty curiosity which is most characteristic of him. He went and studied it, as afterwards he studied his mountains, wandering about, a deeply concerned, yet philosophical observer, through the flames and conflict. Even in the fervour of his youthful sympathy he was still a spectator, held back by an invisible bond of nature from all participation in the events which interested him so deeply. Not till long years after, when the play had been played out, and its hidden meanings revealed, did he put the narrative of his youthful investigation into words; and probably the grave tone of middle age modified that narrative unconsciously; but yet Wordsworth was always Wordsworth, and we recognise the sound of his young footstep, the familiar cadence of his voice amid the tumults which he mused upon. At the time it troubled him to feel that he was not sufficiently moved. When he picked up a stone of the Bastille to keep as a relic, he was conscious of a deficiency somewhere—

> " I looked for something that I could not find,
>   Affecting more emotion than I felt."

and, bewildered by his own tranquillity, compared himself to a plant " glassed in a greenhouse "—

> " That spreads its leaves in unmolested peace,
>   While every bush and tree the country through,
>   Is shaking to its roots."

Himself and his own individuality, and this calm
atmosphere of spectatorship, accompanied him into the
very midst of the flames, where he walked, and talked,
and discussed all things with the young revolutionary
General Beaupris " on the borders of the unhappy Loire,"
as if that river of blood had been a motionless tarn
among his own mountains.   When, however, the wandering observer found himself again in Paris, his composure
gave way, and a troubled attempt to comprehend a
hitherto unsuspected new meaning in the movement which
he had hailed with so much sympathy, obscured his
faculties.   He stood on the scene of the September
massacre a month after it happened, interrogating the
very stones that had so lately run with blood, and gazing
about him

> " As doth a man
> Upon a volume, whose contents he knows
> Are memorable, but for him locked up ;
> Being written in a tongue he cannot read."

This brought him to a dead stop in his profound and
anxious study.   The mystery of this bloody interpolation
into the tale of human enfranchisement and regeneration
was beyond his power of solving.   His imagination
yielded to the terror that was in the air.   When he
reached the high and lonely chamber in the roof, where
his lodging was, he watched all night, trying to read by
intervals, unable to sleep, thinking he heard a voice which
cried aloud to the whole city, " Sleep no more !" and
finding that the place, " all hushed and silent as it was,"
had become

> " Unfit for the repose of night,
> Defenceless as a wood where tigers roam."

It is a wonderful proof of the truthfulness with which Wordsworth, in the calm of after years, reported these sensations and convulsions of youth, that he does not represent himself as changed in his opinion of the main question at issue, even by contact with those terrible consequences of it.   Though the carnage was a mystery and distress to him, and his spirit was overclouded and driven out of the easy certainty of youth by this revelation of cruelties and savage forces unthought of, yet he did not change in his conviction that France, in her passion and agony, was still accomplishing the highest of missions.   " From all doubt," he says,

> " Or trepidation of the end of things,
>   Free was I as the angels are from guilt."

So profound was this faith, that when he returned home and found England excited by discussions about the slave trade (not to speak of the " Hair-powder Tax" on which Coleridge discoursed to his astonished audience), he dismissed the subject almost with contempt, in the strength of his conviction, that if France and the cause of freedom in her prospered, all other questions were involved in that great one, and universal setting right of all wrongs must follow as an inevitable consequence. And when in the process of time the young poet found his own country joined in the alliance against the great rebel of Europe, his dismay and despair had impassioned vent—

> " No shock
>   Given to my inmost nature had I known
>   Down to that very moment,"

he cried out with sharp pain.   No prayer for the success of England, no thanksgiving for her victories, could cross his lips.   He saw the expeditions fitted out, the fleets ready to sail, with tears of indignant passion, " Oh, pity

and shame !" he exclaimed.   To him this intervention
of England in the affairs of the world, so potential as it
turned out to be, so great a subject of national pride as it
has been since, was an act which " tore away "

> " By violence at our decision, rent
> From the best youth in England their dear pride,
> Their joy in England."

This was the opinion of all, at least, of the poets of
the time and many of its most serious thinkers.   Few,
if any, voices now living would echo these indignant
complaints.   We may doubt whether the expedition to
the Crimea was entirely heroic and wise, as we follow,
with a painful and ashamed sense of our national deficiencies, Mr. Kinglake's great philosophical history, so
different from all other martial records.   But we have
no doubt now of the greatness of English action and
influence in the beginning of the century, or of the noble
part our country then played in the world.   To be
sure, the protesters changed their opinion when Napoleon
arose, the enemy of freedom as well as of Europe.   But
at the beginning, notwithstanding all the blood that had
tarnished the progress of the revolution,—the murdered
king and queen, the guillotine, and all its attendant
horrors,—it is curious to be thus brought in sight of the
strenuous opposition of " the best youth in England,"
recorded so long after, and with such seriousness, by one
of the least revolutionary of men.

This was the young man whom Coleridge, in all the
visionary chaos of his thousand plans, had suddenly
stumbled upon.   Wordsworth had been thrown all
astray in his life by that strange revolution episode—
an episode which, notwithstanding much change of
opinion, had the greatest lifelong effect upon his works.
He had come to that moment of doubt as to what was

to become of him, which occurs to so many young men after their early training is over. But already, like all young men of genius, he had found, among his contemporaries, admirers and believers — and one of these, Raisley Calvert, the friend with whom he had travelled, left him at his death a sum of money, expressly with the understanding that it was to enable him to exercise " powers and attainments which might be of use to mankind." On receiving this bequest, Wordsworth, as has been said, took his only sister Dorothy from their uncle's house, and the two went forth together in that delightful union of brother and sister, which is, when it implies such perfect sympathy and agreement as existed between these two, one of the most exquisite of relationships. They took a house called Racedown Lodge, near Crewkerne, on the borders of Dorset and Somerset —" the place dearest to my recollection in the whole world," Miss Wordsworth writes. " It was the first home I had." Without taking his sister into consideration, no just idea can be formed of Wordsworth. He was, as it were, henceforward the spokesman to the world of two souls. It was not that she visibly and consciously aided or stimulated him, but that she was a part of him, a second pair of eyes to see, a second and more delicate intuition to discern. This union was so close, that in many instances it becomes difficult to distinguish which is the brother and which the sister. She was part not only of his life but of his imagination. He saw by her, felt through her ; at her touch the strings of the instrument began to thrill, the great melodies awoke. Her journals are Wordsworth in prose, just as his poems are Dorothy in verse. The one soul kindled at the other. These two young poets took up their life together in an idyllic purity of happiness which it is delightful to think of. No warmer wishes were theirs—the world was

far from them and all its concerns.   The mornings and
evenings, the sunsettings and dews, the sky and atmosphere, were their study, the occupation of their life.
Why those children of the mountains should have chosen
a scene so unlike that which was native to them, we are
not told——but here they had lived for two long years,
happy upon their tiny income, in each other's society,
when Coleridge was wafted their way by a chance breeze
from heaven, or kind suggestion of some wayfaring angel.
It is to be supposed that more earthly means of introduction were employed, and it is even suggested that the
two poets had made each other's acquaintance some time
before ; but they came together and formed a real and
instantaneous alliance at the house of Racedown early
in 1797.   "At first I thought him very plain, that is
for about three minutes," Dorothy Wordsworth says.
"He is pale, thin, has a wide mouth, thick lips, and not
very good teeth, longish, loose-growing, half curling, rough
black hair.   But if you hear him speak for five minutes
you think no more of them."   It is clear from every
testimony that Coleridge thus carried his charter of
genius openly displayed wherever he went.   No one
could be in any doubt about him.   "His forehead was
broad and high, light, as if built of ivory, with large
projecting eyebrows, and his eyes rolling beneath them
like a sea with darkened lustre," says Hazlitt.   He
"dissipated all doubts on the subject by beginning to
talk.   He did not cease while he stayed, nor has he
since that I know of."   At no time of his life did Coleridge require to carry any proofs of his genius about
with him, but it is all the more wonderful that it should
have been so universally acknowledged at this period,
since his little volume published by Cottle had given
little indication of it.   Nor was there much in the
volume of "Descriptive Sketches," tame and smooth,

which Wordsworth had already put forth.   But they recognised each other on the spot.

And from the moment of the meeting the very atmosphere seems to grow luminous about these two great figures,—the group which Dorothy, all soul and emotion, the most wonderful of sympathetic hearers, made complete.   The youthful sublimity and delight of the encounter are mingled with a youthful exaggeration and absurdity which must conciliate the hardest critic. The first evening they spent together is described by Dorothy. . " The first thing," she says, " that was read after he came was William's new poem, the ' Ruined Cottage' (afterwards embodied in the first book of the Excursion—the story of Margaret), with which he was much delighted ; and after tea he repeated to us two acts and a half of his tragedy ' Osorio.'   The next evening William read his tragedy, ' The Borderers.' "   This sudden plunge ten fathom deep into the silver sea of poetry is portentous, yet delightful.   Wordsworth was no critic, and never seems to have known the sublime from the matter-of-fact in his own work, but it is a curious evidence of the incompetence of even the most delicate of critical faculties, when disturbed by influences either of *amour propre* or friendly enthusiasm, that Coleridge should not have discerned any special difference between the wonderful reality and original power of the first of these poems and the commonplace verse of the tragedy.   But though much of what they thus communicated to each other has dropped from the records of fame, it does not less interest us to know that each discovered in the other, with genuine enthusiasm, those secret signs of brotherhood which are more potent than the ties of nature.   Nothing could be more interesting than such a meeting.   Wordsworth was twenty-seven, his new friend two years younger, and great as their

after achievements were, no doubt there shone before
them in the golden mists of these early days many an
impossible triumph such as earthly powers have never
yet realised. They walked about together over the
downs, with their heads in the clouds, disclosing all their
hopes and dreams to each other, visionary philosophers
full of the highest thoughts, as well as poets with the
vision and the faculty divine in their youthful eyes.
Half spectator, half inspirer, the deep-eyed rapid girl
between heard, and saw, and felt, and enhanced every
passing thought and emotion ; and with an enthusiasm
which borders on extravagance, they divined, and understood, and celebrated each other. " He is a wonderful
man," Dorothy wrote ; " his conversation teems with soul,
and mind, and spirit." Coleridge, on his part, describes
" Wordsworth and his exquisite sister" with equal fervour.
" I speak with heartfelt sincerity, and I think unblinded
judgment, when I tell you that I feel a small man by his
side," he writes; and of Dorothy he adds, "In every motion
her innocent soul outbeams so brightly, that who saw her
would think guilt was a thing impossible to her. Her
information is various, her eye watchful in observation of
nature, and her taste a perfect electrometer." It is curious
that Coleridge should have embodied part of these words
in his description of Joan of Arc—whether he was quoting from the already published text, or if he afterwards
added them in his numerous revisions, it is difficult to say.

This rapid conquest of each other made by the three
friends advanced so quickly, that, in a month after the
beginning of their acquaintance, the Wordsworths removed from Racedown to a house called Alfoxden, near
Nether Stowey, in which village Coleridge was living—
" our principal inducement being Coleridge's society."
Here they lived in the closest intercourse, making plans
and verses enough to fill the whole air with echoes.

"Upon smooth Quantock's airy ridge we roam'd,
  Unchecked, or loitered 'mid his sylvan combs ;
  Thou in bewitching words with happy heart
  Didst chant the vision of that ancient man,
  The bright-eyed mariner, and rueful woes
  Didst utter of the Lady Christabel—
  And I, associate with such labours, steeped
  In soft forgetfulness the livelong hours,
  Murmuring of him who, joyous hap, was found
  After the perils of his moonlight ride
  Near the loud waterfall : or her who sate
  In misery near the miserable Thorn."

Hazlitt's account of the pair of poets and the intercourse in which they lived,—a kind of Apostolic life
having all things poetical in common,—affords so complete a picture of their intercourse, and of the real begin-
nings of their memorable works, that it is indispensable
here.

"In the afternoon Coleridge took me over to Alfoxden, a
romantic old family mansion of the St. Aubins, where Wordsworth
lived. It was then in the possession of a friend of the poet's, who
gave him the free use of it. Wordsworth himself was from home,
but his sister kept house, and set before us a frugal repast, and we
had free access to her brother's poems, the 'Lyrical Ballads,' which
were still in manuscript. I dipped into a few of these with great
satisfaction and with the faith of a novice." . . . Next "morning, as
soon as breakfast was over, we strolled out into the park, and
seating ourselves on the trunk of an old ash tree, Coleridge read
aloud, with a sonorous and musical voice, the ballad of 'Betty Foy.'
I was not critically or sceptically inclined. I saw touches of truth
and nature, and took the rest for granted. But in the 'Thorn,' the
'Mad Mother,' and the 'Complaint of a poor Indian Woman,' I felt
that deeper power and pathos which have since been acknowledged
as the characteristics of this author, and the sense of a new style
and a new spirit in poetry came over me. It had to me something
of the effect that arises from the turning up of fresh soil, or of the
first welcome breath of spring. Coleridge and myself walked back
to Stowey that evening, and his voice sounded high

"'Of providence, fore-knowledge, will, and fate,
  Fix'd fate, free will, fore-knowledge absolute.'

"He lamented that Wordsworth was not prone enough to belief in the traditional superstitions of the place, and that there was a something corporeal, a matter-of-factness, a clinging to the palpable or often to the petty in his poetry, in consequence. . . . He said, however, if I remember right, that this objection must be confined to his descriptive pieces, that his philosophic poetry had a grand and comprehensive spirit in it, so that his soul seemed to inhabit the universe like a palace, and to discover truth by intuition rather than by deduction. . . . We went over to Alfoxden again the day following, and Wordsworth read us the story of 'Peter Bell' in the open air. There is a *chant* in the recitation both of Coleridge and Wordsworth, which acts as a spell upon the hearer and disarms the judgment. Perhaps they have deceived themselves by making habitual use of this ambiguous accompaniment. Coleridge's manner is more full, animated, and varied; Wordsworth's more equable, sustained, and internal. Coleridge has told me that he himself liked to compose in walking over uneven ground, or breaking through the straggling branches of a copsewood, whereas Wordsworth always composed walking up and down a straight gravel walk, or in some spot where the continuity of his verse met with no collateral interruptions."

Thus the two poets came to the edge of their first joint publication, a book which, amid all its manifold imperfections, its presumptions, and assumptions, was yet to give the world assurance of two new lights of the greatest magnitude in its firmament. They had, as we have said, all things in common; the "Lyrical Ballads" were the family store to which the young visitor had "free access" as to the bread and butter which Dorothy served him. To take a poem out of the stock, and read it aloud as they sat on the fallen ash tree in these long sweet summer afternoons, was the natural entertainment. What did it matter which of the two communicated that pleasure? It was "Betty Foy," not the "Ancient Mariner," that Coleridge read; but the "Ancient Mariner" too was getting itself chanted forth to the accompaniment of all the winds and storms that swept the seas, and to the sweeter cadence of the rippling calm. As they walked about " for miles and miles on the brown heaths overlooking the Channel," the happy youth, thus admitted into the poet's confidence, "pointed out to Coleridge's notice the bare masts of a vessel on the very edge of the horizon, and within the red-orbed disk of the setting sun, like his own spectre ship in the 'Ancient Mariner.'" Who can doubt that the poet had seen it already, and many a wonder more?

In the meantime Southey had come home, and had begun the course of industry and continuous work from which he never deviated all his after-life. He got employment on the Reviews and newspapers, he wrote and published "Letters from Portugal," he planned innumerable works. Complaining of his dislike to "desultory topics," he reveals his own love of the gigantic with curious simplicity and the same absence of all critical perception in respect to his own works which we have noted in his greater brethren. "Joan of Arc," he says, "was a whole —it was something to think of at every moment of solitude, and to dream of at night: my heart was in the poem; I threw my own feelings into it in my own language, ay, and out of one part of it and another you may find my own character. Seriously, to go on with Madoc is *almost* necessary to my happiness; I had rather leave off eating than poetising." But now these big works had no longer the assistance of Coleridge's enthusiasm and co-operation. There was not apparently any severance of friendship; they had quarrelled, but had been reconciled; and the transference of Charles Lloyd, a young man of wealth and weakness, a poet in his way, who had for some time lived at Nether Stowey with Coleridge, helping to keep the house by the allowance made for his board—to Southey's household instead, was not an element of harmony; but there seems to have been no positive breach. However, Southey expunged the portion written by Coleridge from his "Joan of Arc,"

and Coleridge threw himself entirely into the society of
Wordsworth, publishing conjointly with him. He had a
tendency always to unite his friends with himself in his
books. Poems, both by Charles Lloyd, his temporary
companion, and by his old and faithful friend Charles
Lamb, whose delicate and delightful personality ought to
have come into this sketch ere now, were mingled, to the
confusion of editors, in his second volume of poetry. His
conjunction with Wordsworth went so far as interlinea-
tion. It seems to have been a necessity of his nature to
weave himself in with some more steady, more deeply-
rooted being.

CHAPTER VII.

THE LYRICAL BALLADS.

THIS conjoint volume was published in September 1798. It was the product of those wonderful roamings over "smooth Quantock's airy ridge," and all the long intercourse of the endless summer days, when Coleridge wove the most wonderful dream-tissues of his genius, and Wordsworth produced so much that was immortal— and something, too, that was not worthy of immortality. The book was received by the world not as the revelation of two new poets, but as something like an insult to its own fine taste and lofty standards of excellence. A shout of derision rose from all the critics; and England in general can scarcely be said to have been less than personally offended by this serious and almost solemn attempt to impose a new poetical creed upon her. Few abortive publications have ever raised so great a ferment —for it could not at first be called anything but abortive. The book was so badly received, and sold so poorly, that when Cottle—always generous, who had given Wordsworth thirty guineas for it, his usual measure of what poetic genius was worth—sold his copyrights to Longman in London shortly after, he found that this was considered as of no value at all, and restored it to its original owners. Yet this was the volume which contained the "Ancient Mariner," a poem in which there was no insult-

ing assault upon poetic diction, or selection of the prosaic
and colloquial in language, but which seems to have been
passed over in the ferment raised about Alice Fell's torn
cloak, and the other familiarities of the volume. We
cannot venture to say now that the critics had not some
excuse. The book was a challenge and a defiance. The
young writer was bent not only upon instructing mankind, which was a legitimate aim, by the real message
which he had to deliver, but on revolutionising the very
form and fashion under which poetry had hitherto addressed the world. It was a fantastic as well as a presumptuous attempt; and though one poet was the chief
offender, the system had been settled upon after number-
less discussions between the two, who combined with the
fervour of their personal convictions a contempt for the
opinion of the public, which was heightened by confidence
in its inevitable docility and submission, one time or
another, to themselves, its natural leaders. They knew,
and were rather pleased to think, that the critics would
be puzzled and startled; but they did not perceive how
likely such an attempt was to run into extravagance, or
how good taste and good sense might both be sacrificed
to the polemics of the effort. Coleridge has given us, in
his *Biographia Literaria*, an elaborate description of their
scheme. It was to be " a series of poems, of two sorts."

" In the one the incidents and agents were to be in part at least
supernatural, and the excellence aimed at was to consist in the interesting of the affections by the dramatic truth of such emotions as
would naturally accompany such situations, supposing them real.
And real in this sense they have been to every human being who,
from whatever source of delusion, has at any time believed himself
under supernatural agency. For the second class subjects were to
be chosen from actual life ; the characters and incidents were to be
such as will be found in every village and its vicinity where there
is a meditative and feeling mind to seek after them, or to notice
them when they present themselves. In this idea originated the
plan of the Lyrical Ballads, in which it was agreed that my endea-

vours should be directed to persons and characters supernatural or at least romantic, yet so as to transfer from our inward nature a human interest and a semblance of truth sufficient to procure for these shadows of imagination that willing suspension of disbelief for the moment which constitutes poetic faith. Mr. Wordsworth, on the other hand, was to propose to himself as his object to give the charm of novelty to the things of every day, and to excite a feeling analogous to the supernatural by awakening the mind's attention to the lethargy of custom, and directing it to the loveliness and wonders of the world before us—an inexhaustible treasure, but for which, in consequence of the film of familiarity and selfish solicitude, we have eyes and see not, ears that hear not, and hearts that neither feel nor understand."

These ostentatiously simple means of awakening the public suffered the fate of all that is artificial and factitious. To begin a serious and affecting poem thus—

" A little child, dear brother Jim,"

which was, as originally written, the first line (afterwards left incomplete) of " We are Seven;" to concentrate the interest of a first volume of poetry in a long-winded production like the " Idiot Boy;" to introduce into serious verse

" A household tub, like one of those
Which women use to wash their clothes,"

were sins for which there is very little excuse, and which mere rebellion against the hackneyed medium of poetic diction, of which Cowper and Burns had already broken the spell, does not justify. And when we see that this was not done accidentally but with serious intention, and from a height of superiority, as if something sacred and sublime was in the narrative of Johnny's ride and Harry Gill's shivering, the indignation of the public strikes us as not without reason. This foolish and quite unnecessary attempt was insisted upon as the very essence and soul of his mission by Wordsworth himself, until maturing years improved his perceptions and his taste. Nothing could be more distinctly characteristic of the curious self-absorption of his nature. He was a law to himself; the example of all older poetry and the opinion of the world were nothing to him until time had gradually revealed the fact, which is so often imperceptible to youth, that all things are not equally important; that in poetry, as in life, there are different magnitudes, and that the fullest truth to nature does not demand a slavish adherence to fact. What he intended to demonstrate was, that the feelings of Betty Foy, while her boy was lost, were as deep and tragical, and as worthy of revelation to the world, as would have been those of a queen; and there is no doubt that this is perfectly true : the idea that any one would have ventured to assert the contrary existed only in Wordsworth's fancy. But the choice of such colloquial familiarity of treatment as suggests a jocular rather than a serious meaning, the absolute insignificance of the incident, and the absence of any attempt to give grace and dignity to the story, balked its effect completely as an exposition of nature, while the humour in it was too feeble, too diffuse, to give it a lively comic interest. Cowper had ventured to be quite as colloquial and realistic in John Gilpin, with electrical effect: but then the spirit and pure fun of that performance were inimitable, whereas Wordsworth's fun never rose above a tame reflective banter. Thus in his longest poem he failed, and failed utterly, in the very purpose which he had taken up with such fanatic enthusiasm, and determination to convince and proselytise. He did not " give the charm of novelty to the things of every day," nor " excite a feeling analogous to the supernatural by awaking the mind's attention to the lethargy of custom, and directing it to the loveliness and the wonders of the world before us." This was what he had undertaken to do ; and we do not wonder that the world, always more eager to seize upon a visible

failure than to hail a modest success, should have received
his high profession with incredulity and even with scoffing.
What he did succeed in doing was to give such evidences
of his real genius, that, some choice spirits at once, and
by slow degrees the general public, learnt to appreciate it,
in spite of the fictitious swaddling bands in which it had
been his caprice to bind it; but this was a very different
issue from that which Wordsworth intended and desired.

We may therefore freely acknowledge that the world
was not likely to derive any altogether new revelation of
human nature, or even to acquire a deeper insight into
those manifestations which it saw daily, by means of
Betty Foy and Susan Gale.   This was a mistake, and a
presumptuous mistake, one of the follies of the wise, which
are more foolish than the unconscious imbecilities of
nature.   But alongside of this failure, and even within
it, there appeared certain brief and delicate studies of
humanity which no true soul could disdain.   The child
who "lightly draws her breath, and feels her life in every
limb," dwelling in angelic simplicity on the borders of the
unseen, and knowing no reason for that blank barrier
between, which our less keen faculties come to so dead a
pause before—and the fanciful and innocent philosopher,
grave in his little fiction, as if it were the solemnest
truth, who justifies his preference of one place over another by the first external circumstance that catches his
eye, "at Kilve there was no weather-cock:" were revela-
tions of a very different kind from that of the "Idiot
Boy," made without any ostentation of homeliness, with
all the grace and sweetness of spontaneous verse; yet
certainly calculated to awake "the mind's attention," and
disclose the deeper things of nature lying under our very
eyes, but so little noted.   No one till then, not Shakspeare himself, had so revealed that simplest yet most
complex germ of humanity, separated from us by a dis-

tinction more subtle than any which exists between rich and poor, yet entirely intelligible to us—the mind of a child. The poet, however, would scarcely seem to have been aware that in this way, and not in the other, he was carrying out his promise, by no forced lowliness of subject or diction, but by the penetration of a new and tender insight. In something of the same way he here begins to open up those associations of the mind with natural objects which were henceforward to take so great a place in his philosophy. Burns's "Mouse" and his "Daisy" had given a width of pathetic meaning to the humblest objects, but this was rather by a humanising of the little "timorous cowering beastie," and the crushed flower, than by that luminous contemplation which, without changing in the least degree the outward object, takes it into the human bosom, and makes it a source of gladness or instruction. We cannot better instance this great and novel power than by one of the most lovely of Wordsworth's smaller poems :—

> "I wander'd lonely as a cloud
>   That floats on high o'er vales and hills,
> When all at once I saw a crowd,
>   A host of golden daffodils ;
> Beside the lake, beneath the trees,
> Fluttering and dancing in the breeze.
>
> "Continuous as the stars that shine
>   And twinkle on the milky way,
> They stretch'd in never-ending line
>   Along the margin of a bay :
> Ten thousand saw I at a glance,
> Tossing their heads in sprightly dance.
>
> "The waves beside them danced, but they
>   Outdid the sparkling waves in glee :—
> A poet could not but be gay,
>   In such a jocund company :
> I gazed—and gazed—but little thought
> What wealth this show to me had brought :

> " For oft when on my couch I lie,
>   In vacant or in pensive mood,
> They flash upon that inward eye
>   Which is the bliss of solitude,
> And then my heart with pleasure fills,
> And dances with the daffodils." [1]

Nothing can be more different from this than a flower which is made the type and emblem of human circumstances : " such is the fate of artless maid." No moral reflection, no lesson is in it. It is but a perception, a seeing of something simple and common, yet too delicate and refined to be so much as thought of by the crowd— of the manner in which scenes and accidents of nature enter into us, are hung like pictures upon the walls of our secret chambers, and live to refresh us and recreate us, the most inalienable of all possessions for ever. Here was indeed a stirring of " the lethargy of custom," a thought that might be allowed " to excite a feeling analogous to the supernatural ;" for every musing mind must have felt that its inner pleasures were thus divined, and another happiness added to the list of those for which a man might hope.

But these lovely snatches of profound and simple thought were perhaps too brief and unobtrusive to catch at the first glimpse the public eye, and all were lumped up together in the indiscriminate opprobrium called forth by the inane simplicities of " Goody Blake " and " Betty Foy." What is still more memorable, however, is the fact that the poet himself seems to have been unaware of the difference between them. In the confusion of his youth, amid all the tumult of rising and developing

[1] The poem which we had quoted at random was, as the writer finds on examination, written at a later period. Others, however, to which our remarks will equally apply, will be found in the volume of Lyrical Ballads ; but as this is perhaps the most perfect and the most simple example of one of Wordsworth's noticeable qualities, we prefer to let it stand as the illustration of these remarks.

powers, he knew no more than his audience did which
was the true and which the fictitious metal; nay, it
would almost seem that the inferior work appeared to
him more important and better than the best. He tells
us with simple elation, speaking of the " Idiot Boy "——
" This long poem was composed in the groves of Alfoxden
almost extempore, not a word, I believe, being corrected,
though one stanza was omitted. I mention this in
gratitude to those happy moments, for in truth I never
wrote anything with so much glee." This curious boyish
simplicity, delighted with the thought that its production
was " almost extempore," and that not a word was corrected, blunts the edge of the critic's comment, and melts
him into indulgence. It is doubly strange and doubly
startling to find so singular a delusion in the mind of one
who was so deep a student of his own nature, and had
already so high a theory of his mission and work. But
there are other traces besides this of Wordsworth's youth-
fulness. The " dear brother Jim " of " We are Seven "
was added in the spirit of sheer nonsense, at Coleridge's
urgent prayer. " We all enjoyed the joke of putting in
our friend James Tobin's name," says Wordsworth, with
a boyish delight in mischief, though he objected to the
rhyme as ridiculous. That two of the greatest figures in
modern literature should thus disport themselves is the most
wonderful evidence of that love of fun which exists in every
wholesome youthful breast : but to play such tricks with
the public was not respectful to that great power, which
is the final judge of all excellence, and which exceedingly
resented the liberty. There were people, indeed, who
thought the whole volume a hoax, and who, between the
bewildering mysteries of the " Ancient Mariner " and the
wordy foolishness of " Betty Foy," believed nothing less
than that they were being laughed at——a result which was
the fault of the poets, and not of their astonished audience.

This curious mixture of success and failure appears in about exactly the same proportions in the longer poem produced at the same time, and intended for publication in this volume, the story of "Peter Bell." Here once more the poet breaks down in what he means to be the most important part of his work, and is brilliantly successful at a point which he has considered but little. We know no description of the kind which can bear comparison with the first part of "Peter Bell." The sketch of the potter is one of those extraordinary pictures which, once produced, nothing can obliterate. It is simple fact, true to the individual man in outward appearance, temper, manners, and character, as if it had been a photograph; and at the same time it is absolute truth, embracing a whole race of men, transcending the little limits of the generations, true to-day, and to the end of the world. Nor is it the portrait of the potter alone which is set before us. With a subtle skill, the poet brings in himself, with all his fine perceptions, the vision and faculty divine that is in his own eyes and soul, as painters sometimes put in a tender and visionary background to throw up and bring into full relief the figure that occupies the front of the picture. A certain unexpressed surprise at the thing he has called into being, and comparison of this strange ruffian with himself, is, we can see, visible all through in Wordsworth's thoughts, **a** comparison which makes him both smile and sigh; that such a being should breathe while the other kind, the species of himself, was still existing, how wonderful! Then, with a half-humorous, half-melancholy minuteness, he shows us in glimpses that world so lovely to himself which surrounds the unawakened soul—the hamlets which lie deep and low, each " beneath its little patch of sky and little lot of stars," the tender grass " leading its earliest green along the lane," the primrose,

which is nothing but a yellow primrose to Peter, the soft
blue sky melting through the high branches on the forest's
edge.   All this rises before us, while Peter, unconcerned
and rude, leading his lawless life in the midst, roving
among the vales and streams, sleeping beside his asses on
the hills, couched on the warm heath, below the sunshine
or under the trees, and neither noticing nor caring,
trudges through the landscape with the surly half-con-
tempt of his kind.

> " Though Nature could not touch his heart
>   By lovely forms, and silent weather,
>   And tender sounds, yet you might see
>   At once, that Peter Bell and she
>   Had often been together.
>
> " A savage wildness round him hung
>   As of a dweller out of doors :
>   In his whole figure and his mien
>   A savage character was seen
>   Of mountains and of dreary moors.
>
> " To all the unshaped half-human thoughts
>   That solitary Nature feeds
>   'Mid summer storms or winter's ice,
>   Had Peter joined whatever vice
>   The cruel city breeds.
>
> " His face was keen as is the wind
>   That cuts along the hawthorn fence ;
>   Of courage you saw little there,
>   But, in its stead, a medley air
>   Of cunning and of impudence.
>
> " He had a dark and sidelong walk,
>   And long and slouching was his gait ;
>   Beneath his looks so bare and bold,
>   You might perceive his spirit cold
>   Was playing with some inward bait.
>
> " His forehead wrinkled was and furred ;
>   A work one half of which was done
>   By thinking of his ' whens ' and ' hows ;'

> And half, by knitting of his brows,
> Beneath the glaring sun.

> " There was a hardness in his cheek,
> There was a hardness in his eye,
> As if the man had fixed his face,
> In many a solitary place,
> Against the wind and open sky."

Thus, this portrait is made to expound not only the feelingless and rude character of the subject, but at the same time the poetic nature which has conceived it.   It is the most forcible representation of what is by what is not, and suggestion of a whole world of beauty and meaning by the distinct embodiment of a sphere in which these qualities are altogether absent, which ever was executed.   The force of the picture lies not in sympathy, but antipathy, the writer and his theme standing, as it were, at the opposite poles of existence.   But when the reader turns from this wonderful beginning to the "tale," so called, that follows, he is brought down into dulness and failure with all the luckless force of gravitation, falling like Lucifer from heaven into unspeakable depths.   How Peter found an ass upon the banks of the "murmuring river Swale ;" how the ass,

> " With motion dull,
> Upon the pivot of its skull
> Turned round his long left ear ;"

how he then gave forth, and prolonged to all the echoes,

> " Most ruefully a deep-drawn shout,
> The hard dry see-saw of his terrible bray ;"

how Peter, stopped in his first delighted intention of stealing the beast, discovered the corpse of the pedlar who owned him in the water, and, struck to the heart by the poor animal's faithfulness, was guided by it to the poor man's cottage, carrying the news of his death to his wife and children; and how the stillness and solemnity of the night, and the strange adventure, so wrought upon him that he

> " Forsook his crimes, renounced his folly,
>   And, after ten months' melancholy,
>   Became a good and honest man ;"

is told in page after page of confused and tedious verse, to which even the measure and cadence, so finely adapted to the clear-cut lines of the previous description, is prejudicial, chopping up the story into small morsels, and dissipating the interest—such as it is. No deterioration could be more marked. The beginning is instinct with life and meaning, while all that follows is meandering, diffuse, and obscure—the one a model of continuous thought and happy expression, the other strained into ludicrous simplicity and faithfulness to fact, provoking laughter when it means to be solemn, yet never bold and strong enough to rise into true humour. We reach the climax of strange confusion when we read the poet's own account .of the newspaper anecdote which suggested the poem, and of his close study at Alfoxden of the " habits, traits, and physiognomy of asses." " I have no doubt," he adds, " that I was put upon writing the poem of Peter Bell out of liking for the creature that is so often dreadfully abused." Thus his intention was, to make his tale about an uncouth ruffian and a drowned pedlar a triumphant proof of the power of poetry to instruct the world by the meanest subjects ; and to turn something still less dignified and romantic than an idiot, an ass, into the hero of the epic. In this project he completely failed ; but here genius stepping in set the balance right, and by the way, without any set purpose or heroic meaning, betrayed him into that picture of the wild tramp and wanderer which can never die. We fear, however, so

irredeemable is the tale, that it is only the sworn disciples
of Wordsworth who have ever been fully aware of this
jewel in the toad's head, this matchless preface to a performance, for which, as a whole, no one but a fanatic
could find anything to say.

The contribution of the other member of the poetical
partnership to the "Lyrical Ballads" was in itself much
more memorable than anything produced by Wordsworth
—though the attention of the public never seems to have
been attracted by it, and criticism passed it over in
delighted perception of the opportunities of slaughter
afforded by the other.   The allotment of the supernatural
and mysterious to himself is accounted for by Coleridge
in curious apparent unconsciousness of any bias in himself towards that sphere of poetical contemplation, by
purely arbitrary reasons.   In the long walks and talks
which the Wordsworths and he took together, one of the
chief interests of the beautiful landscape which they sur-
veyed from "Quantock's airy ridge," was the constant
change of light and colour flitting over it, the rhythmic
flight of the shadows and vicissitudes of the atmosphere.
"The sudden charm which accidents of light and shade,
which moonlight or sunshine, diffused over a familiar landscape, appeared to represent the practicability of combin-
ing" those two distinct forces in poetry which they were
so fond of discussing—"the power of exciting the sympathy
of the reader by a faithful adherence to the truth of
nature—and the power of giving the interest of novelty
by the modifying colours of imagination."   Wordsworth's
part was that of the sunshine, dwelling upon and bringing
out into brilliant prominence the minutest detail of some
certain spot in the valley or slopes below.   And Coleridge,
with a readiness which was half loyal submission and
half that consciousness of unbounded faculty which made
him so fertile in plans of every kind, took up the other,

because it was left to him by the distinct natural bias of
his companion.   Such at least is the natural inference to
be drawn from his own account of the matter.   And up
to this time Coleridge had shown no special inclination
towards the supernatural; his poems had been, like his
friend's, descriptive, with an admixture of high moral
sentiment and reflection, but nothing more—when they
were not fiercely political, and concerned with the passions of the day.   Even when he helped to celebrate the
inspired Maiden, the heroine of France, no native instinct
seems to have led him to the means of her inspiration,
the heavenly voices and visions to which he could have
lent a mystic form and reality.   He took up this sphere
of poetry now, because, it would seem, the other was
manifestly preoccupied, and one thing was as easy as
another to his many-sided soul.   Never perhaps was the
preordained instrument put into a great singer's hands in
a manner more accidental.   For his own part he did not
much care which it was; he was as ready to have plunged
into science, into metaphysics, or politics.   But in the
meantime, as the supernatural was wanted to throw up
and complete the real, the supernatural was the subject
he adopted.   His attitude is like that of a man groping
in the darkness for his tools, and finding them by heavenly
guidance, without any prevision or pre-inclination of his
own.

It was in pursuance of this plan that the "Ancient
Mariner" was composed—in those very woods of Alfoxden
perhaps, where Wordsworth, with a beatitude which half
angers, half amuses the reader, was crooning over the
endless verses of "Betty Foy:" or on the road between
that poetical place and the cottage at Nether Stowey, a
road which led over the brown downs, from which the
poet, as we know, could see, by times a spectral ship
gliding athwart the setting sun, or the pilot's boat pushed

out upon the crisp morning waves for the guidance of the
homeward bound.   We can almost perceive the mariner's
mystic progress shaping itself, as in all moods and tempers
the poet looks forth upon the sea, and beholds in imagination not only the lighthouse tower, the kirk and the bay,
but all the wide-spreading wastes of water beyond the
firmament, and the wonders that may be passing there.
Perhaps some white gull winging across the darkness of
a storm cloud suggested to him the bird " that made the
wind to blow "——the friendly wild companion of the seamen's course that

> " Every day for food and play
>   Came to the mariner's hollo ; "

perhaps to himself, straying along with his head in the
clouds, the sight of it was like that of " a Christian soul,"
whom he hailed in God's name ; perhaps the crack of
some heartless rifle, the sudden drop through the gloomy
air of the innocent winged brother thus met on the way,
sent his indignant imagination forth to conceive what
punishment he should deserve who thus sent out of
happy life a fellow-creature who meant him nothing but
friendship.   And thus day by day, as he went and came,
the seas would render up their secrets, and Nature's
revenge for her child extend into all the weird and
mysterious consequences of man's breach of faith with
the subject-creation.   Neither the poet himself nor his
companions seem to have perceived the extraordinary
superiority of this wonderful conception to the other
poems with which it was published ; for not only was its
subject much more elevated, but it possessed in fact all
the completeness of execution and faithfulness to its plan,
which they failed in.   While Wordsworth represented
the light in the landscape chiefly in his imitation of the
prominence sometimes given by the sunshine to the most

insignificant spot, Coleridge carried out the similitude on
his side with a faithfulness of the grandest kind. Like
a great shadow moving noiselessly over the widest sweep
of mountain and plain, a pillar of cloud—or like the
flight of indescribable fleecy hosts of winged vapours
spreading their impalpable influence like a breath, changing the face of the earth, subduing the thoughts of men,
yet nothing, and capable of no interpretation—such was
the great poem destined to represent in the world of
poetry the effect which these mystic cloud-agencies have
upon the daylight and the sky. The life of every day is
going on gaily, the wedding guests are close to the festal
doors, when Mystery and Wonder suddenly interpose in
the way, shutting out everything else around. The
sounds of the other existence are heard through them,
and even by glimpses that life is visible—the merry
minstrels " nodding their heads," the bride in her blushes
—but the unwilling listener has entered into the shadow,
and the unseen has got hold of him. It is a parable, not
only of the ship and the albatross (which is hard of interpretation), but of mankind, a stranger upon earth,
" moving about in worlds not realised," always subject to
be seized upon by powers unknown to which he is of
kin, though he understands them not. " There is more
of the invisible than the visible in the world, *plures· esse
Naturas invisibiles quam visibiles in rerum universitate*," is
the poet's motto, and with a great splendour and force of
imagination he enforces his text. " There was a ship,"
quoth he—and the weird vessel glides before the unwilling listener's eyes, so that he can see nothing else. It
comes between him and the feast, between him and those
figures of his friends which flit like ghosts out of every
door. Which is the real, and which the vision ? The
mind grows giddy, and ceases to be able to judge ; and
while everything tangible disappears, the unseen sweeps

triumphantly in and holds possession, more real, more true, more unquestionable, than anything that eye can see.

This was what Coleridge meant when, seated on the breezy hillside with shadow and sunshine pursuing each other over the broad country at his feet, he took in hand to add to the common volume a poem which should deal with the supernatural and invisible, " so as to transfer from our outward nature a human interest and a semblance of truth sufficient to procure for these shadows of the imagination that willing suspension of disbelief for the moment, which constitutes poetic faith." We might even find a further symbolism in the scene, within which this tale of mystery and fate came into being, and the circumstances which have framed, in a lovely picture of greenness and summer beauty, indulgent skies and youthful happiness, one of the gravest, profoundest, and most lofty utterances of poetry — a song which was " chanted with happy heart," with pleasant breaks of laughter and eager discussion, with glad gazings upon sun and shadow, with many a playful interruption and criticism — out of the heart of as sad a life as ever enacted itself in tragic pain and darkness before the eyes of men.

Nor was the story of the Mariner itself unworthy of its aim, or of the wonderful wealth of poetic resource poured forth upon it. When the struggle between the actual and the invisible is over, and the Mariner is triumphant, what a stillness as of the great deep falls upon the strain ! The sun comes up out of the sea, and goes down into it — grand image of the loneliness, the isolation from all other created things, of that speck upon the boundless noiseless waters. Throughout the poem this sentiment of isolation is preserved with a magical and most impressive reality · all the action is absolutely shut up within the doomed ship. The storm, and the mist, and the snow, the flitting vision of the albatross, the spectre vessel against the sunset, the voices of the spirits, all derive their importance from that one centre of human life, driven before the tyrannous wind or held at the pleasure of the still more terrible calm, yet the only thing that gives meaning to either. The one man who is the chronicler of all, and to whose fate everything refers, is never withdrawn from our attention for a moment. He is, as it were, the epitome of humankind, the emblem of the sinner and sufferer, shut up within those rotting bulwarks, beneath those sails so thin and sere. The awful trance of silence in which his being is involved,—a silence of awe and pain, yet of a dumb enduring unconquerable force,—descends upon us and takes possession of our spirits also : no loud bassoon, no festal procession, can break the charm of that intense yet passive consciousness. We grow silent with him " with throat unslaked, with black lips baked," in a sympathy which is the very climax of poetic pain. And then what touches of tenderness are those that surprise us in this numbness and trance of awful solitude—

> " O happy living things ! no tongue
>   Their beauty might declare :
> A spring of love rushed from my heart,
>   And I blessed them unaware :
> Sure my kind saint took pity on me,
>   And I blessed them unaware "—

or this other which comes after the horror of the reanimated bodies, the ghastly crew of the dead-alive :—

> " For when it dawned, they dropped their arms,
>   And clustered round the mast ;
> Sweet sounds rose slowly through their mouths,
>   And from their bodies passed.
> Around, around, flew each sweet sound,
>   Then darted to the Sun ;
> Slowly the sounds came back again,

> Now mixed, now one by one.
> Sometimes a-dropping from the sky
> I heard the sky-lark sing ;
> Sometimes all little birds that are,
> How they seemed to fill the sea and air
> With their sweet jargoning !
> And now 'twas like all instruments,
> Now like a lonely flute ;
> And now it is an angel's song,
> Which makes the heavens be mute."

When the tale has reached its height of mystery and emotion, a change ensues ; gradually the greater spell is removed, the spirits depart, the strain softens—with a weird yet gentle progress the ship comes " slowly and smoothly," without a breeze, back to the known and visible. As the voyage approaches its conclusion, ordinary instrumentalities appear once more. There is first the rising of the soft familiar wind, " like a meadow gale in spring," then the blessed vision of the lighthouse-top, the hill, the kirk, all those well-known realities which gradually relieve the absorbed excitement of the listener, and favour his slow return to ordinary daylight. And then comes the ineffable half-childish, half-divine simplicity of those soft moralisings at the end, so strangely different from the tenor of the tale, so wonderfully perfecting its visionary strain. After all, the poet seems to say, after this weird excursion into the very deepest, awful heart of the seas and mysteries, here is your child's moral, a tender little half trivial sentiment, yet profound as the blue depths of heaven :—

> " He prayeth best, who loveth best
>   All things both great and small ;
> For the dear God who loveth us,
>   He made and loveth all."

This unexpected gentle conclusion brings our feet back to the common soil with a bewildered sweetness of

relief and soft quiet after the prodigious strain of mental
excitement which is like nothing else we can remember
in poetry. The effect is one rarely produced, and which
few poets have the strength and daring to accomplish,
sinking from the highest notes of spiritual music to the
absolute simplicity of exhausted nature. Thus we are
set down on the soft grass, in a tender bewilderment, out
of the clouds. The visionary voyage is over, we are back
again on the mortal soil from which we started; but
never more, never again, can the visible and invisible
bear to us the same meaning. For once in our lives, if
never before, we have passed the borders of the unseen.

The same period which produced the "Ancient Mariner" produced also "Christabel," as much of it as was
ever written. It is said that Coleridge had planned the
second part of this poem, and meant to finish it, but it is
well that his wayward indolence came in, backed for once
by the voices of judicious friends. Charles Lamb was
one of those who said the fragment should never be completed, and that is something the more which we owe our
beloved Elia. This further investigation into the unknown was not published for years after, but it was read
in the brotherhood, and known, from this happy and
fertile period. It is a more distinct revelation than the
other. The first was, so to speak, introductory, an uplift-
ing of the veil, the disclosure of a vast unseen world full
of struggles and mysteries. The second is the distinct
identification of a mystery of evil, an unseen harm and
bane, working secretly in the dark places of the earth
against white innocence, purity, and truth, and carrying
on, with a new dread and awe, the continual conflict
between good and evil. The poet does not stop to explain
to us how this can be. Philosopher as he is to the depth
of his soul, he is yet so much the more poet as to see
that any theory of spiritual hate against the happiness of

earth would confuse the unity of his strain, and probably transfer our interest, as it has done in the "Paradise Lost," to the despairing spirit whose envy and enmity arise out of that hopeless majesty of wretchedness, great enough to be sublime, which devours his own soul.   But Coleridge gives no reason for the hideous and terrible persecution of which his lovely maiden, "Christabel," symbolical even in name, is the object.   The poem is a romance of Christianity—a legend of the saints.   For no fault of hers, but rather for her virtues, are the powers of evil raised against her: and one of the most subtle and wonderful touches in the poem is that which makes us sensible of the ignorance of her innocence, her want of any knowledge or experience which can make her aware what the evil is, and how she is to deal with it.   The witch Geraldine has all the foul wisdom of her wickedness to help her sorceries, her supernatural knowledge, her spells and cunning.   But "Christabel" has nothing save her purity, and stands defenceless as a lamb, not even knowing what the danger is, exposed at every point in her simplicity, and paralysed, not instructed, by the first gleam of bewildering enlightenment.   Never was there a higher or more beautiful conception.   It is finer in its indefiniteness than the contrast of Una and Duessa, the pure and impure, the false and true, of a more elaborate allegory: Spenser, who lived in a more downright age, keeps himself within a narrower circle, and is compelled by his story to acts and deeds: but his very distinctness limits his power.   The sorceress or disguised demon of Coleridge does not attempt to ruin her victim in any such uncompromising way.   What she does is to throw boundless confusion into the gentle soul, to fill its limpid depths with fear and horror and distrust of all fair appearances, and even of itself—a still more appalling doubt: to undermine the sacred foundations of that love and honour in which Christabel's very name is enshrined, and to establish herself, a subtle enemy, an antagonistic power, at the pure creature's side, turning her existence into chaos.   Una is a foully slandered and innocent maiden, but Christabel is a martyr soul, suffering for her race, without knowing it, struggling in a dumb consternation against the evil that holds her spellbound.   And all the more pathetic, all the more enthralling, is the picture, because the Christ-maiden is entirely human—too young, too childlike, even to understand the high mission which has fallen upon her.   She knows nothing, neither her own position, a sight for angels to watch, nor all that depends upon her steadfast adherence to her white banner of religious faith and purity : but her enemy knows everything, and has an armoury of subtle spiritual weapons at her disposal : " Jesu Maria, shield her well ! "

The contrast between the serene purity of the undisturbed soul and the confusion caused by her unconscious, unwilling contact with evil, is summed up in the following beautiful passage :—

> " It was a lovely sight to see
>   The Lady Christabel, when she
>   Was praying at the old oak tree.
>   Amid the jagged shadows
>   Of mossy leafless boughs,
>   Kneeling in the moonlight,
>   To make her gentle vows ;
>   Her slender palms together prest,
>   Heaving sometimes on her breast ;
>   Her face resigned to bliss or bale—
>   Her face, oh call it fair not pale,
>   And both blue eyes more bright than clear,
>   Each about to have a tear.

> " With open eyes (ah woe is me !)
>   Asleep, and dreaming fearfully,
>   Fearfully dreaming, yet I wis,
>   Dreaming that alone, which is—

O sorrow and shame !   Can this be she,
The lady, who knelt at the old oak tree ?
And lo ! the worker of these harms,
That holds the maiden in her arms,
Seems to slumber still and mild,
As a mother with her child.

" A star hath set, a star hath risen,
O Geraldine ! since arms of thine
Have been the lovely lady's prison.
O Geraldine ! one hour was thine—
Thou'st had thy will !   By tairn and rill,
The night-birds all that hour were still.
But now they are jubilant anew,
From cliff and tower, tu-whoo ! tu-whoo !
Tu-whoo ! tu-whoo ! from wood and fell !
And see ! the lady Christabel
Gathers herself from out her trance ;
Her limbs relax, her countenance
Grows sad and soft ; the smooth thin lids
Close o'er her eyes ; and tears she sheds—
Large tears that leave the lashes bright !
And oft the while she seems to smile
As infants at a sudden light !
Yea, she doth smile, and she doth weep,
Like a youthful hermitess,
Beauteous in a wilderness,
Who, praying always, prays in sleep.
And, if she move unquietly,
Perchance, 'tis but the blood so free,
Comes back and tingles in her feet.
No doubt, she hath a vision sweet.
What if her guardian spirit 'twere ?
What if she knew her mother near ?
But this she knows, in joys and woes,
That saints will aid if men will call :
For the blue sky bends over all ! "

The first part, ending with the above lines, was written
during this happy period at Nether Stowey; the next,
not till several years later, when the poet had removed
to the north country, and the brotherhood had begun to
be known as the " Lake Poets."   But it was not published

until long after, in 1816, when the public, who had
allowed the "Ancient Mariner" to slip into existence
with very little notice, gave to this wonderful fragment
such a reception as few poems have had.   There was no
doubt nor hesitation about it.   Cottle tells us that
Wordsworth attributed the failure of the "Lyrical Ballads" to the appearance in it of the "Ancient Mariner,"
which nobody understood ; but it continued to hold its
place in the next edition, which appeared in 1800, with
a preface in which Wordsworth set forth his theories of
poetry, and in two other successive editions.   The fine
poem called "Love," one of those which we place most
willingly by the side of the "Mariner" and "Christabel,"
was also included in the second edition.

Notwithstanding the unsuccess of this volume, the
universal ridicule with which it was received, and the
very inadequate idea of Wordsworth's genius given by it,
there was, after its publication, very little real question
about the rank of these two brother poets.   How this
should have come about it is difficult to say.   It happens
sometimes that under the great outcry of indignation or
dislike, raised by a certain work or act, there is a subtle
indescribable deposit left by its mere contact with the
mind of the reader, which is the foundation of the fullest
and truest fame.   No better example could be than this
first work of the new brotherhood.   The effect was unequal, but that does not diminish its singularity : though
we think Coleridge was far better represented in it than
Wordsworth, yet the publication had no such effect upon
the reputation of the author of the "Ancient Mariner"
as upon that of his coadjutor.   Wordsworth was the
special object of assault on all hands, but his poetical
fortune was made.   When the book was republished, the
copyright of which had been given back to him as worth-
less, it was no longer an unbroken phalanx of angry or

indignant critics which he found before him.   Here and
there a young outlooker on some watch-tower had seen
the light on the skies, and recognised whence it came.
He got nothing but abuse for his first publication, but yet,
in some strange way, it became his stepping-stone to fame.

The second edition contained two series of poems,
which every lover of Wordsworth turns to instinctively,
as perhaps the most exquisite of his minor productions.
These are the poems which reveal " Lucy "—she of whom
Nature vowed to make " a lady of her own"—she, who
" dwelt among the untrodden ways, besides the springs of
Dove," the most refined, yet most simple of all the half-
revealed dreams of poetry.   Five little poems are all we
have of her.   If she were a real being, or only an imagination, no one can tell; but the little casket of gems,
in which her gentle name is enshrined, is pure and divine
as the stars themselves, though the poems are artless as
so many wild flowers.   Here, indeed, the poet has arrived
at his aim of producing the very highest effect by the
simplest means—yet not as he meant to do it: for his
subject is no grotesque embodiment of lowly love, but a
creature belonging to the order of the Juliets and Desde-
monas, the lawful ladies of our fancy.   The consecration
and the pathos of her story, which is no story, is almost
more sacred, indeed, than that of these queens of the
imagination—for it is wrapped round about in a pensive,
yet penetrating sadness, devoid either of hope or passion.
She is dead before we so much as hear of her.   When
her lover, riding towards her cottage, sees the waning
moon go down, and gloom come over that humble roof,
his heart is struck with an ominous foreboding—

> " What fond and wayward thoughts will slide
>   Into a lover's head !—
> ' O mercy !' to myself I cried,
>   ' If Lucy should be dead !' "

Another step, another little broken outburst of simplest song, and we know that the foreboding has come true—

> " She lived unknown, and few could know
>   When Lucy ceased to be ;
> But she is in her grave, and, oh,
>   The difference to me !"

Never were words more simple, more everyday ; and yet it is hard to read them without tears ; impossible, if the reader's life has ever held a Lucy of its own. Without passion, with no outcry even, more strong than this sense of want, it is heartrending in its quiet despair. The conclusion of all, which touches even patriotism to a deeper tone, we may quote entire. There is the very soul of chastened sorrow and profoundest melancholy faithfulness in every word—

> " I travelled among unknown men,
>   In lands beyond the sea ;
> Nor, England ! did I know till then
>   What love I bore to thee.

> " 'Tis past, that melancholy dream !
>   Nor will I quit thy shore
> A second time ; for still I seem
>   To love thee more and more.

> " Among thy mountains did I feel
>   The joy of my desire ;
> And she I cherished turned her wheel
>   Beside an English fire.

> " Thy mornings showed, thy nights concealed
>   The bowers where Lucy played ;
> And thine, too, is the last green field
>   That Lucy's eyes surveyed."

This wonderful little record of a love and grief unknown, was made in Germany, where the poet had spent a dreary winter. To ourselves it is impossible to imagine that these poems had not a reference to some real history

of the heart; but there is no indication of any such thing
in Wordsworth's life. The exquisite pathos and power
with which the story is conveyed to us was perhaps pur-
posely marred by the poet himself, who separated the
verses, according to some solemn fantasy of his own, into
different classifications. We are glad to see that Mr.
Matthew Arnold, in his recent selection from Wordsworth,
has put them together, and permitted them at last to tell
their own tale.

And by the side of "Lucy" unknown, we place another figure of a different kind, no more than an old
schoolmaster——the Matthew, whose name on a village
tablet calls forth the poet's tender exclamation——

> " —Thou soul of God's best earthly mould !
>   Thou happy Soul ! and can it be
> That these two words of glittering gold
>   Are all that must remain of thee ? "

The "Two April Mornings," and "The Fountain"
contain this humble wayfarer as in some magic globe of
crystal. They are so beautiful that the mere thought of
them is like a strain of music. If Wordsworth had no
more than these to build his fame upon, he would yet be
sure of immortality. The suggestion of a noble human
creature, "a man of mirth," one whose very tears "were
tears of light, the dew of gladness," yet by whom the
mood of "still and serious thought" was "felt with spirit
so profound," is such as, perhaps, no one else, in so brief
a space, and with so little aid of circumstance, could have
given. It is impossible to refrain from setting this gem
of purest ray serene in the humble framework of this
page. Not only literature, but life is the better for anything so exquisite——

> " We walked along, while bright and red
>   Uprose the morning sun ;

And Matthew stopped, he looked and said,
     ' The will of God be done !'

" A village Schoolmaster was he,
     With hair of glittering gray ;
As blithe a man as you could see
     On a spring holiday.

" And on that morning, through the grass
     And by the steaming rills,
We travelled merrily, to pass
     A day among the hills.

" ' Our work,' said I, ' was well begun ;
     Then, from thy breast what thought,
Beneath so beautiful a sun,
     So sad a sigh has brought ?'

" A second time did Matthew stop ;
     And fixing still his eye
Upon the eastern mountain-top,
     To me he made reply :

" ' Yon cloud with that long purple cleft
     Brings fresh into my mind
A day like this which I have left
     Full thirty years behind.

" ' And just above yon slope of corn
     Such colours, and no other,
Where in the sky, that April morn,
     Of this the very brother.

" ' With rod and line I sued the sport
     Which that sweet season gave,
And, coming to the church, stopped short
     Beside my daughter's grave.

" ' Nine summers had she scarcely seen,
     The pride of all the vale ;
And then she sang ;—she would have been
     A very nightingale.

" ' Six feet in earth my Emma lay ;
     And yet I loved her more,
For so it seemed, than till that day
     I e'er had loved before.

" 'And, turning from her grave, I met,
 Beside the churchyard yew,
A blooming girl, whose hair was wet
 With points of morning dew.

" 'A basket on her head she bare ;
 Her brow was smooth and white :
To see a child so very fair,
 It was a pure delight !

" 'No fountain from its rocky cave
 E'er tripped with foot so free ;
She seemed as happy as a wave
 That dances on the sea.

" ' There came from me a sigh of pain
 Which I could ill confine ;
I looked at her, and looked again :
 —And did not wish her mine.'

" Matthew is in his grave, yet now,
 Methinks, I see him stand,
As at that moment, with a bough
 Of wilding in his hand."

Wordsworth has for the present, perhaps, passed the height of his fame. He is less universally appreciated, less beloved, than he was twenty years ago. The failure can only be temporary, but it is grief to those to whom he stands like his own mountains, a glory and power, to catch the echo of a gibe from unlikely quarters now-a-days, repeating the gibes with which the eighteenth century, while it lay a-dying, feebly mocked at the innovation. But even that old century, on the verge of the grave, and with the mock on its bloodless lips, began to feel before it died that the new poet was too many for it, with all its powers of ridicule, and with all the opportunities for their exercise which he gave so boldly. The " Lyrical Ballads," at which every toothless critic sneered, and upon which the new gladiators of literature all fleshed their swords, was nevertheless, as he intended, the sure

foundation of the poet's fame. He insisted, notwithstanding all the jests, that this and no other should be
the first stone, and by sheer strength of genius and
strength of will, succeeded, unlikely though it seemed.

Such were the two young poets who, after all preludes
and symphonies were completed, opened a new and noble
chapter, a great era, of poetry in England. Wordsworth
brought to the sweet, and fair, and real English landscape, rediscovered with all its genial breezes and wholesome freshness by Cowper, his own deeply reasoning
spirit, full of a lofty perception of the mysteries, and
sorrows, and doubts, of nature, and a high sympathetic
philosophical faculty for the solution of these doubts and
mysteries. Instead of the stale moralities and reflections
of which the world had grown so weary, he brought back
to human nature that high vindication of the ways of
God to man which Milton and his angels had held in
Eden, and taking—what mattered the outside?—a poet
or a peasant indifferently, expounded the agency of
human sorrows in the economy of life, and put forth his
hand to grasp " the far-off interest of tears."—Coleridge,
on the other hand, opened up all that mystic world of
suggestion in which the human spirit lives conscious but
bewildered, " the world not realised," the wonderful
unknown to which no soul is a stranger, which no man
has ever interpreted, but which, breathing mysteriously
upon us in tremors of the blood and thrills of spiritual
curiosity, attracts more or less every conscious soul. The
mystic wanderer who has lived among the dead, and
carries about the world the burden of his strange punishment : the undisclosed secret of that darkness out of
which the lady who is " beautiful exceedingly," the
" angel beautiful and bright," who is nevertheless a fiend,
glides suddenly when the victim thinks no evil : and
all the powers of the heights and the depths thus came

back upon the world which had forgotten any spiritual creatures more entrancing or mysterious than the Nymphs and Muses, and those little vulgar spirits that managed Belinda's petticoat. New voices were yet to rise, and new lights to appear, in the firmament before the epoch was accomplished, but it had come to its full and splendid beginning, with all its paths made straight and all its foundations laid, when Wordsworth and Coleridge published the "Lyrical Ballads," and came forth from their solitudes upon the world.

In poetry Coleridge made no advance upon the work of those early days. His philosophy did not affect the world as his poetry did, notwithstanding the glamour of impression rather than influence which it produced afterwards, or which his personal presence and discourse produced, when he was no longer young, upon those who were. It will, however, demand notice elsewhere. With Wordsworth the result of years was very different. When he settled in his native north country at Grasmere, and finally at Rydal, where he lived the greater part of his life, and died an old man, it was with the settled intention of devoting himself and all his powers to poetry, and the records of the earlier portion of this retired life are entirely poetical. His sister was still his sole and constant companion, and her diary, full of many gleams of poetic description and insight, is yet an almost matter-of-fact account of incidents which her keen eyes and ready perception noted, or which friends related to the steady and diligent workman, whose whole soul was bent upon his noble trade, and who immediately made use of the material, and reproduced it in verse. They met upon the road " an old man bent nearly double," whose trade it was to gather leeches—and straightway " William wrote the ' Leech-Gatherer,'" one of the noblest of his lesser poems ; or Dorothy encountered a party of

wandering beggars—parents and children ; or " we saw
a few daffodils close to the waterside." Nothing was
neglected between them ; no unusual effect either of
mind or matter, no incident of life, but found a place.
These swallow flights of song, however, were not enough
to satisfy the conscientious mind of the man who had
determined not only to be a poet, but a great one, and
who felt the pressure of his mission upon him. Wordsworth was a lover of system and theory. The wild
simplicities of the Lyrical Ballads, as we have seen, were
all severely resolved upon, and he was now not less, but
more, bent upon impressing his poetical creed upon the
world. He began, therefore, as soon as he had settled
himself in the north, to look about him for a subject
great enough for his handling, and very soon came to the
decision, with something of the large and lofty egotism
which was one of the inspirations of his life, that nothing
more profoundly interesting than the " history of his own
mind " could be given to the world. He describes his
intention, and all the farspreading results that were to
follow, with a sort of simple grandiloquence, in his preface
to the " Excursion," published in 1814.

" When the Author retired to his native mountains with the
hope of being able to construct a literary Work that might live,
it was a reasonable thing that he should take a review of his own
mind, and examine how far Nature and Education had qualified
him for such employment. As subsidiary to this preparation, he
undertook to record, in verse, the origin and progress of his own
powers, as far as he was acquainted with them. That Work,
addressed to a dear Friend, most distinguished for his knowledge
and genius, and to whom the Author's Intellect is deeply indebted,
. . . and the result of the investigation which gave rise to it was a
determination to compose a philosophical poem, containing views of
Man, Nature, and Society, and to be entitled the 'Recluse ;' as
having for its principal subject the sensations and opinions of a
poet living in retirement. The preparatory poem is biographical,
and conducts the history of the Author's mind to the point when

he was emboldened to hope that his faculties were sufficiently matured for entering upon the arduous labour which he had proposed to himself; and the two Works have the same kind of relation to each other, if he may so express himself, as the ante-chapel has to the body of a Gothic church. Continuing this allusion, he may be permitted to add that his minor Pieces, . . . when they shall be properly arranged, will be found by the attentive Reader to have such connection with the main Work, as may give them claim to be likened to the little cells, oratories, and sepulchral recesses ordinarily included in those edifices."

The artificial solemnity of this scheme, given forth with a sublime unconsciousness of all possibilities of derision, is not, perhaps, more remarkable than the arrogant humility of the theories with which the Lyrical Ballads were issued to the world. Never was there a more curious demonstration of the foolishness of wisdom. He who proclaimed himself as the emancipator of the poetic art would have fitted her into the most rigid machinery if he could have had his will, and the elaborate system in which every part was adapted to the other, and all together were to form a temple of glory great as Solomon's own, and worthy to be the centre of earth, was almost more dear to him than the poetry itself, though that was the breath of his nostrils. But nature which loves no such elaboration, and wayward genius which scorns machinery, and human liking which will none of it, had the better of Wordsworth. He had vanquished the age with his Lyrical Ballads, returning again and again to the charge with the selfsame weapon, till his despised arms had won the battle; but not even his obstinate valour and steady pertinacity could achieve this second triumph. Poetry blew away his systems like the mere foam of fancy they were. No one, even among his worshippers, has thought of his work as of a " Gothic church." Most people whose opinion is worth having —backed by that general multitude which pretends to little discrimination, yet has a commanding instinct superior to criticism—would rather lose both " Excursion" and " Prelude," than consent to part with the "Leech-Gatherer," or that great " Ode " which also belongs to these peaceful prefatory years.   Even Wordsworth's enormous force of will, united to his genius, could not succeed in making the history of a poet's mind a subject of absorbing interest to the world.   But he himself must have so far felt this that he never carried out his majestic intention. ' The " Prelude " was indeed finished, but it was not given to the world till after Wordsworth's death, when it was received with the reverential respect due to a posthumous work from such a hand, but not with any enthusiasm of appreciation.   The friend to whom it was addressed was Coleridge, who speaks of it with rapturous admiration, declaring that this dedication was the only thing in the world which could give him an hour's vanity ; and perhaps the warmest, certainly the most touching, link of human interest which we have with the poem is the effect it produced upon him when, on his return from Malta in 1806, the completed manuscript was read to him by his friend.   By that time he had entered upon the downward part of his career.   Bad health, combined, no doubt, with the restlessness of a mind unsatisfied, and a conscience already sick and burdened with weakness it could not overcome, had sent him away wandering in search of health and peace two years before.   At Malta he had fallen fortuitously into public employment, which gave some meaning to his detention, but he was uneasy and restless under these bonds as under all other.   When he arrived in England, after this long absence, his first visit was to the Wordsworths at Coleorton, the house of Sir George Beaumont ; and here it was that this poetical autobiography, full of so many noble passages, and at all points overflowing with interest to Wordsworth's contemporary and brother-in-arms, was read to him.   Coleridge was greatly moved. He felt the contrast to his very heart : his friend had gone steadily and solemnly on in his career, and seemed now sure of that starry crown of immortality which, a little while before, had appeared more near Coleridge's head than his ; while he had dropped away into ways which were not ways of blessedness, into a melancholy oblivion of his own highest aims and powers.   It is not difficult to imagine what must have been the thoughts of the worn and weary traveller, conscious of many a slip and back-sliding.   How different the situation then from their conjunction at the time of which the poem had just reminded him, when, from " Quantock's airy ridge " the entire world of life and poetry lay at the feet of the two brethren in genius.   In the stillness of the summer night, the unfortunate, the unsuccessful, the erring and suffering wanderer, addressed his friend in lines which betray the swelling of a full heart.   " An Orphic song indeed," he cries—

> " A song divine, of high and passionate thoughts
>   To their own music chanted ! "

He gazes upon the writer with a new-born awe, viewing him " in the choir of ever-enduring men," one of those " truly great " who—

> " Have all one age, and from one visible space
>   Shed influence ! "

But he himself, the poet's peer and comrade, how strangely, how sadly different, how deeply departed from their common aims !

> " Ah ! as I listened with a heart forlorn,
>   The pulses of my being beat anew :
>   And even as life returns upon the drowned
>   Life's joy rekindling roused a throng of pains,

> Keen pangs of love, awakening as a babe,
> Turbulent with an outcry in the heart ;
> And fears self-willed that shunned the eye of hope,
> And hope that scarce would know itself from fear ;
> Sense of past youth, and manhood come in vain,
> And genius given and knowledge won in vain ;
> And all which I had culled in woodwalks wild,
> And all which patient toil had reared, and all,
> Commune with thee had opened out—but flowers
> Strewed on my corse, and borne upon my bier,
> In the same coffin, for the self same grave ! "

The growth of a poet's mind, developing itself serene and lofty, amid all the still and sublime influences of virtue and domestic calm, affords room for many an elevated thought : but as long as humanity is as now, this other figure coming in, no conqueror but sadly worsted in the life-battle, his bosom strained with a sob of self-compassion, yet generous voice of enthusiasm, proclaiming the triumph of the victor, will gain from us a very different regard. Wordsworth in his self-determined greatness has our respect and admiration, but it is with that anguish of sympathy which stirs the very depths of our being, that we turn to the other, with his weird and wonderful insight into the mysteries of creation, and his helpless incapacity to hold his own against the vulgarest forces of evil. The contrast is heartrending yet ever-recurring. And it is one of the most affecting of compensations, that the soul which fails in the fight should so often possess that magnanimity and generous power of appreciation which Coleridge thus manifested. We cannot but doubt whether Wordsworth, the pure and strong, had he failed like his brother, could have borne the comparison with anything like the same noble candour and humility.

The " Prelude," perhaps, was too long delayed to have its due effect upon the public mind. In 1850, which was the date of its publication, the French Revolution, and all the convulsions which attended it, were so far away, and the feelings of hope, of wonder, of dismay, with which its progress was watched, had by that time fallen too entirely into the calm of historical contemplation to stir the lively sympathy of the reader : but the value of the poem as a picture of the mental history of the period can scarcely be over-estimated.   The philosophical yet sympathetic spectator, curious, anxious, and full of the deepest interest, watching the historic scroll roll out before him with all a contemporary's certainty of under-standing, yet bewildered half knowledge of those hieroglyphics which only Time interprets fully—eluci-dates, if not the stirring story of the time, yet his own generation, with all its hopes and aspirations and disappointments, better than any other historian has done.   It is not, however, to this part of the record that the poetical reader will turn, but to the earlier scenes, the poet's childhood among his " native mountains," his schoolboy feats and adventures—still Esthwaite, in the midst of its valley, " the moon in splendour couched among the leaves of a tall ash that near our cottage stood,' and these questionings of nature and silence which arose in the heart of the growing boy.   This school-boy story is full of the freshness of the mountains, and the thrill of simple life and nature.   Perhaps a picture more vivid and real, yet more finely imaginative, was never drawn than that of the frozen lake and the band of boyish skaters careless of the summons to home and the fireside which " the cottage windows blazed through twilight gloom."

> . . " not a voice was idle : with the din
> Smitten, the precipices rang aloud ;
> The leafless trees and every icy crag
> Tinkled like iron ; while far distant hills

> Into the tumult sent an alien sound
> Of melancholy, not unnoticed, while the stars,
> Eastward, were sparkling clear, and in the west
> The orange sky of evening died away.
> Not seldom from the uproar I retired
> Into a silent bay,—or sportively
> Glanced sideway, leaving the tumultuous throng,
> To cut across the reflex of a star
> That fled, and, flying still before me, gleamed
> Upon the glassy plain ; and oftentimes,
> When we had given our bodies to the wind,
> And all the shadowy banks on either side
> Came sweeping through the darkness, spinning still
> The rapid line of motion, then at once
> Have I, reclining back upon my heels,
> Stopped short ; yet still the solitary cliffs
> Wheeled by me—even as if the earth had rolled
> With visible motion her diurnal round !
> Behind me did they stretch in solemn train,
> Feebler and feebler, and I stood and watched
> Till all was tranquil as a dreamless sleep."

It would be impossible to find a description more true to fact, yet more instinct with the wonder and the mystery of existence and this " world not realised," which is its scene.

The " Excursion," which is the only part of the proposed great poem of the " Recluse" which got into being, was published in 1814, while the controversies, excited by the " Lyrical Ballads," were still in force. And though the poet had by that time a devoted band of disciples, and had so far conquered public attention that nothing could come from his hand which the critics dared venture to neglect, yet the treatment of this long poem was not much more genial than that with which its predecessors had been entertained. Jeffrey, to his own confusion, hailed it, as everybody knows, with that, " This will never do," which has served the world for an example of light-hearted audacity ever since. We are doubtful, however, whether, had it been published now, even the more wary critics of our own days, warned by such examples, might not have given a very similar verdict. No poem so long, so monotonous, and at the same time so unequal, was ever popular. That there are many passages in it of the noblest poetry does not in any way affect this fact ; and both in its nobleness and in its heaviness, the atmosphere was too elevated for common man. Without the relief of story, or of any variety of character, with nothing but the highest rarefied air of the mountains about the three or four austere philoso-phical figures reasoning among themselves of the ways of God to man, nothing was left to attract the lighter part of nature, or to beguile the careless reader into the high fare thus set before him. We doubt if the lowliness of the chief character, the still half-ostentatious selection of the trade of pedlar to distinguish him, was half the drawback it was supposed to be ; but the unbroken gravity of the strain, its lofty dialogue almost entirely occupied with the philosophy of sorrow,—that lofty and abstruse argument by which the poet and the creatures of his fancy endeavour to prove the advantages to humanity of individual grief and misfortune,—touched only here and there a note to which the heart could respond. The first book contains a picture of extra-ordinary pathos and power, from which it results that there are many who know the story of Margaret, just as there are many who are acquainted with the episode of Paolo and Francesca in the *Inferno*, without venturing farther in a way too high for them. This story has furnished English poetry with one of the most touching pictures of the anguish of suspense and the long heart-breaking vigil of vain expectation, to be found in any language. The wistful, patient woman sitting at her cottage door, with her long scrutinising gaze directed

along the vacant road, her eyes " busy in the distance,
shaping things that make her heart beat quick," her
habitual pause in her work to give another and another
glance to that vacany out of which the beloved, long-
looked-for wanderer might at any moment come,—her
infant that " from its mother caught the trick of grief
and sighed among its playthings,"—her wide wanderings
afield when her heart grew too sick to rest, and the
gradual desperate yielding of heart and hope, of comfort
and all its outside semblances—are placed before us with
a reality of sadness which is heartrending. This figure
appears in the foreground of the picture with a humble
majesty of woe which recalls the cry of another sufferer—

> " Here I and Sorrow sit ;
>   This is my throne, let kings come bow to it."

There is no other figure in the poem so real or so fine.
The Priest and the Pedlar, who join in the excursion of
the poet by the village churchyard and among the
surrounding hills, are but so many Wordsworths taking
up the different tones of his argument——the Solitary a
feebler objector, equally philosophical, whose bitterness
is made to be overcome. How evil itself can be turned
to good, how the great patience of suffering ennobles the
earth and the race, and how all that is painful passes
away, leaving an immortal tranquillity and confidence as
the supreme mood of nature, is the argument of the
whole. It is a very lofty argument, worth a poet's while ;
but it is hard to seize, and needs a mind of kindred
peacefulness and faith. When the poet has heard
Margaret's melancholy story his heart goes out towards
her in all the tenderness of sympathy. " It seemed,"
he says,

> " To comfort me, while with a brother's love
>   I blessed her in the impotence of grief."

He feels himself solaced and strengthened by this flood
of natural feeling.   The tale of grief impresses and
solemnises his own soul.

" Then towards the cottage I returned ; and traced
   Fondly, though with an interest more mild,
   That secret spirit of humanity
   Which, 'mid the calm oblivious tendencies
   Of nature, 'mid her plants, and weeds, and flowers,
   And silent overgrowings, still survived.
   The old Man, noting this, resumed, and said,
' My Friend ! enough to sorrow you have given,
   The purposes of wisdom ask no more :
         .   .   .
   She sleeps in the calm earth, and peace is here.
   I well remember that those very plumes,
   Those weeds, and the high spear-grass on that wall,
   By mist and silent rain-drops silvered o'er,
   As once I passed into my heart conveyed
   So still an image of tranquillity,
   So calm and still, and looked so beautiful
   Amid the uneasy thoughts which filled my mind,
   That what we feel of sorrow and despair
   From ruin and from change, and all the grief
   That passing shows of Being leave behind,
   Appeared an idle dream, that could maintain,
   Nowhere, dominion o'er the enlightened spirit
   Whose meditative sympathies repose
   Upon the breast of Faith.   I turned away,
   And walked along my road in happiness.' "

In all his mature work this is always the lesson
which Wordsworth labours to enforce.   Perhaps the early
shock given to his mind by the failure of the visionary
hopes, of which France was the centre, first turned his
deeply searching and patient intelligence to draw some
sort of goodness, if he could, out of things evil—and as
his mind ripened and occupied itself more and more with
the great questions of human life, the so frequent failure
of all hopes, the incessant disappointments and miseries
of men, this was the consolation which he gathered to

himself: that sorrow was temporary but peace eternal, and that Nature's continual work is to bind up wounds and cover over graves. This constant process of renovation and the perpetual survival of the general calm, whatsoever may be the adversities of the individual, which appals the minds of some observers, and makes Nature, in their eyes, a cruel automaton altogether indifferent to the fortunes of mankind, was to Wordsworth a sacred and hopeful patience, an assurance of that everlasting composure and satisfaction that is in the bosom of God. It is easier, perhaps, to give to this doctrine a large adhesion, and to preach it to men, when the soul of the speaker dwells in peace as Wordsworth's did, and disappointment and calamity do not come his way. But it is a noble burden of prophecy; and nowhere could it have had a fitter atmosphere than in that presence of the hills which pervades this great poem. The mountains are all about us, as we read, raising their great shadows against the sky, opening out into blue distance, with many a misty peak, and half-seen valley, or closing in the scene with serried rank of cliff on cliff, and rock piled above rock—

> "The silence that is in the starry sky,
> The sleep that is among the lonely hills,"

an air chill and pure; a sweep of uncontaminated wind, the hush of half-heard streams, and inarticulate movement spread all about. This sentiment of the mountains is in itself a poem, and the "Excursion" is instinct with it. The long reasonings, the over-serious argument, may weary the reader, but even the most careless will find that he has been swept away into a land of mists and mountains, amid influences of the clouds and winds, and lyric outbursts of sunshine and light, such as come nowhere else. It is more than descriptive poetry. The poet's intense realisation of those beloved landscapes carries us with him into the very bosom of his hills.

But of all the poems to which this wonderful season of fruitfulness gave birth, perhaps the one which we would least willingly let die is the " Ode"—to which we hardly require to add its long-sounding descriptive title, " On the Intimations of Immortality." Most of the other odes in the English language are prized for their fidelity to the rules of an exotic production, but no one has any leisure to think of Strophe or Antistrophe, when this divinest utterance of modern poetry carries him away on its sea of silver melody and wondrous thought. The child, the new-born creature, unfamiliar with earth, " trailing clouds of glory " from the unknown whence he came, and feeling all about him a world not realised, the dangerous deadly sphere in which he is to play out the part which, with a thousand joyous mockeries and gleams of bewildering insight, he rehearses unawares—stands out before us, the tenderest unconscious hero of humankind. Never was there so wonderful a picture drawn all in lines of light : and never were thoughts so profound revealed in a more limpid strain of perfect poetry. If it may be permitted to bring in a personal recollection, the writer can scarcely refrain from recalling the silent uncommunicated rapture with which this wonderful poem swept into her mind in the early years, when feeling is more near the infinite than maturity can realise. Books were not to be had in those days at every corner, and she still retains, with a half-amused, half-regretful tenderness, a little sheaf of yellow leaflets, how carefully written out ! containing the " Ode " which was a revelation of inconceivable beauty and emotion.

> " The thought of our past years in me doth breed
>   Perpetual benediction : not indeed
>   For that which is most worthy to be blest ;

 Delight and liberty, the simple creed
Of childhood, whether busy or at rest,
With new-fledged hope still fluttering in his breast:—
          Not for these I raise
          The song of thanks and praise ;
          But for those obstinate questionings
          Of sense and outward things,
          Fallings from us, vanishings ;
          Blank misgivings of a Creature
Moving about in worlds not realised,
High instincts before which our mortal Nature
Did tremble like a guilty thing surprised :
          But for those first affections,
          Those shadowy recollections,
     Which, be they what they may,
Are yet the fountain light of all our day,
Are yet a master light of all our seeing ;
     Uphold us, cherish, and have power to make
Our noisy years seem moments in the being
Of the eternal Silence : truths that wake,
          To perish never ;
Which neither listlessness, nor mad endeavour,
          Nor Man nor Boy,
Nor all that is at enmity with joy,
Can utterly abolish or destroy !
          Hence in a season of calm weather,
          Though inland far we be,
Our souls have sight of that immortal sea
          Which brought us hither
          Can in a moment travel thither,
And see the children sport upon the shore,
And hear the mighty waters rolling evermore."

Wordsworth lived a gentle, retired, and dignified life
among his " native mountains " from this time forward.
He was what so few poets are—or perhaps it is more
just to say were—prosperous and well off during all the
rest of his life ; his own steadfast and determined nature
forcing, one might almost think, the gifts of the external
world, as well as that full acknowledgment of his genius
which his age was at first so unwilling to give. The
reader who loves Wordsworth will, in most cases, prefer

not to read his own commentaries upon himself, a subject upon which he was too solemnly eloquent ; and we have already endeavoured to point out in what way the poetical theories with which he began his life were strained and unnatural. He kept to them in so far as to make the hero of his longest poem a Pedlar ; but the language of the " Excursion " is as far from the bald simplicity which he recommended at the outset, as it is possible to imagine ; and that poem, as well as the " Prelude," is markedly addressed, not to the " huts where poor men lie," but to a specially elect and chosen audience—the few who are able to appreciate efforts so continuous and lofty.

We refrain from any criticism of the poems on classical subjects which, by some critics, are invested, it seems to us, with an entirely undue importance, principally because they *are* upon classical subjects — those themes which have been proclaimed so well and so much by their own poets as to leave little inducement, we think, for their re-treatment by the sons of an age so remote and so different. The " Laodameia," however beautiful, shows none of the characteristic qualities of Wordsworth, and it is Wordsworth, and not an abstract poet, whom we are here to deal with. Neither shall we attempt to wade through the waste of sonnets in which, with painfully systematic zeal, he has expressed a multitude of sentiments, not very original, upon various subjects. Some dozen of these are worthy of the highest rank, and will recur at once to the recollection of the reader ; the rest we would willingly dispense with altogether. But our venerated poet was no critic. He had a certain religious regard for his work, whatever it was, and sometimes liked the worst best, with a simplicity of human foolishness which might endear his wisdom to us, if it were not uncomfortably mixed with that solemn egotism which was his greatest defect.

Wordsworth lived to be acknowledged the greatest living name in literature, and at the end of his life he received that graceful tribute of public honour, the laureateship, which before then had been soiled by much ignoble use, but which Southey had gathered out of the mud, and which has been actually as well as formally, the meed of the greatest since then. He lived a prosperous, and serene, and untroubled life until the end, when natural sorrows clouded over " the eye which had kept watch o'er man's mortality." When it came to be his turn to see his best-beloved go to the grave before him, the poet bore his sorrows with a noble and touching patience. He died in April 1850, the last of the great brotherhood—at once of his own companions and of the younger band who, among them, had raised the end of one century and the beginning of the next, into a great poetic age—one of the greatest in English history; he survived all, as he was in many respects the greatest and most influential of all—the strongest nature and the most steadfast soul.

Of Coleridge we can make no such record. While Wordsworth was devoting himself to his great art, in determined withdrawal from everything that he thought likely to debase or distract his mind, Coleridge was wandering uneasily from place to place, seldom appearing in the spot which he had chosen as his home. His health was the reason commonly alleged, and it is added by some that the constant society of so well-regulated and orderly a companion as Southey, was more than this much-proposing and little-accomplishing soul could bear. But at least he was constantly absent: for two years in Malta, as has been seen; at other times in different parts of England; sometimes in London, fitfully engaging in newspaper work; neither well nor happy at any time; falling daily more and more under the sway of a deadly

habit; losing hope, and courage, and self-respect; a sort
of discrowned king, never without the signs of inalienable
royalty, but without a subject, even in himself; with all
his learning wasted, and all his wonderful faculties
running to seed. In 1809 we find him at Grasmere,
under the inspiring influence of Wordsworth, and there
he published, through the hands of a local bookseller,
The Friend, a little weekly periodical, in which his own
fine and abstruse thinkings, and the contributions of his
brethren and immediate disciples in literature, made up
a publication as entirely caviare to the general as ever
issued from the press. It lived for some months, appearing at irregular intervals, and was, so far as popularity
went, an entire failure, which, indeed, might have been
looked for. In 1810 he finally left the Lakes and his
family, returning to them no more. It was with Mr.
Basil Montague, the genial friend and helper of so many
men of letters, whose house and heart were open to
generations of writers, from Godwin down to Carlyle, and
who was not always recompensed by the gratitude of his
guests, that Coleridge went to London, and he lived for
some time in the house of this kind friend and brother,
whose society and care were, no doubt, supposed likely
to be salutary to the unfortunate poet. For the next
half-dozen years we can follow Coleridge but dimly
through the shadows of his unhappy life. Now and then
he reappeared in the daylight, notably in 1813, when
his tragedy " Remorse " was produced at Drury Lane.
It had been submitted to Sheridan many years before,
but had been by him laughed out of hearing. It was to
Lord Byron now that its reception was owing. He, then
in the height of his early popularity, a young demigod,
beloved alike of fashion and genius, was all-influential in
the theatre, for which, after the failure of the competition
(which produced the genial mockery of the " Rejected

Addresses "), he had been requested to write an opening Ode—and was generally in the ascendant. He had libelled Coleridge in the " English Bards and Scotch Reviewers," and was to do so again : but though he was so little qualified to judge the poet as to speak of the author of the " Ancient Mariner," as " to turgid ode and tumid stanza dear," yet his deeds were better than his words, and it was his generous interposition which procured this drama a hearing. " The success was immediate and decisive, and the play had a run of twenty nights ;" then, to all appearance, it dropped from the stage, and was heard of no more. It was published, however, shortly afterwards, and a large number sold at once. During this period, too, Coleridge reappeared as a lecturer discoursing upon poetry—upon Shakspeare, and Milton, and the earlier dramatists—lectures which were attended by some eager auditors, intent on seeing, almost more than hearing, the poet, one of whom was young Keats. Crabb Robinson's account of these lectures is, however, entirely in keeping with the melancholy circumstances and mind of the poet. " I do hope he will have steadiness to go on with the lectures to the end. It would be so great a point gained if he could but pursue one object without interruption," a friend writes of him to this deeply concerned and interested spectator ; and Robinson, in return, furnished a description of the curious irregularity and inequality of these performances. Of one, he says that Coleridge " surpassed himself in the art of talking in a very interesting way without speaking at all on the subject announced. According to advertisement, he was to lecture on ' Romeo and Juliet,' and Shakspeare's female characters. Instead of this, he began with a defence of school-flogging, in preference, at least, to Lancaster's mode of punishing, without pretending to find the least connection between that topic and poetry.

. . . On another occasion, however, he declaimed with great eloquence about love without wandering from his subject. . . . As evidence of splendid talent, original thought, and rare powers of expression and fancy, they are all his admirers can wish; but as a discharge of his undertaking, a fulfilment of his promise to the public, they give his friends great uneasiness." " He has about one hundred and fifty hearers on an average," says the same writer. Thus the light which was in him gleamed fitfully, showing chiefly its own eclipse. In 1814 he visited Bristol for the same purpose of delivering lectures, and there his unhappy condition aroused the pained and troubled comments of his faithful friend Cottle, he who had been the providence of his youth. It is very natural that Coleridge's family should have resented this good man's maunderings on so painful a subject: and yet it would have been a very unusual stretch of virtue had he refrained, and he had, he assures us, the injunction of Coleridge himself, always full of that facile but ineffectual penitence which rends the hearts of friends, always pious and desirous of affording help to his fellow-creatures, to justify the publication of the poet's own melancholy letter as a warning and an example to others. In 1816 this painful period of his life came to an end, and he was received into the house of Mr. Gillman at Highgate, who treated him at once as a medical attendant and devoted friend, and procured him some comfort and tranquillity in the later years of his life. His " Christabel " was published only at this period; but it had been so well known in literary circles before,—so often read, recited, and quoted,—that its final introduction to the public seems but an insignificant incident in the story of this wonderful poem. It had instant and immense acceptance among all who loved poetry. The easy strain, the facile verse, which Scott had so brilliantly, yet so simply,

introduced, and which almost every poet of the age had
used more or less, came to its apotheosis in this mystic
and lovely spiritual romance.   The " consecration and the
poet's dream ; " the "light that never was on sea and
land," had at last penetrated through and through this
artless web of poetry and given it its highest development.
During these latter years in the sheltered retreat at
Highgate, where he was at least free from the storms and
shames of an unhappy existence, Coleridge collected and
published several volumes, and in 1828 an entire edition
of his poetical works ; but all his finest utterances belong
to the period of his early intercourse with Wordsworth.
" The Ancient Mariner," " Christabel," and that exquisite
poem called " Love," which of all the others is, perhaps, the
one which his true disciples like the best, belong to these
all-golden and hopeful morning hours.   Had he never
written a line in poetry after the beginning of the century,
it would not have materially affected his fame.   His
" Biographia Literaria," and several of his philosophical
works, belonged to the painful period, between 1810 and
1816, when his fortunes were at the lowest, and his life
the saddest.   These were published after he had reached
the final haven of his declining days.

There is, however, no aspect of Coleridge's life so
well known to the public as that of his later life at
Highgate—we cannot call it his old age, for he died at
sixty-two on the edge only of that period.   There, in his
seclusion, he drew all manner of intelligences towards
him ; enthusiastic young men went out to sit at his feet
——Edward Irving, John Sterling—the former taking
with him a certain young Scotsman in the rough husk
of a genius still undeveloped, future preacher of Hero-
worship, but in himself little addicted to that religion,
and judging all things with a sort of relentless Gothic
eyesight, intolerant of all that was unusual to him.   But

Carlyle's description of the poet-sage, if not reverential, is in all its circumstances more picturesque and vivid than any other we can supply to the reader. "Coleridge," he says, "sat on the brow of Highgate Hill in those years, looking down on London and its smoke-tumult like a sage escaped from the inanity of life's battle, attracting towards him the thoughts of innumerable brave souls still engaged there." He of whom Southey first of all, and afterwards the Wordsworths, and such differing witnesses as gossipy Mr. Cottle in his Bristol shop, and young Hazlitt acute and bitter, had but one word to say in the days of his strength—that never man had produced such an impression of infinite faculty and many-sided soul—appeared under a different light to the natural scepticism, the half-defiant, all-inquiring gaze of the young and stubborn Scot. He continues :—

"He was thought to hold, he alone in England, the key of German and other Transcendentalisms; knew the sublime secret of believing by the 'reason' what the 'understanding' had been obliged to fling out as incredible; and could still, after Hume and Voltaire had done their best and worst with him, profess himself an orthodox Christian, and say and print to the Church of England, with its singular old rubrics and surplices at Allhallowtide, *Esto Perpetua.* A sublime man; who alone in those dark days had saved his crown of spiritual manhood; escaping from the black materialisms and revolutionary deluges with 'God, Freedom, Immortality' still his : a king of men. The practical intellects of the world did not much heed him, or carelessly reckoned him a metaphysical dreamer; but to the rising spirits of the young generation he had this dusky sublime character, and sat there as a kind of Magus, girt in mystery and enigma : his Dodona oak-grove, Mr. Gillman's house at Highgate—whispering strange things, uncertain whether oracles or jargon. The Gillmans did not encourage much company or excitation of any sort round their sage ; nevertheless, access to him, if a youth did reverently wish it, was not difficult. He would stroll about the pleasant garden with you, sit in the pleasant rooms of the place—perhaps take you to his own peculiar room high up, with a rearward view, which was the chief view of all. A really charming outlook in fine weather. Close at hand wide sweep of flowery leafy gardens, their few houses mostly hidden, the very chimney pots veiled under blossomy umbrage, flowed gloriously down hill, gloriously issuing in wide-tufted undulating plain-country, rich in all charms of field and town. Waving blooming country of the brightest green, dotted all over with handsome villas, handsome groves, crossed by roads and human traffic here inaudible or heard only as a musical hum, and behind all, swam, under olive-tinted haze, the illimitable limitary ocean of London, with its domes and steeples definite in the sun, big Paul's and the many memories attached to it hanging high over all. Nowhere of its kind could you see a grander prospect on a bright summer day with the set of the air going southward—southward, and so draping with the city smoke not *you* but the city. Here for hours would Coleridge talk concerning all conceivable or inconceivable things ; and liked nothing better than to have an intelligent, or failing that, even a silent and patient human listener. He distinguished himself to all that ever heard him as the most surprising talker extant in this world—and to some small minority, by no means to all, as the most excellent. The good man, he was now getting old, towards sixty perhaps ; and gave you the idea of a life that had been full of sufferings ; a life heavy laden, half vanquished, still swimming painfully in seas of manifold physical and other bewilderment. Brow and head were round and of massive weight, but the face was flabby and irresolute. The deep eyes of a light hazel were as full of sorrow as of inspiration ; confused pain looked mildly from them, as in a kind of mild astonishment. . . . I have heard Coleridge talk with eager musical energy two stricken hours, his face radiant and moist, and communicate no meaning whatsoever to any individual of his hearers, certain of whom, I for one, still kept eagerly listening in hope ; the most had long before given up and formed, if the room were large enough, secondary humming groups of their own. . . . You swam and fluttered in the mistiest, wide, unintelligible deluge of things, for most part in a rather profitless uncomfortable manner. Glorious islets too I have seen rise out of the haze ; but they were few, and soon swallowed in the general element again. Balmy sunny islets, islets of the blest and the intelligible ;—on which occasions those secondary humming groups would all cease humming and hang breathless upon the eloquent words, till once your islet got wrapt in the mist again, and they would recommence humming. Eloquent, artistically expressive words you always had ; piercing radiances of a most subtle insight came at intervals ; tones of noble pious sympathy, recognisable as pious, though strangely coloured, were never wanting long."

This is not a reverential description, but no doubt, taking into consideration the keen doubting unawed vision of the gazer, coming from latitudes so different, a true one, and amazingly vivid and real. There are still traces even in this picture of the same man who entranced the audience in the stage-coach, and made known his identity wherever he went by holding all bystanders suspended, as was the image in those days, on his breath.

He died in 1834 still under the charge of the pair to whose very name a grateful sentiment clings. After all, it is but little Coleridge has left behind him of real importance, less than any one of his contemporaries : and yet for fine poetical fame, the highest ethereal crown which mankind can bestow, there is no one in English literature who has gained a more delicate laurel, or one more unanimously accorded. Far more subtle and spontaneous in the intuitions of spiritual life than Wordsworth, with a sense of mystic meaning infinitely more penetrating and universal than Shelley, there are no others to be compared to him in his generation. The three poems upon which his reputation rests are among the most perfect of the great productions of the age.

WILLIAM WORDSWORTH, born 1770 ; died 1850.

Published Descriptive Sketches, 1793.
    Lyrical Ballads, 1 vol., 1798.
    Lyrical Ballads, 2 vols., with many additions, 1800.
    Poems in two volumes, 1807.

        These included, among many others of his finest poems, the "Ode," and the "Leech-Gatherer" called "Resolution and Independence."

    Tract on the "Convention of Cintra," 1809.
    Contributions to the *Friend*, 1809-10.
    (Advice to the Young ; Essays on Epitaphs.)

Published Guide to the Lake Country, 1810.

The Excursion, 1814.

The White Doe of Rylstone, 1815.

Peter Bell (written in 1799), 1819.

The Waggoner, 1819.

Sonnets on the River Duddon, 1819.

Memorials of a Tour on the Continent (chiefly Sonnets), 1822.

Ecclesiastical Sonnets, 1823.

Yarrow Revisited and other Poems, 1835.

Poems chiefly of Early and Later Years (including Memorials of Tour in Italy), 1842.

The Prelude (after the Poet's death), 1850.

SAMUEL TAYLOR COLERIDGE, born 1772 ; died 1834.

Published Moral and Political Lectures ; Conciones ad Populum, etc., 1795.

The Watchman, 1796.

Poems on Various Subjects, 1796.

Second edition, with additions and various poems of Charles Lamb and Charles Lloyd, 1797; third edition, 1803.

Ode to the Departing Year, 1796.

Rhyme of the Ancient Mariner (in Lyrical Ballads), 1798.

Various Poems, including Fire, Famine, and Slaughter, in *Morning Post ;* reprinted in pamphlet form, 1800.

Translation of Wallenstein, 1800.

Poems originally published in *Morning Post,* reprinted in Southey's Annual Anthology, 1800.

The Friend, 1809-10 ; another edition in 1818.

The Remorse, 1813.

Christabel, 1816.

A Lay Sermon, 1816.

Another Lay Sermon, 1817.

Biographia Literaria, 1817.

Sibylline Leaves, 1817.

Zapolya, 1817.

Aids to Reflection, 1825.

First collected edition of Poetical and Dramatic works, 1828 ; another, 1829.

On the Constitution of Church and State, 1830.

CHAPTER VIII.

ROBERT SOUTHEY——WALTER SAVAGE LANDOR.

THERE are few stranger accidents in the history of literature than that which has linked the name of Southey
to those of the two greater brethren whom we have just
discussed. His early association with Coleridge ended
so soon that the two poets could have had but little
influence upon each other, and though their connection
by marriage kept up relations of friendship between
them, their minds were as different as day and night.
With Wordsworth, Southey had no early connection, and
though a sober friendship united them in maturer life,
there was no conjoint work, or even literary sympathy,
to justify the common appellation of the Lake Poets, by
which they were known, in spite of many protests, all
their lives, and still to some degree continue to be known.
It was not, however, only in poetry that the new age had
developed new powers. A new school of critics had
sprung up side by side with the new poets, animated by
such an impulse of opposition and resistance as gave new
force to the name and new importance to the profession.
It was their business to require from the men of genius,
whom they did their best to quell and overwhelm and
keep in bounds, full proof of their divine commission, and
this ungracious but useful office they performed *con amore*,
fighting every step of that way to Fame, of which they

were the volunteer and often officious guardians. It was in the exercise of this task, and among other skilful ways of depreciating and offending the objects of their care, that the above nickname (always so easy a weapon and so generally popular) was invented. Afterwards there was a " Satanic school," which was not equally effective, but yet had its day.

To compare the philosophical and dreamy Coleridge, with his rare and strange poetical inspirations, the austere and self-absorbed Wordsworth, with his obstinate poetic creed—and that able, precise, and laborious intelligence, always busy and never exhausted, which distinguished the best man of the three, the support and stay of all who trusted in him, the noble, generous, and blameless Southey, is an invidious task. It is not only that one star differeth from another star in glory, but that there is a difference of kind more visible now than when they stood together, putting a gulf between them which neither of them was aware of, and which the critics themselves, for all their acuteness of vision, missed. In life, neither of these, his great contemporaries, was Southey's equal ; but in poetry there can be little doubt that this most admirable and excellent of men occupied a very different and a very much lower standing ground. We make the admission with a certain grudge and sense of injustice in the arrangements of Providence. Why should not the most excellent have had the highest gifts ? but there is no answer to this question. Southey bore the burdens of all connected with him. He was the friend of all who were in need ; his purse and his heart were alike open to all suppliants, and his helping hand never wanting to any one whom he could aid. He worked early and late, well and ill, with a cheerful devotion which no man has ever surpassed, and, though not wiser than other men, was better than other men, both in purity of soul and noble use of his talents. But he did not get the prize from heaven. In his excellence he was left low down in the lower room, and no one said to him, "Come up higher." The others were not so learned nor so pains-taking, any more than they were as good. One of them wasted his existence, and was unfaithful to all his duties. The other shut himself up within himself, within the closest domestic circle, and, doing his duty there, did no more. Strange favouritism of heaven! They did not deserve the supreme gift as he did who never got it. But Southey, let us be thankful, was quite unaware of the injustice. He was as sure as either of them of his own immortality,—much more sure, indeed, than Cole-ridge, whose faulty life and lost opportunities kept him humble. "One overwhelming propensity," the excellent Southey says, "has formed my destiny, and marred all prospects of rank or wealth; but it has made me happy, and *it will make me immortal*. . . . Every gener-ation will afford me some half-dozen admirers, and the everlasting column of Dante's praise does not stand upon a wider basis." Blessed delusion! he went to his grave with it; but it is strange and humiliating to the interested bystander, who cannot but love Southey, to note the extraordinary misapprehension of his own powers and absence of literary discrimination, which could make it possible for him to compare his fame with the "everlast-ing praise" of Dante. It was well for his own comfort, however, that he could do so.

Southey parted company with Coleridge when he went to Lisbon in 1795. He was there for six months, and on his return plunged at once into the life of a hard-working writer. A similar kind of appointment to that which enabled Coleridge to keep up his cottage at Nether Stowey, an engagement upon a daily newspaper, with chance contributions to the *Monthly Magazine*, etc.,

afforded to Southey a little certainty of income,—a
certainty supplemented by the annuity of £160 a year
secured to him by his friend Mr. Wynn on coming of age.
Nearly the same sum was given to Coleridge by the
Wedgewoods ; indeed, all the three poets had a sustenance
steady if small, thus provided for them by private friendship, a fine relic of the days when the fortunes of the
poet became the special care of his patron.   We doubt
whether the same generosity would occur to any one now.
Southey wandered for some time before deciding upon
his home.   He began to read law reluctantly, having no
liking for anything but literature.   Finally, in 1802,
after another visit to Portugal, and much wandering, he
settled in the Lake district, where Coleridge was then
living.   Though they had fallen so much apart, they still
kept up an affectionate friendship, and Southey had
repeatedly planned in his letters the possibility of a
joint household somewhere in the south, where he then
hoped to get diplomatic employment.   " I shall have so
little to do," he writes, speculating on this subject in
something of the spirit of the old Pantisocracy, " that my
time may be counted my own, and our joint amusements
will easily supply all expenses."   These joint amusements
were the sonnets and occasional verses which made the
Morning Post and *Courier* of the period memorable.   But
no diplomatic appointment turned up ; and after a second
visit to Portugal, and a gradual increase of literary
engagements, all ideas of any profession but literature
were relinquished.   Coleridge had settled for the time in
Greta Hall, on the banks of the Greta, near Keswick, and
the description which he sent of his house to his brother-
in-law was very tempting to a poet.   It was a house
" on a low hill," commanding beautiful views, the river
Greta winding round the slope, and " catching the evening lights in front of the house."   Before it lay " a

giant's camp, an encamped army of tent-like mountains."
Southey had been wandering about Wales, verifying the
scenery of his Madoc, when this description reached him.
He had just failed in securing a house there, and
Coleridge's company was a great temptation to him, as
that of her sister was to his wife. They went accordingly, though with some doubts, to the north country,
and there remained for the rest of their lives ; there all
their children were born, except the first, who died
shortly after her birth : and all Southey's joys and
sorrows and his endless labours, and his life of cheerful
excellence, belong to this odd establishment, where there
were three families under one roof, besides the quaint
little bachelor apartments of the owner of the house, who
occupied one portion of it with his housekeeper till his
death.

Coleridge's wanderings have been already described.
He was never at home for any lengthened period ; and
in 1810 finally disappeared from their society ; but
the three Bristol beauties, who had married the young
enthusiasts on the eve of starting for the Pantisocracy
on the banks of the Susquehannah, were all collected
there,—Mrs. Lovell, a widow, with one child ; Sara, once
celebrated in tenderest verse, but soon left behind, with
her beautiful girl and her infant boys, not much better
than a widow, though her husband lived. The happy
one was Edith Southey, whose tender and faithful mate
never left her side when he could help it, and was the
kind brother and helper of the others, the head of this
strangely mingled household. Here brothers, friends,
everybody who wanted a temporary home, came as to the
headquarters of the clan. When the old landlord died,
it was a matter of course that his old housekeeper, the
beloved of the children, should stay, a member of the
overflowing household, till the end. Why should any

one leave it?   Kindness and love were in the house and
radiated from it.   Southey was always busy, but never
too busy to have a cheerful greeting for all who came,
and that tender courtesy of ready attention even to the
irrelevant, which is the genius of the heart.   There is
no more beautiful sight than that of this good man in the
midst of the group, the greater part of which, strictly
speaking, did not belong to him——the children who had
but a secondary claim at the best, and yet were all his,
mingled and undistinguishable, in the love and cheerful
warmth of the domestic centre, the lovely and serious
Sara Coleridge growing up the very twin of his own gay
Edith; and, among the rest, that strange and elvish boy,
"whose fancies from afar were brought,"——the quaint
little "Moses" of whom Southey's letters when he is
absent are full, the unfortunate and gentle Hartley, whose
life was wrecked by some mysterious reflection of the
sins of his fathers before he was born.   The house, with
that "encampment of mountains" before it, and the
river at its feet catching the evening lights: the book-
shelves gradually spreading over all the rooms: and the
happy voices and soft family commotion surrounding that
heart of gentle silence and tranquillity, the study——is
delightful to think of.   Sorrow came to it, bitter and
hard to bear; but yet for years a happier home, a more
ideal shelter and refuge and centre of all the charities,
was not on earth.

Southey had taken no part in the "Lyrical Ballads,"
nor does he seem, any more than the merest Philistine
of the moment, to have understood or appreciated this
publication, which its authors were so anxious to prove
to be a new departure.   He scarcely knew Wordsworth,
indeed, at the time of its publication; and Coleridge's
devotion to the society of his new friend had probably
kept him apart from his older connections, and given a

shade of prejudice to their minds.   A certain impatience
and almost intolerance of their crusade against the
previous faith and poetical dogmas of England, appears
by times, involuntarily, unconsciously, in Southey.   He
was so busy a man, and had his mind so teeming with
schemes and plots for new work, that the obstinate return
of Wordsworth to the charge, and his determination to
conquer with the very same volume, little enlarged, which
had provoked such a storm of disapproval, must naturally
have exasperated the buoyant and fertile mind which had
so much always ready to pour forth.   Coleridge, he
thought, had made " the clumsiest attempt at German
mysticism I ever saw " in the " Ancient Mariner ; " and
he had scarcely patience with the men who, full of genius
as he knew them to be, did so little, while he was overflowing with work.   As for the revolution which was
finally accomplished by that publication, Southey was
unacquainted with it.   He is like a man arranging his
books or classifying his antiquities in a library or museum
while governments are being overthrown and kingdoms
upset outside.   He knows nothing about these revolutions ; he had not been aware of the want of them, and
he did not see the effect when it was accomplished.   In
Wordsworth's theories at a later period he partially agreed,
but he never seems to have perceived that, side by side
with the busy wheels of his always working imagination, a power greater than his own was changing altogether
the aspect of affairs.

Southey, however, might have taken credit, had he
been aware of what was going on, for the fact that he
alone of all his contemporaries had never bowed the knee
to Baal.   Both Wordsworth and Coleridge had begun to
write in the recognised poetical style, in the couplets and
mechanic tune of which Cowper had complained even
while employing it.   But Southey, so far, had been

original from the beginning; he had spurned that
bondage. He was of an orthodox nature, notwithstanding his youthful vagaries; but at the same time he had
less reverence than the more truly poetical spirits, and
evidently felt no bond of allegiance to those who had
gone before. His mind had the independence of extreme
energy and activity, an independence which was at once
a fault and a virtue—a fault because it gave him over-
confidence in his own way, and made his own taste his
only real standard. Thus he had no eye for what was
wanting at the crisis, no consciousness of a change of
current in the stream of literature. He had got into a
wild eddy of his own, and was ready to stake his existence on its flow: but he did not even perceive the sweep
of the larger river. He was, indeed—at a time, so to
speak, of great legislative changes—only a rebel and
nothing more. By the fact that he preferred freedom—
nay, lawlessness—for himself, he gave a certain aid to
the final strokes of the emancipators, but inadvertently
and without any real sympathy in their work. He
himself never could have belonged to any school, unless
he had originated one. We could imagine him, indeed,
at the head of a band of young *collaborateurs*, setting
them literary tasks by the dozen, and never so pleased as
when devising plots and constructing skeletons of endless
dramas, epics, fables, and histories, plans which only the
limit of individual faculty prevented him from carrying
out himself; but it is impossible to conceive of him as
working in harmony with other equal or superior minds,
or in subordination to a greater purpose than his own.

The following extract from a letter to one of his
faithful friends will show how his " barmy noddle " was
continually at work :—

" I have some plots maturing in my head, but none ripe. My
wish is to make something better than love the mainspring, and I

have one or two sketches ; but all my plots seem rather calculated
to produce one or two great scenes than a general effect.   My mind
has been turned too much to the epic, which admits a longer action
and passes over the uninteresting parts.

   " The escape of the Pythoness with a young Thessalian seems
to afford most spectacle.   If you have ' Diodorus Siculus ' at hand,
and will refer to Lib. 16, p. 428, you may find all the story, for I
know no more than the fact.   Pedro the Just pleases me best ; this
is my outline " (then follows a detailed description) . . . " This is
a half-plot, you see, capable of powerful scenes, but defective in
general interest, I fear.   I have thought of a domestic story, founded
on the persecution under Queen Mary.   To this my objection is
that I cannot well conclude it without burning my hero, or making
the queen die very *à propos*, which is cutting the knot and not
letting the catastrophe necessarily arise from previous circumstances.
However, the story pleases me, because I have a fine Catholic
woman and her confessor in it.

   " For feudal times something might be made, perhaps, of a fief
(feud ?) with a wicked lord, or of the wardship oppressions ; but
what will young Colman's play be ?   It may forestall me.

   " Then I have thought of Sparta, of the Crypteia, and a Helot
hero ; but this would be interpreted into sedition.   Of Florida and
the customary sacrifice of the first-born male ; in this case to have
a European father and an escape.   Sebastian comes into my thoughts,
and Beatrix of Milan accused by Oronbello on the rack and executed.
A Welsh or English story would be better ; but fix where I will, I
will be well acquainted with country, manners, etc. . . . You have
these views as they float before me."

   It is scarcely possible that a man with all these plans
in his head should have had much sympathy with the
method of the others, who meant to change the face of
literature with " Alice Fell " and " Lucy Gray."   He
went along his nimble way while they were musing,
always in earnest, always at full strain of production,
elaborating notes when he was not writing poetry, and
with his eyes ever open on old bookstalls and new
publications for facts, which might verify the details of
his old subjects, or suggest new.   His workmanship
was as conscientious as his invention was boundless.
" Yesterday I finished ' Madoc,' thank God," he writes,

" and thoroughly to my satisfaction. But I have resolved on one great laborious and radical alteration. It was my design to identify ' Madoc ' with ' Mango Capoc,' the legislator of Peru. In this I have totally failed ; therefore ' *Mango Capoc is to be the hero of another poem*, and instead of carrying ' Madoc' down the Marañon I shall follow the more probable opinion and land him in Florida. Here, instead of the Peruvians, who have no striking manners for my poem, we get among the wild North American Indians. On their customs and superstitions facts must be grounded and woven into the work, spliced so neatly as not to betray the junction. So much for ' Madoc ;' it is a great work done, and my brain is now ready for the Dom Daniel, the next labour in succession." Thus the wheels go round and one subject succeeds another.

Southey accomplished in the midst of all his other labours five long and important poems—three belonging to the vague world of mediæval life, where picturesque effects abound, and where fact is capable of transmutation—and two to the region of pure fable. Through all a serious and lofty purpose flows, though with a certain monotony. In all we are called to attend a heroic deliverer, or still more heroic penitent, through all that the powers of evil can do against him. In " Joan of Arc " the struggle is single. It is against the enemies of her country. But Madoc, the emigrant prince, has two phases, and after we have got him safely delivered from trouble in his own country, he has a savage conflict to go through in the new world before his power is established and his colony consolidated. The struggle of " Roderick the Goth " ends only in death. He is a despairing sinner when we see him first on the field of a lost battle ; but soon the most sublime of penitents. In all the motive is the same ; virtue almost superhuman, courage of the most dauntless kind, love of the purest—even Roderick, though it is supposed to have been by the most dastardly of vices that he brought down Count Julian's vengeance and the Moors upon him, is washed white not only by his repentance, but by extenuating circumstances, which take all the darker shades out of his offence, and make it indeed no greater than that of Paolo and Francesca, the pair for whom all the world mourns. There is no divided purpose, no contending sympathies in these poems; they are straightforward moral romances, in which heroic virtue always gains the day. The wild eastern framework of " Thalaba " and " Kehama " gives a new aspect to the same old conclusion, but the purpose is still the same. Here, however, the poet goes wildly into waters unexplored and wastes unknown. They are the productions most characteristic of him, as being like nothing else in the range of English verse. In no way can we show so clearly the difference between Southey and his great contemporaries, as by comparing one of these poems with Coleridge's first memorable production : the purpose of which, professedly, was so to suspend the reader's judgment in respect to probabilities, that the supernatural should take hold of his mind with all the force of reality. To accomplish this he required no magic, no unearthly spells or terrors. " There was a ship, said he "—and forthwith the mists that veil the unseen trembled, and the great spiritual world outside of us—which every human soul is conscious of, or at the least suspects, became somehow apparent in glimpses, in touches, though without either contact or sight, a something wider and stranger than even the wide and terrible sea which opened like a picture before every reader. But Southey's method is not like this. His imagination has nothing to do with common existence, nor can he open those secret portals which go straight

into the darkness.   What he does to awaken our wonder
and our curiosity is to make a wild and strange picture
of life, in which none of the circumstances are recognisable, and fill it with magical appliances not more strange
or unknown than itself.   If we are once persuaded to
take any interest in the romantic existence of a Thalaba,
we can have no difficulty in receiving along with him all
the magicians that plot against him, for they are at least
as real and in no way more unlike ordinary experience
than he.   Here is no question of that contact between
the visible and invisible which at once excites and
bewilders the faculties, and confuses our mind with a
vain endeavour to discriminate, to keep hold upon the
real, while the unreal grows before us in a truth that is
more convincing than fact, yet is fiction.   These are
efforts altogether beyond the simple straightforward
agencies of the lesser poet.   The practical character of
his mind, instead of weakening the romance in him, or
subduing a very wilful and fantastic imagination, sup-
ports both as by an iron framework, working out these
visionary creations into matter of fact details, and making the wildest machinery of invention " practicable."
Thalaba and Kehama are both of the straightforward
character of fairy tales — they are homogeneous, their
most simple figures being as little like ordinary humanity
as the incidents of their career are like the facts of life.
Probability has nothing to do with them ; they are
wildly unreal, but always matter of fact.   Coleridge,
though he holds us breathless, takes no trouble to make
us understand why so many and such terrible penalties
were exacted from the Mariner, and the gentle moral
into which he drops at the end of his mystic narrative
falls upon us with the most confusing sense of incom-
pleteness, without in the least breaking the extraordinary
spell of that dream which is inexplainable—which we

have no wish to have explained. But about Southey
there is no such difficulty. We understand it all
perfectly. There is nothing left for our imagination, no
uncertainty, nothing inadequate or without balance. We
are prepared for all the magicians and the enchantments:
none of these things ever surprise us. Spells are
uttered freely which move earth and heaven; but they
do not move us. We accompany the hero quite placidly
to the foreseen adventure at the end of his career, and
are not in the least astonished even by the Dom Daniel
caves, though Southey, with his usual practical-romantic
and elephantine-humorous style, thinks of setting on foot
a calculation as to how much our earth would be affected
by the destruction of those caverns supposed to lie at its
centre. This was the kind of elaborate joke that pleased
him. At his wildest his foot never abandons the earth.
There is no flight in him, nor is there any world un-
fathomed into which even for a moment he can carry us
in a trance of suspended living, in a lightning gleam of
sudden discovery; nothing of that ethereal kind: but for
sorceries and charms and straightforward magic, there is
nobody like him. He could tell us the very shape of
the shovel with which fuel is piled on to those central
fires.

Kehama is still more matter of fact in its wildness
than Thalaba. We are here in the presence of an almost
almighty man, who, by his magic, is gradually getting
possession not only of earth but heaven. But heaven
and earth are indistinguishable, and our minds are
wearied, not excited, by the monotonous wonders which
accumulate so steadily and fit in so exactly into the
elaborate tale. It is in this poem that one of those few
pieces of verse occurs, which alone, of all Southey's
voluminous works, have taken the ear of the world. Of
the many volumes he has left behind him besides, only

one or two ballads have secured a place in the general
memory, and, so far as we are aware, no child learns, no
memory retains, any of the scenes of Madoc or Roderick,
though some of these are picturesque enough to deserve
a better fate. The address to Love in Kehama, he himself declared to be clap-trap, and resented the selection of
it as an example of the poem; in which he was right
enough, for it is no fair example of the poem, and it does
partake of the nature of clap-trap, that sublimated
mixture of commonplace and sentiment which always
delights the multitude :—

> " They sin who tell us Love can die.
>   With life all other passions fly,
>   All others are but vanity.
> In Heaven Ambition cannot dwell,
> Nor Avarice in the vaults of Hell ;
> Earthly these passions of the Earth,
> They perish where they have their birth ;
>   But Love is indestructible.
>   Its holy flame for ever burneth,
> From Heaven it came, to Heaven returneth ;
>   Too oft on Earth a troubled Guest,
>   At times deceived, at times opprest,
>   It here is tried and purified,
>   Then hath in Heaven its perfect rest :
>   It soweth here with toil and care,
> But the harvest time of Love is there.
>
> Oh ! when a Mother meets on high
>   The Babe she lost in infancy,
> Hath she not then, for pains and fears,
> The day of woe, the watchful night,
> For all her sorrow, all her tears,
>   An over-payment of delight ?"

There are many Englishmen, not too ignorant, who
know this and nothing more, of Robert Southey's long
and elaborate poem, which he constructed with such care,
and for which he hoped not the vulgar fame of popularity,
but an audience fit though few, extending downward

through the generations. The reader will feel a certain shame yet pleasure to know that in his own mind he had no doubt on this point. He believed that his fame would go on increasing and rest upon as wide a basis as Dante's. He chid his friend for calling him the most sublime poet of the age, not that he had any difficulty in accepting the title, but because "both Wordsworth and Landor are at least my equals." Poor Southey! One smiles yet weeps over the delusion.

And it is difficult to believe that Southey aided in any perceptible way in the poetical revolution of the time. His freedom of poetic diction was as entirely unlike that for which Wordsworth contended, as his Oriental magic was like the mystic and visionary insight of Coleridge. The *Edinburgh Review*, in its first number, begins a critical notice of Thalaba by a disquisition upon the style of the *sect*, of which the author of Thalaba was, it believed, "one of the chief apostles and champions," which, while evidently aimed at Wordsworth and his theory, was ludicrously inappropriate to Southey, who had never professed any belief in homeliness of expression, and never abandoned the elevated language usually adopted in poetry. But the critic concludes by a more real identification of the kind of lawlessness in which Southey did indulge. Thalaba, he allows, is entirely free from the simplicities of the "Lyrical Ballads;" but it has at the same time a freedom of its own, much more extravagant in license, and still less justified by precedent.

"The first thing that strikes the reader of Thalaba," says Jeffrey (after he has ended his discourse upon the peculiarities of a totally different style), "is the singular structure of the versification, which is a jumble of all the measures that are known in English poetry (and a few more), without rhyme, and without any sort of regularity in their arrangement. . . . Every combination of different measures is apt to perplex and disturb the reader who is not familiar with it, and we are never reconciled to a sentence of a new structure till we have accustomed our ear to it by two or three repetitions. This is the case even where we have the assistance of rhyme to direct us in our search after regularity, and where the definite form and appearance of a stanza assures us that regularity is to be found. When both of these are wanting, it may be imagined that our condition will be still more deplorable, and a compassionate author might even excuse us if we were unable to distinguish this kind of verse from prose. . . . The author, however, entertains a different opinion of it. . . . He is persuaded that its melody is more obvious and perceptible than that of our vulgar measures. ' One advantage,' says Mr. Southey, ' this metre assuredly possesses,—the dullest reader cannot distort it into discord ; he may read it with a *prose mouth*, but its flow and fall will still be perceptible.'"

The writer proceeds with characteristic malice to quote various passages in which "the flow and fall" are very confusing and eccentric. Thus Southey demonstrates once more what we have called, for want of a better term, the imaginative matter-of-factness of his mind. It was not for him to see the beauty that lay in the simplest untaught phrases of nature, which Wordsworth, though with many mistakes and much lack of critical discrimination—as well as a certain arrogance of belief that he was the first to see and use them—had divined : but he caught the principle by a side twist, and adopted it in his own way, turning the freedom into lawlessness, yet of this very license making once more a rigid machinery of odd and strained and unnatural measures, distinguished less for beauty than for defiance of all previous custom and harmony. Like all spurious freedom, it seemed to go farther and cut itself adrift more completely from previous bondage than the real and moderate emancipation which is founded upon a genuine principle. It is possible that thus in its dash and bravado of irregularity, the poetry of Thalaba and Kehama assisted, especially with the vulgar, in detaching the last of the chains of Pope and precedent.

This mixture of daring independence and impatience of control, with a certain innate orthodoxy of mind, was very characteristic of Southey. In the method which struck his fancy he would have his fling regardless who opposed him, but he could not construct anything that was not built upon an actual foundation. His scenery and enchantments are not only, as we have said, always "practicable," to use theatrical language, but they are all punctiliously founded on fact, not a cantrip that does not hold its footing on some legend, not a spell that has not been got out of some tradition. Yet the language in which these wild yet perfectly matter-of-fact operations are narrated is beyond rule, and put together in defiance both of precedent and English custom. The measure was his own invention, and he held by it notwithstanding his certainty that it would not please the public, nor commend itself to the English ear. In "Kehama," indeed, he went even farther, mixing this novel measure with interjections of rhyme at his will, and content, if he pleased his own ear, to leave his readers to make the best they could of the unfamiliar medley. This lawlessness and caprice, existing along with the most dutiful subordination to fact and knowledge, are apparent in no other poet of the day. Southey's sympathy with the conventionally wild and weird, with the eccentric and fantastic, wherever he found them, is exceedingly curious. One of the liveliest friendships of his life, the tie which we must shortly discuss, which bound him to Walter Savage Landor, a man whose strange personality has disappeared but a short time since from among us, and who of all the men of his time was perhaps the most lawless, the most undisciplined, the wildest embodiment of human caprice known to recent times, is a case in point.

Southey's other long poems stand upon a different footing; their length itself is perhaps the most remark-

able thing about them. They have faded away notwithstanding some beauty of description and much tenderness
of sentiment, more completely perhaps than they deserve.
" Joan of Arc " is so long-winded in expression, and so
inadequate in conception, that nobody can regret it, and
it was a very youthful production and might well have
been sacrificed had its successors profited by its fall.
But this unfortunately is what they did not do. They
were all composed with care and pains unspeakable.
" So very laboriously was ' Madoc ' re-written and corrected time after time, that I will pledge myself, if you
ask me in any instance why one word stands in the
place of another . . . to give you a reason which will
convince you that I had previously weighed both in the
balance." And Southey went to Wales on purpose to
make himself sure of the scenery, and accumulated as
much learning in his notes as would not have misbecome
the most authentic and dignified history. We can but
say alas ! when all is done. How is it that the effect
does not follow ? . Here there is everything but one
thing, the altar laid, the sacrifice extended, the faggots
ready as in that famous offering prepared by the priests of
Baal : but the divine spark is wanting, and no touch from
heaven sets it alight. Roderick is a little more vigorous,
but the wild and guilty Goth is made into so exemplary
a penitent, and even his crime is so smoothed down and
pared away, that the fierce story is turned into a pathetic
romance of the sentimental-religious kind, and though
happiness is indeed postponed until the heavenly meeting
to which all look forward, it is so certain that the most
exacting stickler for a good end must be satisfied. The
story of Roderick was in favour at this particular moment.
It was taken as the subject of a drama by Savage Landor,
and Scott also made use of one incident in the tale.
Landor's " Count Julian " has been greatly applauded

though little read, but we think we need not hesitate to
give the palm, such as it is, to Southey.   Scott's poem is
little more than a rhetorical account of the revolutions
which were to run over Spain, with special reference to
the heroes of the Peninsular war, and Roderick has very
little to do with it.   But of the two friends who treated
this tragical episode of history, neither has succeeded in
impressing it upon the mind of the reader.   Southey's
poem is one to be read in the leisure of youth, when the
soul has an unbounded capacity for verse, if indeed now
in these days of examinations youth has any more leisure
than the rest of us for reading which "does not pay ;"
but it will never out of that gentle obscurity lay hands
upon any one, or compel the alteration of the world's
verdict.   The half-dozen *âmes d'élite*, who were to be
Southey's ever-increasing audience, and make him immortal, have disappointed his expectations, and all those
labours and hopes, and that ardour of poetic energy, are
but so much waste.   "Few persons will like 'Kehama,'"
he says himself : "everybody will wonder at it ; it will
increase my reputation without increasing my popularity.
A general remark will be, what a pity that I have wasted
so much power."   And then he consoles himself with the
thought of the half-dozen admirers which "every generation" would afford him.   We grudge their non-existence,
and our own inability to be one of them, for Southey's
sake ; but, on earth at least, he never knew : and if he
became aware of it aftewards, probably he had learned by
that time the secret of greater poetry.   We must hope
that *amour propre*, and vanity, whatever may be said for
more lofty sentiments, do not outlive the grave.

   In the very end of the century, when Southey, out of
health and out of spirits, but busy, as always, was preparing for a second expedition to Lisbon, he fell upon a
small and flimsy publication printed "by a small book-

seller at Warwick, in the form of a sixpenny pamphlet,"
which took him by storm. It was called "Gebir," and
was the work of a young man who had shared something
of his own fate at the University, an unruly youth who
had left his college in disgrace, and was already an
Ishmael of private life, with his hand against every man,
and a strong conviction that every man's hand was against
him. The poem was a very strange one, wildly unintelligible and confused, so far as its story goes, but with
gleams of strange beauty in it like "flashes of lightning
at midnight," as Southey afterwards said. It charmed his
congenial mind at once. With eager generosity he hailed
the advent of the new poet, in the *Critical Review*, to
which he was then a contributor, and spread its reputation privately among all his friends. " You will find in
it some of the most exquisite poetry in the language," he
says to one; to another, that "it has miraculous beauties.
I would go a hundred miles to see the anonymous author."
When he went off upon his journey he took " Gebir "
among his few books. A sort of love at first sight moved
him towards the brother-soul who had produced it.
When he heard the name of the author, he cudgelled his
brains to remember him at Oxford, where all he could
recollect was that he had the character of being a "mad
Jacobin." Southey was not clear that there was not
even now something not quite sound in the brain of the
new writer. The poem was like "the miraculous work
of a madman," he said to William Taylor, probably feeling less safe in his enthusiasm with that excellent
bourgeois-critic. For nobody else whom he encountered
in his maturer life does he express the same interest.
When he met at last, several years later, with this friend
of his imagination, he speaks of the encounter with almost
rapturous satisfaction.

"At Bristol I met the man, of all others, whom I was most desirous of meeting—Savage Landor, the author of 'Gebir.' I never saw any one more unlike myself in every prominent part of human character, nor any one who so cordially and instinctively agreed with me on so many of the most important subjects. I have often said before we met that I would walk forty miles to see him, and having seen him, I would gladly walk fourscore to see him again. He talked of 'Thalaba,' and I told him of the series of mythological poems which I had planned, mentioned some of the leading incidents on which they were to have been formed, and also told him for what reason they were laid aside—in plain English, that I could not afford to write them. Landor's reply was, 'Go on with them, and I will pay for printing them, as many as you will write, and as many copies as you please.' 'I had reconciled myself' (says Southey, in a burst of mingled pride and humility, and grateful enthusiasm) 'to my abdication, if the phrase may be allowed, and am not sure that this princely offer has not done me mischief: for it has awakened in me old dreams and hopes which have been laid aside, and a stinging desire to go on, for the sake of showing him poem after poem, and saying—I need not accept your offer, but I have done this because you made it. It is something to be praised by one's peers.'"

This proposal of generous extravagance is the best manner of introduction which we could find for Landor. It was entirely characteristic of the man. Born to a good estate, and with the habits of wealth, he was ready to lavish assistance—at least in intention—upon all with whom he sympathised; and if it seldom came about that his intentions could be realised, that was less his fault than the fault of circumstances, of unkind fortune which deprived him of the means, but never of the will to aid. Landor's biographer, Mr. John Forster, suggests, with great ingenuity, that Southey admired in Landor the terseness and concentration of thought which were so wanting in himself, the rich conglomerate of fancy too closely pressed and heaped together to give fair play to all its beauties, which formed such a contrast to his own natural diffuseness and long-drawn fluency. But the friendship was far more than a merely poetical one, and there can be little doubt, we think, that that latent love of the strange and extravagant, which had so little outlet in his own dutiful and self-controlled life, attracted Southey to the most bizarre of all the many eccentrics who have borne the name of men of letters. There were various more reasonable points of meeting between them; they were both fond of learning, of out-of-the-way studies, of books in the fullest sense of the word—both running over with impetuous activity and independence, both generous and hasty. But the one who had tamed himself into steady work, and weighted himself with unusual burdens, and set aside the fantastic occupation he loved for the less delightful trade by which he lived—felt his imagination emancipated from all these bondages when he saw a man bound by none of them, who had flung off all restraints and behaved as he liked, in a subject and wondering world. From the beginning to the end of his career, Southey seems never to have indulged in a laugh at his friend's wild explosions, or at the ups and downs of a mind so precariously balanced that every breath affected its equilibrium. He was always respectful, even of Landor's wildest vagaries, and treated his fits of overwhelming despair and of passionate offence with equal seriousness, refusing to look at the ridiculous side. Southey was equally loyal to his early friendship for Coleridge, and had the most undoubting faith in his genius, and admiration for it; but Coleridge's weaknesses were not of a kind with which he had any sympathy; and with none of the "peers," whose applause was so sweet to him, did the author of "Thalaba" stand on such an invariably tender and brotherly footing as with this wild and uncontrolled rebel against all the respectabilities. It does not seem too bold an assumption to say that here once more the extravagant-practical, the imaginative matter-of-fact, which was a characteristic of Southey's mind, affected his

liking.   Landor was an embodiment such as he loved of
the poetic nature.   He was romance made into fact, a
sort of naked and unveiled genius, with all the movements
of his inspired soul visible to the eye, and no coverings
of reason or common sense, or any other of the draperies
with which ordinary persons conceal themselves from the
world, to make him like other men.

This extraordinary being was the son of a race of
country gentlemen possessing ease and breeding, and a
comfortable standing ground upon the soil.   His own
father had adopted the profession of a doctor, in those
days when every local district had its own little metropolis, and Warwick was to Warwickshire what London is
now to every county in England.   Dr. Landor occupied
the largest house in the little town, and was more than
a professional man — a person of local importance, heir to
a good estate, the husband in succession of two heiresses,
and altogether a dignified figure in the little world, more
individual, more independent, than any provincial society
now-a-days, to which he belonged.   He had a number·of
children, the eldest of whom was the future poet — a boy
very soon to make himself remarkable, and the greatest
plague that a sober-minded household could have had.
He was heir of entail both to his father's and mother's
property; and no doubt, in his restless vivacity, wild
temper, and budding genius, a very important member of
the doctor's household.   Fabulous stories are told of his
feats of strength and athletic skill, and reckless vagaries
at school; but these seem to merit little attention.   In-
subordinate, undisciplined, yielding to every fancy that
crossed his mind, and plunging into every unreasonable
freak that tempted him, he evidently was, and continued
to be all his life.   His manners were as eccentric as his
mind.   He was greatly given to "riotous laughter," "a
long loud laugh hardly less than leonine," sounding

"higher and higher, peal after peal, in continuous and increasing volleys until regions of sound were reached very far beyond ordinary human lungs;" but the jokes that produced this hurricane of mirth do not seem to have been remarkable for brilliancy. He was distinguished at school, where "Playday for Landor's Latin verses" was a pleasure which his old school-fellows long remembered —but was too fastidious and proud ever to compete for any distinction. At Oxford he spent only a year and a half, retiring compulsorily from his college (Trinity) in consequence of a foolish freak. Nothing can be more strange than to note (once more) how entirely independent of those influences of the Universities which are considered of sovereign importance to English youth was the generation of poets to which Landor belonged. They were none of them devoid of a love of learning, yet of the four mentioned up to this time—Wordsworth, Coleridge, Southey, and Landor—only one took his degree, and he the least learned, the least academical, of all. One wonders if the next generation of poets will be more inclined towards those regions in which they "wear the gown."

Landor was "a mad Jacobin," according to Southey's recollection, in his college days. He was wildly excited, like all the rest, by the French Revolution and American independence, and the fever of freedom that was in the air. "I was about the first student who wore his hair without powder," he says. "'Take care,' said my tutor; 'they will stone you for a republican.'" Southey, too, took this wildly revolutionary step. They were at Oxford at the same time—next door to each other, so to speak, in Balliol and Trinity, the two powderless long-haired youths. Young men of genius, real or supposed, seem to have a curious propensity towards long hair. These haunts of learning are not destitute of them now; but they talk art at this moment more than poetry, and know little of the fervid energy of politics, the more manly inspiration which then fired every youthful soul, and promised Utopias, if not Paradises, of freedom and emancipation to come. Landor was as little disposed to produce his acquirements in public, or to acquire prizes by them, at Oxford as at Rugby. When he composed some more than usually exquisite piece of Latin verse, he read it to his chosen friends, and concealed it from the authorities. His first poem, " Gebir," already alluded to, which belongs to the period after he left college, while he was still only twenty, was composed partly in Latin, with a curious indifference to, or ignorance of, any larger world than that to which Latin would be as acceptable as English. This strange recklessness and contempt of general appreciation was conjoined in after times with much violent and bitter resentment of the indifference of the public, though he had himself so very broadly evidenced his contempt of its opinion. But Landor attained what Southey has failed to attain, if not the appreciation of the general reader, at least a considerable degree of enthusiasm and worship from that higher class which has the honours of literary reputation in its hands—if not, perhaps, the simpler universal crown of fame.

" Gebir" was written in the course of some wild wanderings in Wales, whither he strayed after his college disgrace, when his father's displeasure, and his own excited and restless spirit, made home little attractive to him. It was founded upon an Eastern tale, which he picked up accidentally out of a chance volume ; but, indeed, it is to be hoped that this nameless book gave the incidents more clearly than the young poet interpreted them. Even Southey, the one admirer who stood its champion, did not make any boast of understanding it. He was content to admire the "exquisite

poetry" in it, the gleams of miraculous beauty. His
description of it as " a picture in whose obscure colour-
ing no plan was discoverable, but in whose every distinct
touch the master hand was visible," is sufficiently true.
The common reader is harder to please in this respect
than the expert; he wants to know what he is reading
about, what is the story, and who are the personages
of the tale, if it is a tale. This is only to be gleaned
by intense application, by the "flashes of lightning at
midnight" to which Southey compared the intelligible
passages. By these the reader makes out two male
personages—a mysterious Prince Gebir, who has invaded
Egypt, and an equally mysterious shepherd, his brother,
who is keeping the prince's flocks hard by. How it
was that the flocks accompanied the army in so peaceful
and pastoral a manner is as little explained to us as how
it was that the brother of the prince was the shepherd.
So it is, and that is enough in those realms of fancy and
impetuous youth, above all interpretations. The female
personages are Charoba, Queen of Egypt, a visionary
ancestress, we should suppose, of Cleopatra, and a sea-
nymph, who woos Tamor, the shepherd, by a wrestling
match, and at last carries him off to her home of bliss in
the sea; while Gebir, less fortunate, is killed in the
midst of his bridal feast by a poisoned mantle which
Charoba's nurse has sought in a magical city of antiquity
for the destruction of the invader—the idea being that
peaceful love attains what war and violence forfeit. All
this, however, is beyond the grasp of the ordinary reader,
who has no clue to guide him through the waste; but
" the flashes of lightning " are fine, and if not "the most
exquisite poetry in the language," are still very well
worth looking at. There is very little difference of
opinion as to which passages embody the flashes thus
described. The same quotation reappears wherever this

strange poem is referred to. There is one in particular
in regard to which Landor was very fond of congratu-
lating himself in after days, that Wordsworth had put
it in his pocket and made use of the pretty notion. It
is very pretty, like a delicate bit of workmanship in
alabaster, or some such fairy material, but we doubt
whether it has become one of "the priceless possessions
of English poetry," as Mr. Forster says :—

> " And I have sinuous shells of pearly hue
> Within, and they that lustre have imbibed
> In the sun's palace porch, where when unyoked
> His chariot-wheel stands midway in the wave.
> Shake one, and it awakens, then apply
> Its polished lips to your attentive ear,
> And it remembers its august abodes
> And murmurs as the ocean murmurs there."

This is charmingly pretty, much as the shell itself is,
a curiosity to be put in the daintiest collection—but we
think not much more. Anything which it is so easy to
detach from its setting, and hand about for the admiration of the assistants, is always of doubtful excellence in
poetry. A much finer effect, and one indeed which
touches upon the sublime of human feeling, is that in
which the disappointment of Charoba with one of the
greatest sights in nature—great yet so much less than
infinite imagination expected—is expressed :

> "Past are three summers since she first beheld
> The ocean ; all around the child await
> Some exclamation of amazement : here
> She coldly said, her long-lash't eyes abased,
> Is *this the mighty ocean?* is *this all!*"

The sickness of the wondrous soul which was

> " Capacious then as earth or heaven could hold
> Soul discontented with capacity—"

never able to see, or hear, or fathom half enough to

satisfy its larger requirements, is a perception far beyond
any graceful metaphor or delicate description. It is
more like the mystic insight of Coleridge, to whom all
those depths were native, than anything in Southey's
more precise and limited nature. So far as we are able
to judge, this note struck by chance at twenty is one of
the highest notes Landor ever struck. He produced a
full-grown drama afterwards, a good deal of verse, and
much poetical prose—but he scarcely ever attained this
height of delicate insight again.

"Hardly a hundred copies were sold" of the book,
and De Quincey boasted that he and Southey were the
only two people who had read it, an assertion which,
much as Landor loved Southey, irritated him and his
friends. It was afterwards republished "in a much
better edition, with a Latin translation;" Latin or
English, the vehicle was indifferent to the boy poet,
who perhaps was most confident on the whole of his
powers in the older language, and indifferent to the
limitation which this would have made in his audience
—nay, rather pleased with the limitation. He would
have scorned the vulgarity of a fame which was in everybody's mouth.

The career of Landor was full of storm and tumult,
and it must be added of the strangest sincere braggadocio,
vanity, generosity, and extravagance throughout. When
his father died, he sold all that could be sold of his
inheritance to buy a romantic property in Wales, Llanthony Abbey, where he believed himself to have planted
a million of trees, and began to built an impracticable
never-to-be finished house. Here he quarrelled with all
his surroundings, and did everything that in him lay to
make the neighbourhood too hot to hold him, while at
the same time his hasty and unpractical nature was im-
posed upon on all sides. He soon found the Welsh

peasants about him to be savages, and the country
gentlemen to be without a spark of public feeling.
Every class of society joined in league to persecute and
disturb him; his farmers did not pay their rent (though
no theory of justification for that omission existed in
those days), and Landor, after throwing away the greater
part of his fortune, went off in profound offence and
bitterness to Italy, where he lived for most of the
remainder of his life. His stormy progress through the
world was without any of the dignity which sometimes
attends a passionate rebel against the ways of the world.
He was too noisy, too eccentric, for any pomp of injured
feeling or intellectual suffering. He stormed through his
life, with violent puffs of smoke and fire, more like a
runaway steam-engine fuming, creaking, snorting, explod-
ing, tearing along the resounding way, than any grander
fugitive. He married, rather, apparently, because he had
been lucky enough to find a perfectly unsuitable person,
than for any other motive. In after years, long after
Llanthony had ceased to be anything but a burden and a
trouble to him, he stumbled into a lovely spot upon his
own natural inheritance, and asked passionately why he
had not been persuaded to buy that instead of Llanthony,
altogether unaware that he had himself sold it in order
to purchase the imaginary paradise of the other. It
would be difficult to find a better example of the hotheaded haste and confusion of the mind, which never saw
anything but what it happened to be gazing at for the
moment, and saw that through a wild illumination of
impetuous fancy.

His only other important poetical work was the drama
of " Count Julian," written shortly after. This is praised
in terms so lofty by various excellent critics, that the
simple reader, if the drama ever gained any such, would
find it difficult to account for his disappointment in pre-

sence of their enthusiasm. "Landor's style is here at
its best, and contemporary poetry has nothing to show
beyond 'Count Julian' in purity or in grandeur," says
Mr. Forster. "Mr. Landor," says de Quincey, "who
always rises with his subject, . . . is probably the one
man in Europe that has adequately conceived the situation, the stern self-dependency, and the monumental
misery of Count Julian. That sublimity of penitential
grief which cannot accept consolation from man, cannot
bear external reproach, cannot condescend to notice
insult, cannot so much as see the curiosity of bystanders ;
that awful carelessness of all but the troubled deeps within
his own heart and of God's spirit, brooding upon their
surface, and searching their abysses, never was so majestically described." This is very high praise, but we find it
difficult to assent to it. The position of Count Julian
is one which might indeed be "majestically described,"
and is worthy of the hand which showed us Hamlet and
Othello, each in the centre of a world which had crumbled
about him, undermined by that falsehood which is the
death of every possibility. A powerful Spanish noble,
next to the king in dignity and influence, who in an hour
of agonised fury, finding his daughter outraged by the
monarch, calls in the aid of the Moors to revenge his
quarrel and overthrow his enemy—but this done, sees
for the first time that his frenzy of personal vengeance
has lost his country, and that in driving Roderick from
the field, he has put the yoke of the unbeliever upon the
neck of Spain—is such a hero as demands the hand of
the highest genius. After the last terrible battle, in
which not only Roderick but his country is destroyed,
the fugitive king puts himself into the power of his
enemy. But Julian is too noble, too merciful, and at
the same time too magnanimous, too contemptuous, to
take the life of the wretched and vanquished fugitive.

The Moors, when they know that the king has escaped
by his permission, fall upon him as a traitor, and Muza,
their chief, condemns him to death.   We quote a part of
this scene, for the book is in few hands, and the reader
otherwise might find it difficult to form an opinion of his
own on the subject—

"MUZA.

Away with him!

JULIAN.

       Slaves! not before I lift
My voice to heaven and man: though enemies
Surround me, and none else, yet other men
And other times shall hear: the agony
Of an opprest and of a bursting heart
No violence can silence; at its voice
The trumpet is o'erpower'd, and glory mute,
And peace and war hide all their charms alike.
Surely the guests and ministers of heaven
Scatter it forth through all the elements,
So suddenly, so widely, it extends,
So fearfully men breathe it, shuddering
To ask or fancy how it first arose.

MUZA.

Yes, they shall shudder : but will that, henceforth,
Molest my privacy, or shake my power?

JULIAN.

Guilt hath pavilions, but no privacy.
The very engine of his hatred checks
The torturer in his transport of revenge,
Which, while it swells his bosom, shakes his power,
And raises friends to his worst enemy.

MUZA.

Where now are thine? will they not curse the day
That gave thee birth, and hiss thy funeral!
Thou hast left none that could have pitied thee.

JULIAN.

Many, nor those alone of tenderer mould,
For me will weep; many, alas, through me!
Already I behold my funeral;
The turbid cities wave and swell with it,
And wrongs are lost in that day's pageantry:
Opprest and desolate, the countryman
Receives it like a gift; he hastens home,
Shows where the hoof of Moorish horse laid waste
His narrow croft and winter garden-plot,
Sweetens with fallen pride his children's loss,
And points their hatred, but applauds their tears.
Justice, who came not up to us through life,
Loves to survey our likeness on our tombs,
When rivalry, malevolence, and wrath,
And every passion that once storm'd around,
Is calm alike without them as within.
Our very chains make the whole world our own,
Bind those to us who else had past us by,
Those at whose call brought down to us, the light
Of future ages lives upon our name.

MUZA.

I may accelerate that meteor's fall,
And quench that idle ineffectual light
Without the knowledge of thy distant world.

JULIAN.

My world and thine are not that distant one.
Is age less wise, less merciful, than grief,
To keep this secret from thee, poor old man?
Thou canst not lessen, canst not aggravate
My sufferings, canst not shorten or extend
Half a sword's length between my God and me.
I thank thee for that better thought than fame,
Which none however, who deserve, despise,
Nor lose from view till all things else are lost.

. . . . . .

Yet we, alive or dead, have fellow-men
If ever we have served them, who collect

> From prisons and from dungeons our remains,
> And bear them in their bosoms to their sons.
> Man's only relics are his benefits;
> These, be there ages, be there worlds, between,
> Retain him in communion with his kind:
> Hence is our solace, our security,
> Our sustenance, till heavenly truth descends,
> Covering with brightness and beatitude
> The frail foundations of these humbler hopes,
> And, like an angel guiding us, at once
> Leaves the loose chain and iron gate behind."

This idea is fine, but we think dwelt on at much too great length. The emancipation of the wronged and injured the moment they have received the fatal blow— the remorseful compensation which the world offers them, when there is nothing else left to give—is too consolatory and gentle a thought to have been the last thought of a man, conscious not only of great wrongs and sorrows, but of having been the instrument, by his own vengeance, of his country's calamity. Neither at such a tremendous moment is so long a strain of level verse enough for the necessities of the crisis. Even allowing that passion is swallowed up in the calm of supreme misery, yet no misery can be supreme which retains this consolation. It is the language of noble resignation and virtue, not the confused and bewildering death-song of a man, who heedlessly, without thought, has brought down, in avenging his own wrongs, a torrent of ruin upon the innocent, and finds it out to give bitterness to his end before he dies.

Landor, however, as well as his critics, was satisfied with " Count Julian," and the negotiations about its publication are amusing and characteristic. He described its writing to Southey with a little of his favourite and habitual brag. " I believe I am the first man who ever wrote the better part of a tragedy in a concert-room. . . . It cannot be well done, written with such amazing

rapidity; in forty hours I have *done* a thousand lines."
Soon, however, he modifies this statement. "My rapidity
in the composition was not so great as I led you to
imagine. My hours were four or five together after long
walks, in which I brought before me the various characters, the very tones of their voices, their forms, com-
plexions, and step. In the daytime I laboured, and at
night unburdened my mind, shedding many tears." But
what was to be done with it was now the question. It
ought to be printed—or perhaps rather produced on the
stage. It was supposed that the character of "Count
Julian" would suit Kemble—and at last Southey suggested that he should take it to London and offer it.
Then Landor's pride took fire. "'Count Julian' shall never
lie at Kemble's feet. It must not be offered for representation. I will print it, and immediately." It was then
sent to Longman, with the following tragical result.

"I sent 'Count Julian' to your bookseller, Mr. Longman, and
gave him to understand, though not in so many words, as people
say, that you thought not unfavourably of it. I would have been
glad to have given it up to him for half-a-dozen copies. . . . This
would not do. I then proposed to print it at my own expense.
This also failed. They would have nothing to do with it. We
have lately had cold weather here, and fires. On receiving the last
letter of Mr. Longman to this purport, I committed to the flames
my tragedy of 'Ferranti and Giulio,' with which I intended to surprise you, and am resolved that never verse of mine hereafter shall
be committed to anything else. My literary career has been a very
curious one. You cannot imagine how I feel relieved at laying
down its burden and abandoning this tissue of humiliations."

This is Landor all over. Because one tragedy is not
to be printed, to rush to the fire with another is carrying
despite to the farthest limit of hotheaded folly. Perhaps,
however, after all, it was but the plan of "Ferranti and
Giulio" which went into the fire, which would be the
less damage.

In 1816 Landor went to Italy, from whence he sent forth the *Imaginary Conversations*, by which he will be chiefly known to posterity. These works have been greatly applauded by the best judges; but they have not penetrated the public mind. Perhaps, however worthy they had been, the effect on the general mass could never have been great; for how were the ignorant, who scarcely knew more than the names of the great personages introduced, to understand the fine points of character which were supposed to be unfolded in their imaginary talk? And works which are by their nature beyond the comprehension of the general reader must be content with a limited appreciation. Scholarship, like everything else that is human, has its disadvantages. It is narrowing, like ignorance. It keeps the mind within a certain circle; teaches it to prefer conventional themes; and to rank perfection of expression higher than truth to nature, Landor's system and inspiration were opposed in every principle to those which Wordsworth had spent his life in expounding, and consequently to the new fountain of literary life which belonged to the age; but they have always found the audience he would himself have most desired, and will probably continue to do so. They range over a wide extent of history from the great Greeks and Romans, mediæval nobles, Italian poets, reformers, statesmen, courtiers, and great ladies of the picturesque ages, down to contemporaries of his own; and embrace almost as large a range of topics. For our own part, we find character deficient in these generally very able, and sometimes brilliant little scenes. In many of them, naturally enough, the man who is not of Landor's way of thinking has a very poor part in the discussion, being put up as a sort of foil to the eloquence of the other, who entertains the same faith as his creator; and in this way it is curious to see Melancthon, for example, that mild man of com-

promises, crushing Calvin in argument, with an ease
which makes the victory scarcely worth having. In some
cases the familiarity of the dialogue between historical
personages takes the reader aback, and in almost all we
are forced against our will to see the ideas and tendencies
of the nineteenth century painfully masquerading in robes
of other days. But at the same time these curious historical studies have been approved and applauded by
many of the most perfectly qualified critics ; and Landor
himself has been undoubtingly received to all the honours
of the poetic craft by all the poets who were his contemporaries. He lived to be the *doyen* of his art, the old
man eloquent, at whose feet every ardent youth was
proud to sit. Not Southey alone, but all the fraternity,
applauded his productions and sought his friendship.
When his first volume of *Imaginary Conversations* appeared, Wordsworth added a postscript of thanks and
approbation to Southey's letter. He had " the praise of
his peers " in no limited degree : but he never penetrated
to the general heart, consequently he will never be capable
of the highest fame.

To give a catalogue of the miscellaneous works of
Southey would be almost impossible. He produced perhaps a larger body of literature than any other man living,
making his income by reviews and critical articles, by
histories and biographies, few of which merit higher praise
than that of being excellent and conscientious work done
without prejudice or partiality. One of these at least, his
Life of Nelson, has become a classic. His own purpose
in its composition is explained in his preface. He found
that a life of the great seaman was wanted, " clear and
concise enough to become a manual for the young sailor,
which he may carry about with him till he has treasured
up the example in his memory and heart." The book
admirably carries out this intention. Its clear, direct,

and brilliant narrative has something in it of the power
of the minstrel as well as the skill of the historian; and
the complicated story of the age never confuses the simple,
lambent vigour, the heroic unity of the principal figure.
There is no superfluity in it, but a picturesque fulness of
detail. The same can scarcely be said for the lives of
Wesley and Cowper, though both are important and
valuable works. They are perhaps too long drawn out,
especially that of the unhappy poet, in which there is so
little incident: yet both remain standard books, and no
subsequent performance has superseded them. Southey
planned other and greater historical works, and contemplated with some melancholy, yet not without a certain
pleasure, the idea of being chiefly remembered by those
productions; but he did not live to carry his larger conceptions out. The elaborate and elephantine humour of
the *Doctor* gave himself a great deal of pleasure; but the
world has no longer leisure for pleasantries, even when
mingled with wisdom, so lengthened and so laborious.

He put nothing out of his hand—curiously enough
except his poems, which were what he loved the best and
devoted himself most enthusiastically to—which was not
creditable and good. The minor poems, however, are
many of them very little worthy of his reputation, and
some, even of those which he himself thought well of,
and which his friends praised, are of no advantage to
it. William Taylor of Norwich, a name which intrudes
itself continually into the literature of that time, refers
in letter after letter to a certain "Old Woman of
Berkeley," which Southey modestly allows to be a success; but we doubt whether any jury even of the gentlest
readers would vote for its preservation. His weekly
engagement to produce a set of verses for the *Morning
Post* is no doubt the cause of the existence of many
of these minor poems. They did very good service by

furnishing a little income to the young and frugal pair
at the commencement of their life; but it seems a pity
to preserve, in a permanent form, so much verse that has
so little merit in it.

Towards the end of Southey's life there happened to
him what we can call nothing less than a great literary
misfortune. He had been made Poet Laureate some time
before, owing much to the good offices of Scott, to whom
the appointment had been offered, and who resigned it, if
we may so speak, in his favour. Southey tried to make
a condition beforehand that the usual Odes and birthday
salutations should not be required of him, but somehow
this arrangement fell through, and he was called upon
after all to supply, like his predecessors, the tedious tale
of verse. When old King George died, it would seem
that he thought some special effort was required of him.
In the course of the years he had changed his politics
entirely, and the young republican and revolutionary had
turned into a thorough and sound Conservative and sup-
porter of Church and King. Nobody will believe now
that Southey had any interested motive in making this
change. The wonder is rather that he could ever have
been anything but that which he ended by being. It
was the natural atmosphere of his mind, the natural condition of his perfectly regulated and sober life. But in
those days of excited politics any change of the kind was
branded as an apostasy, and there were many who accused
Southey of being a turncoat, a " rat," a deserter from the
cause of the people by reason of his pension and the
favour of the great. Some time before, his early production, the dramatic sketch called " Wat Tyler," which he
had never published, and had considered entirely abolished
and done away with, was brought out suddenly by some
scoundrel into whose hands it had fallen, with the intention
of covering him with confusion, and also shaming the

Government which was supposed to have bought him. Southey accepted the consequences with courage, and added the boyish effort to the collection of his works with a manly acknowledgment that life had taught him various lessons between the ages of eighteen and forty, "and that it may not be supposed I think it any reproach to have written it, or that I am more ashamed of having been a republican than of having been a boy." But it cannot be supposed that this passage of arms had been pleasant to him, or the discussions of which it was the cause. How his good sense and judgment could have so far and entirely forsaken him, however, as to lead him to throw himself into the hands of his adversaries without shield or protection, as he did when he produced the poem with which he intended to do honour to poor old George III., it is impossible to understand. To make the matter a little more fatal, he prefixed to the "Vision of Judgment" a preface, in which he attacked with the sternest vigour the "Satanic School" newly arisen in poetry, with reference too clear to be mistaken to Lord Byron. Thus he delivered himself over with an extraordinary blindness of self-assertion and solemn vanity into the very hands of his slayers. The retaliation of the poet whom he thus assailed was made only too easy. It will be more properly treated when we have reached the corresponding point in the story of Byron and the younger brethren of poetry. But the "Vision of Judgment" itself is one of Southey's misfortunes in every way. It was an attempt to gain a footing for the hexameter in English verse, and even in that was not successful; but when we have said that Southey avows his poem to have been suggested by the great work of Dante, and does not shrink or tremble before the inevitable comparison, we have given all the proof necessary of his extraordinary temerity and blindness. "The reader," he says, "will so surely think of the admirable passage in Dante, which was in the writer's mind when these lines were composed, that I should not think it necessary to notice the imitation were it not that we live in an age of plagiarism. . . . I have never contracted an obligation of this kind either to contemporary or predecessor without acknowledging it." Thus Southey does not hesitate on the threshold of his profane political paradise to call forth the great image of one of the Sovran poets of the world, to put himself by Dante's side, and treat him with respectful brotherhood and no alarm as his " predecessor." The audacity takes away our breath.

In the unfortunate poem itself, from a pretty twilight picture of his mountains and the shining evening skies behind them, we are suddenly transported into a visionary world where the aged shadow of poor old George,—pathetic, helpless, wrong-headed, mad king,— rises to judgment, and all heaven and hell are roused to receive him. But hell can bring no accusers against him; neither is there a voice in heaven or earth to condemn him; and with a great retinue of former statesmen and courtiers advancing in state to meet him, he is led upward to the reserved seats appointed for kings in that polite and considerate heaven. The curious spectacle of the reverential spirit-courtier, evidently hat in hand, and with bowed head, giving to his king a highly satisfactory account of the future of England, would be amusing were we not too sorry to see Southey committing himself so terribly. No poem ever written is more entirely indefensible or threw all his stronghold more unguardedly open to the enemy. It was a terrible and inexplainable mistake, due to the absence of perception which had made him choose so many strange subjects, to the self-will which had always been in Southey's poetical work, and to a self-confidence which had grown with years.

We must conclude with something more agreeable

than this unfortunate production.   One of the minor
poems which increase the bulk of his works, without
adding in any way to his fame, was a "Pilgrimage to
Waterloo," which was the product of a holiday spent
abroad.   The following verses from the proem to this work,
and which describe his return home, are among the most
beautiful and touching he ever wrote :—

> " O joyful hour, when to our longing home
>   The long-expected wheels at length drew nigh !
>   When the first sound went forth, ' They come, they come !'
>   And hope's impatience quicken'd every eye !
>   ' Never had man whom Heaven would heap with bliss
>   More glad return, more happy hour than this.'
>
> " Aloft on yonder bench, with arms dispread,
>   My boy stood, shouting there his father's name,
>   Waving his hat around his happy head ;
>   And there, a younger group, his sisters came :
>   Smiling they stood with looks of pleased surprise,
>   While tears of joy were seen in elder eyes.
>
> " Soon each and all came crowding round to share
>   The cordial greeting, the beloved sight ;
>   What welcomings of hand and lip were there !
>   And when those overflowings of delight
>   Subsided to a sense of quiet bliss,
>   Life hath no purer deeper happiness.
>
> .   .   .   .   .   .
>
> " But there stood one whose heart could entertain
>   And comprehend the fulness of the joy ;
>   The father, teacher, playmate, was again
>   Come to his only and his studious boy :
>   And he beheld again that mother's eye
>   Which with such ceaseless care had watch'd his infancy."

Poor Southey ! this boy, "waving his hat around his
happy head" was the dearest object of his life.   The
poem was scarcely printed in which this fond description
is given, when Herbert, the beloved, the only and studious
boy, was taken away from him.   He came to a blank

and terrible pause in his life, such darkness of anguish as only parents know ; and though he lived long after, and had another son given him as if to replace the lost, Southey never "got over" this crushing blow, or was the same man again. Printed among his later poems is a curious broken page, mingled of verses from the Bible and fragmentary lines of his own.

No more great attempts, only a few autumnal flowers, like second primroses—

> " That name
> In sacred silence buried, which was still,
> At noon and eve, the never-wearying theme
> Of dear discourse,"

> ———" playful thoughts
> Turned now to gall and evil."

> " They who look for me in our Father's Kingdom
> Will look for *him* also : inseparably
> Shall we be so remembered."

Such are the detached and broken lines, like sobs that gave utterance to his sorrow. An " In Memoriam " full of tender art and pains could not have been written by a father over the grave of his only son. These broken notes touch the reader's heart, if he has ever suffered in a similar way, with that pang of keen and almost intolerable fellow-feeling which is the profoundest form of sympathy. And thus we leave Southey, with our hearts bleeding for him——he whose heart had been open to forsaken children, to the weak and the needy, all his life,——yet out of his arms his own was taken, inscrutable and terrible recompense of a good man's life.

It will be suitable to name here a young and hapless poet whose brief story can never be dissociated from Southey's name. Henry Kirke White, who died in the beginning of the century, October 1806, at the age of twenty-one, a poor youth so far in advance of his age that he died of examinations and over-cramming, by the kind but injudicious hands of the college authorities of St. John's, Cambridge, where he had gained a sizorship. He was one of those saintly youths whose religious blameless lives will aways be reverentially read by the simple public, and whose gentle, devotional verses charm and awe and touch, perhaps, a larger number of minds than are ever affected by the highest voices of poetry. An early volume of poetry, which he published at seventeen, received the honours of a kind of martyrdom from a bitter critic; and the consumptive and suffering young poet almost died of the cruel assault. Southey, always kind, was moved by this to an indignant championship of the dying youth, consoled him with tender praise, and afterwards published his little biography and innocent pious "Remains," which became dear to many a young and innocent reader.

Other young names of promise never carried out, which the always generous and tender hand of the gentle Laureate did its best to crown, might be added; perhaps that of Herbert Knowles is the only one which has lingered in any reader's memory. His "Verses in the Churchyard at Richmond" used to appear in those curious receptacles of little-known verse—school reading-books, and other collections. And Southey's name is still more closely connected with that of Caroline Bowles, whom he married in the end of his life—an event which, as so often happens, disturbs the perfection of his domestic story, without having resulted in any special personal advantage. She was the author of various stories, poems, and essays—the latter of which, in the form of a series of "Chapters on Churchyards," published in *Blackwood's Magazine*, are almost the only relics of her that have a faint survival.

ROBERT SOUTHEY, born 1774 ; died 1843.

Published Joan of Arc, 1795 ; second edition, 1798.
    Letters from Spain and Portugal, 1797.
    Thalaba, 1801.
    Metrical Tales, 1804.
    Madoc, 1805.
    Letters from England by Don Manuel Espriella, 1807.
    Curse of Kehama, 1810.
    Roderic, the Last of the Goths, 1814.
    Life of Nelson, 1813.
    Life of Wesley.
    Life of Cowper, 1837.
    The Doctor, 1834.
He accepted the office of Poet-Laureate in 1813, and wrote the Vision of Judgment in 1821.

WALTER SAVAGE LANDOR, born 1775 ; died 1864.

Published Early Poems, in 1795.
    Gebir, 1802.
    Simonidia, etc., 1805.
    Count Julian, 1812.
    Idyllia Heroica (Latin), 1814.
    Imaginary Conversations, 1824 to 1846.
    Letters of a Conservative, 1836.
    Satin on Satirists, 1837.
    Dramas, 1839.
    Last Fruit off an Old Tree, 1853.
    Dry Sticks Fagoted, 1858.

HENRY KIRKE WHITE, born 1785 ; died 1806.

CAROLINE BOWLES (afterwards Southey), born 1787 ; died 1854.
Published Chapters on Churchyards, 1829.

END OF VOL. I.